D1291335

A MARC CORPORATION BOOK

This series in Urban and Ethnic Affairs is sponsored
by the Metropolitan Applied Research Center, Inc.,
Kenneth B. Clark, President.

OTHER MARC CORPORATION BOOKS

A *Relevant War Against Poverty*, Kenneth B. Clark
and Jeannette Hopkins

W. E. B. Du Bois: A Reader, edited and with an
introduction by Meyer Weinberg

Racism and American Education, Harold Howe,
Kenneth B. Clark, James E. Allen, *et al.*

*White Terror: The Ku Klux Klan Conspiracy
and Southern Reconstruction*, Allen W. Trelease

*The Black Image in the White Mind: The Debate
on Afro-American Character and Destiny 1817–1914*,
George M. Fredrickson

Aztlan: An Anthology of Mexican American Literature,
edited by Luis Valdez and Stan Steiner

The Way: An Anthology of American Indian Literature,
edited by Shirley Hill Witt and Stan Steiner

BORINQUEN

BORINQUEN

An Anthology
of Puerto Rican
Literature

EDITED BY
MARÍA TERESA BABÍN
AND STAN STEINER

Vintage Books
A Division of Random House,   New York

108828

TRANSLATIONS BY BARRY JAY LUBY
John Jay College Of Criminal Justice (CUNY)

VINTAGE BOOKS EDITION, November 1974

Copyright © 1974 by Alfred A. Knopf, Inc.
All rights reserved under International and Pan-
American Copyright Conventions. Published in
the United States by Random House, Inc., New York,
and simultaneously in Canada by Random House of
Canada Limited, Toronto. Originally published by
Alfred A. Knopf, Inc., in November 1974.

Library of Congress Cataloging in Publication Data:

Babín, María Teresa, date, comp.
Borinquen; an anthology of Puerto Rican literature.

(A Marc Corporation book)
1. Puerto Rican literature (Selections: Extracts, etc.) I. Steiner, Stanley, joint
comp. II. Title.
PQ7433.B3   1974b   860   73-20926
ISBN 0-394-71020-7

COVER PHOTOGRAPH BY JERRY FRANK
Manufactured in the United States of America
FIRST EDITION

CONTENTS

V. EUGENIO MARÍA de HOSTOS: "CITIZEN OF AMERICA"

VI. LA VIRGEN de BORINQUEN

VII. THE CRY OF LARES

VIII. LA BORINQUEÑA

IX. THE ROMANTIC POETS

X. "CHRONICLES OF A SICK WORLD": THE NOVELS OF MANUEL ZENO GANDÍA

XI. "WE ARE ALL MERCHANDISE"

INTRODUCTION: THE PATH AND THE VOICE

by María Teresa Babín

"The Good of the Good We Lost"
—AGÜEYBANA'S SPEECH IN CASTELLANOS' ELEGY

The call of the wild, mingled with the sea breezes and the aroma emanating from the hillside flowers, signaled the path through the *yucayeques*. The turbulent crest of the watching hurricane and the tremor of hearts and limbs in the primitive *areyto* enlivened the verses entwined with the voices of warriors and sages of the Antilles, weaving in song and dance the tapestry of our myths with dreams of love. The historical destiny of the Greater Antilles was at this early time a vague expectation chanted and danced in the unwritten poetry of movement and color, sounds and rhythms, the ancient language of the wisdom of the people who inhabited the land. The Renaissance and the aborigines of the Caribbean were discovering their own mystery. Mortality versus the immortal soul. Diego de Salcedo was the experiment beyond any doubts . . . and the blood and suffering of conquest and resistance made the land somber until the dawn of a new day in which the surviving forces of man and nature gave rise to the first generation born on our soil, the offspring of the Spanish, the Taino, and the African. Their unifying language became the Castilian, their baptism in the Catholic faith made them Christians, and the ancestor who cradled their infancy worshiped in silence the Cemí as well as Santiago, the mystery of the woods and the solemn fear of the unknown and the world of the dead. Music and dance were part of this ritual initiation. Masks and saints, reality and unreality, hell and purgatory, the talisman of witchcraft and the miracles of holy images began to adorn the altars in the hearts of these Borinquen islanders who lived in *bohíos,* played in the *batey,* and ate *casabe.* The flowers of the *maga* tree were already in bloom in the countryside, and the Guajataca looked splendid in its colorful rainbow arch embracing the seashore.

It all happened around the year 1511. The remnants of the birth of our national culture are present today in caves, in ruins, in the land itself in all its splendor, and in the people whose ancestors came from Spain, from Africa, or from the Tainos.

A legendary vein flows from that perennial fountain of Borinquen ancestry. Tasting it is unavoidable, in the subtle *achiote* coloring our favorite foods, as is hearing it in the vibrant notes of a *güiro* or a *cuatro,* or seeing it in the steps and figures of a *bomba* in the palm forests of the most hidden places encircling the small towns. From the heart of the Plata or the Río Grande, through the Asomante and the Tres Picachos, scattered here and there, the written testimony of our creative being seems to be dictated by the echo of the voice of millions whose sound has been made part of the wind, the waves, the air, and the earth under our feet. Puerto Rican literature is only a partial testimony of the existence of a much vaster and deeper creativity. The *jíbaro* and the slum dweller continue to tell stories orally, stories in which the experience of daily life and the nightmares and the dreams of bright nights sparkled by the *coquí* and the *cucubanos* awaken the imagination to invent the legends that beautify the historical reality of the island's past and present life. This persistent trait seems to gain momentum instead of waning as the centuries pass, as if we had made a secret pact to communicate with each other in this search for our image in all the sources of our inner self. Puerto Rico is the most homogeneous and the most congenial country in terms of spiritual and emotional communication among its people. The intellectual and the ignorant, the man from the city and the man from the mountains, the university student and the sophisticated poet are one in their unanimity of being. The poor and the rich, the well-educated and the humble peasants understand the same signs and respond to the same silent emotions, they like and dislike the same flavors, and their language of love, of despair, of hope, and of rage carries the message with the same semantic meaning through the many social and economic levels of our insular human geography.

The writers of Puerto Rico have succeeded in printing this truth (of our oneness as a people) in Romantic and Realistic expressions, with strong colors and lines. At other times, in a watercolor or in a silent prayer to a rustic wooden saint, they have merely suggested a shade of grief and melancholy. Infinite litanies in poetic prose, and stanzas in which absence from the native soil kindles the imagination, trace a Borinquen landscape or revive a memory in which the fantasy of love creates a superreality. The Puerto Rico invented by the writers, the utopia of a Gautier Benítez or a Lloréns Torres, continues to make its presence known in many of the poets who have lived away from their homeland since the beginning of the twentieth century.

Through language and movement, the style of a culture dating from pre-Columbian days acquires the depth and scope that depict the identity of a country described by the first visitors and chroniclers with awe and amazement. In the stronghold of the mountainous region of the central towns—Maricao, Jayuya, Lares, Barranquitas—folklore abounds: tales of the dead who roam the fields after sundown and guard hidden treasures buried long ago in secret places, ghosts of pirates who roam the coastal towns, sandy beaches that echo the roaring sound of the waves and the chains of heavy treasure chests, and the Carimbo irons that burn the tongue of *décima* singers who improvise lyrics telling of the infamy of slavery and the struggle for freedom. . . . Witchcraft and fairy tales blend in a hurly-burly of lunatic fantasy and transform the island and the life of its people to give a dimension of unreality to ordinary and repetitious actions. The pervading force of history in the tropics through the centuries, the menace of heavy rains, devastating floods, swarms of mosquitos, thunder and lightning, earth tremors, and mysterious beings with long hair, pale faces, and moaning voices make sporadic incursions in the life and death of our towns, contributing to the rich and varied world of literature enlightening the metaphors and the rhetoric of the Puerto Rican poet.

The body of the totality of our cultural manifestations has been shaped by the nutrient sap of the Spanish vernacular. The first persons who heard Indian folk tales and retold them to others were the conquerors and settlers from the Iberian peninsula, and the first witnesses who captured the saga of the island's entry into the realm of a New World concept were soldiers and priests like Juan de Castellanos (1522–1607) and Fray Damián López de Haro (1581–1648). Indeed, our Taino heritage remained in a state of silent underground lethargy until very recently. The awakening of the poets and the dramatists who are incorporating this dormant aspect of our culture in their work in recent times echo the *areyto* and pay homage to the herbs, the trees, the flowers, and the historical sites of the Taino culture in Puerto Rico. The oral literature of the island offers glimpses of pre-Columbian Indian poetry in anecdotes, proverbs, and legends, and the most relevant of all the sources emanating from the Taino heritage is preserved in the linguistic treasure of our everyday experience. Poets imbued with the essence of sophisticated tendencies often have a faithful and even reverent attitude, which is manifested in their choice of words of Indian extraction. Glimpses of the *bohío*, the *casabe*, the *güiro*, the *batey*, appear in sketches and lyrical compositions. The desire to recover the spirit of the primitive Borinqueños is also visible in pottery, in painting, in music, and in dance. As a tribute to the Taino culture, a native ceremonial center has been restored in the Caguana district of Utuado.

The Taino vocabulary gives a special flavor and color to the Spanish language, with reminiscences of the indigenous prehistory of the Caribbean. It is believed that the language of the Tainos became extinct toward the year 1550 in Puerto Rico as well as in Santo Domingo. The isolation of certain mountainous zones in Puerto Rico resulted in nuclei of Indian families that maintained consciousness of their origin till the end of the eighteenth century. The indigenous element has persisted in the districts of Indiera Fría, Indiera Baja, and Indiera Alta, situated in the mountain range of San Germán, within the limits of Maricao. The distinguished Spanish scholar Tomás Navarro believes the mountains of Maricao, where the Indieras' enclave is, to be the location of the greater part of the legends and traditions of Puerto Rican folklore.

The suggestive lines of Agüeybana's voice lamenting "the good of the good we lost" and the sense of grief and protest interwoven in the quest for liberty and the clamor for love and endurance to achieve immortality, flow without interruption from the early cantos of the sixteenth century to the most recent outbursts of passionate existentialist neo-Romanticism. These voices utter their laments or their insults, their frustrations or their denunciations of social and political evils on literary fronts everywhere. In plays and fiction, in poetry and essays, the Puerto Rican writer on the island and in the barrios of New York, Chicago, and other places has revived the memory of the hidden Taino stamina to strengthen the path toward the future.[1]

From the Enchanted Garden to the Lost Eden

The writers who left letters, verses, and diaries were fine observers of the environment, describing the landscape, the flora and fauna, the customs, the "great heat and shade of the coconut trees," and that gentle and refreshing breeze, bequeathed in a sonnet that is a social vignette. The step taken by these seventeenth-century exponents of literary acumen in the Americas was bold and courageous. By then Puerto Rico had established a close relationship with Mexico, and the names of two men from the island became famous in the literature of the period: the Gongorist poet Francisco de Ayerra y Santamaría (1630–1708), whose fame as a Latin scholar and intricate and elegant style was admired by his contemporaries, and Alonso Ramírez (1622–1700), the son of a carpenter, whose adventures and misfortunes are the theme of a novel by the Mexican writer Sigüenza y Góngora (1645–1700). Another interesting relation with Mexico was established when the eminent Spanish poet Bernardo de Balbuena (1568–1627) came to Puerto

1. I refer the reader to these sources in Spanish: M. T. Babín, *Panorama de la Cultura Puertorriqueña* (New York: Las Americas Pub. Co., 1958); *La Cultura de Puerto Rico* (San Juan: Instituto de Cultura Puertorriqueña, 1970); *The Puerto Ricans' Spirit* (New York: Collier-Macmillan, 1971); Tomás Navarro, *El Español en Puerto Rico: Contribución a la geografía lingüística hispanoamericana* (San Juan: Editorial Universitaria, UPR, Río Piedras, 2da edición, 1966).

Rico as Bishop after having lived in Mexico, bringing with him a library that became the research center and intellectual symbol of the Church in San Juan, and that was destroyed by the Dutch in 1625 when they attacked the capital of Puerto Rico. The brilliance and the glory of Balbuena, who wrote some of his books in Puerto Rico, were exalted by Lope de Vega in his *Laurel de Apolo*.

José Campeche (1752–1809) left a graphic testimony of the eighteenth century in beautiful portraits and landscapes, descriptive tableaux of customs and traditional sketches. Poetry became a chant to the "eternal spring" of the island. Abbad y Lasierra (1745–1815), the pious friar and poetic historian, wrote the first history of Puerto Rico, giving an account of three centuries of colonization with a fine perception of pre-Columbian culture and a clear understanding of the social and anthropological components of historical development. Tapia y Rivera (1826–1882) followed his steps in the nineteenth century. In collaboration with a group of classmates and professors in Spain, Tapia collected the *Biblioteca Histórica (Historical Library)*. The period of Romantic patriotic literature exposes the intricate and mixed ties between the Borinquen colony and the Mother Country, as they used to call the land of their forefathers. Thus the struggle for independence and the quest for freedom of the slaves became at the same time the fight for liberalism and progress within the frontiers of the Spanish monarchy. The Puerto Rican patriots were the defenders of the rights of the people of Borinquen as well as the defenders of the rights of the people of Spain. A common language, a traditional pattern of culture, a single faith, the family relations with the "uncles," the "cousins," the "in-laws," and the "godchildren" that all Puerto Ricans and all Spaniards shared as a bond of cultural continuity gave unity to the nineteenth-century Puerto Rico, a unity whose purpose was to eradi-

cate the stigma of colonialism without disrupting the essence of the island's inner self.

By this time the population had already attained that balance of ethnic components—Indian, African, Spaniard—
symbolized in the official seal used by the Institute of Puerto
Rican Culture since its founding in 1955. (The seal depicts
the spiritual domain of the "cosmic race," proclaimed by
the Mexican thinker José Vasconcelos as the epitome of the
cultural amalgam in Latin America.) Puerto Rico was approaching the final years of the nineteenth century wrapped
in the mantle of Spanish colonial colors within the frame of
reference characteristic of the vast Spanish-speaking Latin
American "continent." The Atheneum was created in 1876.
The total abolition of slavery had been proclaimed in 1873,
while a few years earlier, on September 23, 1868, the "Cry
of Lares" had taken place. In 1887 the Autonomist Party
was founded under the leadership of Baldorioty de Castro
(1822–1890), while Governor Palacios ordered the Com-
ponte to punish the revolutionaries. In 1895 a group of
eighteen patriots residing in New York established the
"Puerto Rican section of the Governing Body of the Cuban
Revolutionary Party." Poets and patriots became soldiers.
The life of Pachín Marín (1863–1897) came to a tragic and
glorious end on the battlefield of Cuba, and the Antillean
revolution was enlivened by the Puerto Rican voices of men
like Hostos (1839–1903) in South America and Betances
(1827–1898) in Paris. . . . In November 1897 the royal decree granting autonomy to Puerto Rico was signed, and on
February 9 of that year the island's autonomous government
was inaugurated.

Literature offers through the nineteenth century a magnificent array of tales and anecdotes, poems and plays, short
stories and novels, essays and reconstructions of legends and
traditional stories. This heritage was bequeathed by men

and women who participated actively in the political and social changes of the century. The lyrical and romantic feeling Santiago Vidarte (1827–1848) and Manuel Alonso (1822–1889) experienced for the homeland while they were students in Spain may very well represent the early impulse of the Puerto Rican, absent from the country, yearning to immortalize his birthplace. The hidden secret talisman guarding the faith and love of the sons of Borinquen for that Caribbean Eden was personified in the *jíbaro*—Hostos, Lola, Gautier—and transcended the literary circles of the San Juan Atheneum, where Elzaburu and Tapia were inciting the creative minds to rebel against the mediocre and to step forward in rhythm with the new intellectual trends. These great voices merged in the crossroads of two centuries with other writers—Luis Muñoz Rivera, Manuel Zeno Gandía, José de Diego—who had survived the traumatic experience of 1898.

The Spanish traditional folklore brought by the settlers from the different regions of Spain, the religious elements inspired by the Church, and the remnants of the Indian heritage, besides the magical charm embodied in the dances and songs of the Negro slaves and their descendants, mingled together and bloomed in the literature of the nineteenth century. The criollista national theme represented by such books as *El Gíbaro* (1849) had its counterpart in those writers who aspired to direct our literature through the path of a universal culture, within the Romantic and Realistic ideals, while the oral source of folklore remained unabated in the tales of Juan Bobo, in the ballads and the *aguinaldos*, the *coplas* and the *décimas* of the *jíbaros*—Salvador Brau, José Mercado, Hostos, Tapia, Meléndez Muñoz. Born before the Spanish-American War changed the historical destiny of their homeland, each one of them was going to bring to the attention of the younger writers the substance of a past, rich in its intensity of passions and unforgettable in its painful and sentimental depth. For many years the nineteenth century was called the Golden Age of Puerto Rican culture.

Between 1898 and the First World War (1914–1918) a dramatic suspense existed in the cultural life of this Caribbean island. The mature writers realized that their country had come under the influence of a different language and a new concept of traditions and beliefs, foreign to the Hispanic sources on which they had been nurtured. Their reaction was both pathetic and heroic. There is a wealth of information in the literature of that period depicting the trials and errors of the country while it was adjusting to its new role in history. The Puerto Rican writer kept the Romantic spirit alive during that trying period to safeguard his heritage and his most cherished emotions. But gradually, during those moving years, the island felt isolated from the rest of Spanish America. While Rubén Darío, the immortal Nicaraguan poet, was proudly proclaiming his liberation from the shackles of traditional versification to become the inspiration for all poets throughout the Spanish-speaking world, admonishing Roosevelt-the-hunter for his audacity and pleading to Don Quixote for guidance and fortitude, the life of Puerto Rico was shaken by the Spanish-American War and the military occupation of that country.

Thus the Puerto Rican man of letters was faced with the task of survival, not as an ordinary person, but as the personification of this grave moment in his homeland: the transfer of Puerto Rico from what Américo Castro, the Spanish essayist, has termed the "vital dwelling," to a strange house of immense and empty galleries where the native tongue, Holy Ghost of all literary creation, was neither spoken nor heard. Indeed, it was the dread of extinction of the country's language and mores that gave the literature written during the first decades of the twentieth century its basic strength. A deep patriotic concern for the land and its destiny and the credo embodied in the aesthetic philosophy of Luis Lloréns Torres (1878–1944)—"Beauty is the compenetration and unity of man with nature"—characterized most of the writings by Virgilio Dávila (1869–1943), Nemesio Canales (1878–1923), and other contemporary poets. At the same time Puerto Rican Modernism was a great hymn of pride and glory to awaken the Puerto Rican conscience, to defend and perpetuate the language, traditions, and customs of a country that was faced with a transformation and a menacing expectation of losing its identity.

This period of revival gave the national sentiment a lift, and the writers were the heralds who chanted the glories of the symbols embodied in the flag, the coat of arms, the language, the Hispanic components of our heritage, the beauty of the landscape, the discovery of Puerto Rico and the four hundred years of civilization that had shaped the culture of the country. The fervent appeal to these roots countered the assault made by the imposition of the English language in the schools of the island, and the patronage and humiliation with which the United States' laws and governors imposed their power on the people. It was a time that called for heroic will power to suppress the anguish and despair of the generation of 1898. And at this crucial moment the leaders in politics were also poets and orators. Lloréns Torres, whose chants in verse (*Song of the Antilles* and *Mare Nostrum*) were spiritual messages of great emotional impact, and Nemesio Canales, a humorist with a profound feeling for the causes of the humble ordinary people, were at the same time active in the political arena. In a wave of extraordinary solidarity Puerto Rican literature and political ideals were unified.

The Vanguard March

Around the 1930s the younger writers of Puerto Rico ventured through the new vanguard ways. The movements called "diepalism," "noism," "euphorism," "atalayism," and so on, all short lived, were impressive in their theories and manifestos, and in varied degrees of intensity they were related to the nationalist and independent ideal whose most prominent leader was Albizu Campos. The garb, the loudness, the eccentric attitudes, and the grandiloquent style of some of these writers—many of whom went to jail for their political ideals—constitute the original core and the fertile soil from which many of the so-called new ventures in literary patterns had their beginnings. In the New York City barrios and in other cities of the United States, the influence left by the poets and the fiction writers of that period has flourished in recent manifestations of dramatic and lyric poetry. The names of Luis Palés Matos (1899–1959), Vicente Géigel Polanco (1904–   ), Emilio Delgado (1904–1967), Graciany Miranda Archilla (1910–   ), Clemente Soto Vélez (1905–   ), Juan Antonio Corretjer (1908–   ), and Julia de Burgos (1916–1953) are known for their active participation in a poetic and nationalistic endeavor that expanded and extended its tentacles into a variety of actions. The foremost poet of the period was Luis Palés Matos, who created a magic reality in which the senses of odor and taste acquire a movement and a visual and emotional power. Palés mysteriously enters into the Negro's soul and feels its vitality in the innermost depths of his people. He reaches the soul of Negritude through his land, and the spirit of his land through the Negro, in an earthy and vital mingling of their essences.

The present wave of essays, novels, plays, short stories, and poems dealing with Puerto Rico itself as a literary theme had its definite point of departure around the year that marks the publication of one of the most influential books written in this century, *Insularismo* (1934), by Antonio S. Pedreira (1899–1939). Since then there has been a release of energy directed toward the creation of a literature inspired by the landscape, the people, the traditions, and the self-identity of the Puerto Ricans. But instead of a Romantic platitude for the lost paradise, this literature carries the drama of our historical tribulations, the suffering and the degradation of our innermost personality, the protest and the condemnation of a political system that is considered obsolete and humiliating, and a search for the reconquest of our lost image. The return to the soil, the quest for Taino and African inspiration in song and poetry, the rupture with the accepted status quo, and the revolt against the established acceptance of evils with a docile attitude are expressions of a brave and vertical position. The Institute of Puerto Rican Culture has been an extraordinary incentive to channel these forces toward the reconstruction of our history and the renewal and dissemination of cultural values through the theater festivals, the art and musical programs, and the exhibitions of important artists. At the same time the Puerto Rican exiles, as we may call the thousands of compatriots living in New York and other places, are displaying a forceful approach to literary expression in many ways. They are represented in this anthology with a sampling of moving and beautiful things created with pain and sorrow, in a flash of anger as victims of repression and discrimination on foreign soil, witnesses of a system of life and death that has left its Carimbo mark in their flesh and in their souls.

The patriotic and national theme of liberty, imbued with a deep feeling for the promises and hopes of the homeland, tempers the tragic sense of life. The original name of the island—Borinquen—and the adjectives derived from it (Boricua, Borinqueño) carry the essence of the Puerto Rican spirit.

The literary expression of Puerto Rico has a long and rich tradition. The ideological theme throughout this book is the love of freedom and independence as manifested in lyrical verses, in the dialogue created by the narrators in the novel, the short story, and the theatrical pieces as well as in the essay. The inner development of our creative and intellectual life ever since the period of struggle and conquest during the Spanish Golden Age and the echo of Agüeybana's voice urging his people to defend the land where they were born and raised as Tainos, is still present in the Spanish language of the contemporary men and women whose feelings, dreams, and desires are represented through these pages. Beautiful and romantic descriptions of the Puerto Rican landscape, the suffering, the pride and the will power to survive as a nation are evident in the language and the style of the writers, in the gradation of literary movements and the change of aesthetic attitude and sensibility through the centuries. The drama of a colony debating its destiny within the orbit of the Spanish domain until 1898, its cultural anxiety during the twentieth century as a possession of the United States, the defense of the Spanish language, the educational dilemma, the social and economic crisis and the political debates constitute an important part of the literary scene. The Puerto Rican experience in the United States is captured in dramatic and tragic moments through the short sketches and stories, plays, and novels that describe them.

The quality of the works by the poets and prose writers of Puerto Rico during the nineteenth and twentieth century rank as high as those of the best Spanish and Latin American writers of the same period. Romanticism, Realism, and Modernism are vividly represented in a wide variety of selections. In some instances the Spanish language is flavored with Caribbean and Puerto Rican idiosyncrasy, and throughout the translation we hope to maintain this characteristic as faithfully as possible.

Although the literature of Puerto Rico far surpasses that of the Neo-Rican, or self-styled Rican, in the United States, the latter represents a continuity of the island heritage. Since it is so much older and richer, it is naturally more complex and sophisticated. El Barrio or Los Barrios selections, no matter how crude and young, in a cultural sense, have a vitality that demands recognition; for it is a literature in the process of creation, whose forms and goals have already begun to affect those of the Mother Culture on the island. Among the 107 selections included in the anthology, representative of writers belonging to the past and the present literary trends, there are a few that represent the Neo-Rican modality.

The literature of culture being larger than the literature of the literati, we have included some speeches and articles written by our intellectual political writers, and at the same time we regret the absence from this book of other voices who are as significant as those that are included. But after all, the book aims to offer a mere sampling of a much vaster and deeper reality, and we only wish to give the readers a taste of what they can expect to discover by themselves in the poetry, the prose, the essays, legends, and drama of Puerto Rican life as the writer has interpreted and re-created its meaning.

The notes on authors (pages 481–506), by order of appearance in the text, are meant to satisfy the curiosity of the reader who wants to identify the men and women whose selections we have gathered. Although the titles are given in English, their works, with a few exceptions, have never been translated. Our anthology is, thus, the first attempt to offer in English a representative selection of important

Puerto Rican poetry and prose writings from the sixteenth century to the present day.

Spanish being the tongue of the people of Puerto Rico, it has been painful and difficult to translate into English without altering the inner meaning of the language. The editors appreciate the efforts of Dr. Barry Luby, who translated the main body of the manuscript. Our deep recognition also to other translators mentioned through the text, whose contribution has been very valuable.

The literature of Puerto Rico has been organized following the mood and rhythm of space and time, with emphasis on those topics that have prevailed in the life of the country, instead of adhering to a chronological and historical sequence. Nevertheless, the path of Borinquen from remote pre-Columbian days to the present-day confusion and despair in search of a new dawn is traced in these pages with emotion and sophistication. The book is an invitation to those who wish to listen to the voice of the people in verse and prose.

Let us rejoice in this encounter!

I. THE BORINQUEÑOS

On the isles of the Caribbean, the Admiral Christopher Columbus was welcomed, in 1496, by a "gentle and loving" people. "They exhibit great love toward others in preference to themselves," said the astounded Columbus. Seeing his ships, these Indians yelled in greeting, *"Taino! Taino!"*; it meant "Good! Good!" And so, the Spaniards called them the Tainos, as the Indians of Puerto Rico are called to this day. It was not, and is not, their name; for they clearly told the Spaniards they were the people of Borinquen, the Borinqueños, which they pronounced *Borican* and which the Spaniards mispronounced and misspelled.

In one generation the Conquistadores took their lands and enslaved their men and children. By 1511 the Borinqueños had revolted, so successfully that the Spanish Empire and Catholic Church policy toward the Indians of the Americas was changed forever. The Borinqueños' tribal memory of that revolt is retold by a *jíbaro* in the hills ("Let Me Tell You the Story," *The Islands: The Worlds of the Puerto Ricans*, by Stan Steiner, New York, Harper & Row, 1974) while the Spaniards' imaginative version was told by the poet, Juan de Castellanos (1522–1607), in his *Elegies of Illustrious Men of the Indies*, the longest epic poem in the Spanish language. The selection from the Sixth Elegy, dedicated to Ponce de León, is excerpted from the translation by Muna Lee ("Revolt of the Borinqueños"), as it appears in Babín's edition of the Elegy, *La Gesta de Puerto Rico*, 1967.

LET ME TELL YOU THE STORY

by a Jíbaro

Let me tell you the story of the *cacique* Guarionex. It is not historically recognized. But, it is what I have gathered out of the stories of the old people of this land, where I was born, and where my forebearers have been born, for five, six, or more generations. . . .

All this land of Utuado, Adjuntas, Jayuya and Lares (town in the Central Highlands, ed.) were known as the lands of Otoao, in the beginning, when the Spaniards came. The story goes that it was the name of an Indian chief, Otoao. In the Indian language *otoao* means a "Valley Between Mountains." But appealing to technology it means Otoao was the ruler of the "Valley Between Mountains." So, Otoao happens to be the name of the Indian chief in the land known as Otoao, itself.

In the beginning, as I said, Otoao was the ruler. So take it that way.

Our Indians were very hospitable. They were people of peace. And they were not skeptical of the Spaniards. But, the Spaniards came to conquer. In fact, they came after riches. The Indians did not think about it that way. So they made friends with the Spaniards.

Among the Indians there was a sacrament that we call *compadrazgo*, in Spanish. In the Catholic way. In the Indian way, it was named *guaitiao*. By the way of *compadrazgo* two people become related by a church sacrament. By way of *guaitiao* two people become related by blood. They make a small cut in the wrists, under the wrists, and they cross both wrists, so the blood of one mixes with the blood of the other.

In that way, by the sacrament of the *guaitiao*, they become *guaitiaos*. That means "brothers of blood."

The Indians believed in this. But the Spaniards looked at it as a way to gain control of the Indians, morally and spiritually. In that way Otoao became the *guaitiao* of Ponce de León [the first Spanish Governor of Puerto Rico]. He changed his faith to the Catholic faith. He changed his name to the Christian name of Don Alfonso.

And the Indians became skeptical of the Spaniards. They had been mistreated. They had been robbed of their land. They had been abused of their friendship. They had been made to work in the mines as slaves. But, more than that, their women had been abused by the Spaniards.

So, the *cacique* Otoao fell in the estimation of the Indians by changing his name and his religion.

It was then that the Indians had a new leader by the name of Guarionex. He had come to Borinquen from Santo Domingo, where he had experience fighting against the Spaniards. He had to flee there. So, he came and established himself in the land of Otoao, where Caguana is, actually. The *yucayeque* (village) of Guarionex has never been discovered. But, if you study the geography of Caguana you have to concede this was the place the old people talked about. Anyway, Guarionex became the chieftain of the whole land that had been the domain of Otoao. That was how Guarionex was accepted as the leader of the Indians and was recognized by the Spaniards as their true foe.

Guarionex was the one who led the Indians in their battle against the town of Sotomayor (in 1511). They burned the town.

But he did not die in warfare in Puerto Rico. As a matter of fact there is no tale of Guarionex being killed in battle. He was captured and taken on a ship to Spain, to show to the King that the rebellion had been finished. While the ship in which he was being taken to Spain was anchored outside the port of the Ozama River in Santo Domingo, a hurricane blew it out. The ship was wrecked in the hurricane. All the crew and passengers drowned, except Guarionex and two Indian chieftains from Borinquen, prisoners like him, who escaped. They swam to safety. They gained the shore. They escaped.

They escaped to the Virgin Islands and escaped capture. And that's about all that can be known about the great *cacique* Guarionex.

All these stories I heard from old people. Who are already dead. Who have died. My grandfathers. I recall them. As a little boy, I heard some of them. As a grown man, I heard some. The old people used to tell legends and stories I recall. From these things the old people told me, I gathered these stories about our history.

REVOLT OF THE BORINQUEÑOS
by Juan de Castellanos

Juan Ponce having readied men and store,
Under the powers given to his hand,
Made the journey without delaying more,

With interpreters from Haiti in his command
And since on St. John's Day he went ashore,
San Juan de Puerto Rico he called the land.
The men that he brought with him on that day
Stepped forth on sandy beaches of a bay.

Salcedo

As the Chief was pondering how best to play
His game ensuring the success he planned,
Diego de Salcedo passed that way,
Unaccompanied by any of his band;
Whereat Urayoan, hospitable and gay,
Giving no hint of what he had in hand,
Every attention to Salcedo showed,
And sent men to companion him on the road.
He set out with those Indians and their scheme,
He who wotted not what might betide.
And most courteously when they neared a stream,
They offered to bear him to the other side
Upon their shoulders; best way it would seem,
To keep his clothes dry from the river's tide.
He should have known such promises not to keep.
They flung him in where the water runs most deep.

Watching him flounder as the waters rose
Above where two or three had let him lour,
All the Indians beset him now with blows,
And kept him under water a full hour,
Till seeing him still dead, at last each knows
He had been mortal, with but a mortal's power.
Yet even then remained with them a dread
Lest 'spite all seeming, he be not wholly dead.

And so they waited there till the third day,
Fearful of what that drowned corpse yet might do.
Begging its pardon, they would softly say
How their ill action toward him they must rue,
Until the corpse was putrefying in such way
That by its look and smell at last they knew
Truth could no longer be doubted nor denied:
Here was no feigning: this man indeed had died . . .
I am not shocked by this, their show of might,
Nor by the evil deeds they had in mind;
For they had seen their pleasures vanish quite,
Nor security nor any hope could find.
Their wives and children, each unhappy wight
Knew a life-long servitude would bind.
They had all seen those precious freedoms fly
Which no amount of money can ever buy.

Agüeybana

When in one place they were at last aligned,
In a town-meeting there, as you might say,
Agüeybana, who has the master mind
And planned in everything to have his way,
Addressed that gathering in a speech designed
To give his eloquent argument full sway.
His words not many, but he chose them well,
This, more or less, is what he had to tell:

"If extremes of frenzy cease at long last,
If thinking man feels thought begin to fail,
If you can still remember the good past:
Then no man here can check an anguished wail
For abject wretchedness that holds us fast

In this fell present where all woes assail.
How much we suffer, how bitter is our bread,
How many of us are failing, fleeing—dead!

"While suffering such evils night and day,
We serve these foreigners in our land of birth;
And this our only freedom is: we may
Work their mines and till for them the earth.
Our fields, our plains, our coastlands—and it is they
Who possess all, and leave us to our dearth
Here in the land that always was our own,
Where we were born and wherein we have grown.

"Each of us to a master now belongs,
And must render him complete obedience;
Useless it is to tell you of your wrongs,
Who make no effort in your own defense.
So meekly now do you endure your thongs
It seems that suffering has benumbed your sense.
You let your master as he will enjoy
Your wife, your child, as past-time or as toy.

"Before the shame and evil that they do,
We like vile cowards have only given way,
I have no knowledge any one of you
Is planning aught such injuries to withstay.
Men who no more than cowed endurance show
When suffering or disgraced, what breed are they
If not ourselves, for whom shame has no sting,
We who it seems put up with anything!

"Speak up, forgetful dwellers in this land,
Snoring at ease, who not e'en in sleep complain.
Were you not born with weapons in your hand?

Rather than headlong flight across the plain
Were it not better in the hills to stand?
Speaking of war, must I speak to you in vain?
How is it we have not in all our host
One voice to tell the good of the good we lost?

"The Caribs in their fierce and wild estate
—The man that daunts them never casts a shade—
Whose cruelties are so many and so great
That even recounting them makes men afraid,
At a high value do your friendship rate,
And tremble when Borinquen's name is said.
And we, shall we in our turn tremble then
Before two hundred worn-out, crippled, starving men?

"My grandmother, that old bestial crone,
And my uncle, dull and slow of wit,
Gave us to believe a fiction all their own,
Which I held monstrous, always doubting it.
By now at last the simple truth is shown
By our own river, the Gurabo. This is it:
Christians are not immortal. Understand
At last that they can meet death by your hand!"

II. MYTHS AND TRUTHS OF BORINQUEN

For so small an island, Borinquen was surprisingly rich in natural beauty and wealth. And the people gave to the Spanish and English languages a remarkable lexicon of words for things that came to symbolize the Americas: *maiz* (maize, or corn), *tabaco* (tobacco), *yuca* (yucca), *cacique* (chieftain), *canoa* (canoe), *hamaca* (hammock), *sabana* (savanna), *cayo* (key), *hurakán* (hurricane). All of these were Borinqueño Indian words. Less well known, but as rich, is the heritage of legends and myths of these people. One of the distinguished historians of the folk legends and tribal history of the island was Cayetano Coll y Toste (1850–1930), the poet and politician, who edited *Boletín Historico de Puerto Rico* (*Historical Bulletin of Puerto Rico*), and whose masterwork, *Leyendas Puertorriqueñas* (*Puerto Rican Legends*), from which the story "Guanina" is taken, was a pioneering book of cultural rediscovery in 1925. The work of Coll y Toste has inspired many writers. In recent times the anthropologist Ricardo E. Alegría (1921–   ), director of the Institute of Puerto Rican Culture in San Juan, has written numerous books about the history and culture of the Indians, blacks, and *jíbaros* of the island, as told in their folk tales. Some of these were influenced by European and African folk tales, some by the religious morality tales of Catholicism, and some remain uniquely and indigenously Indian. ("The Renegades," by Ricardo E. Alegría, from *The Island Times*, November 8, 1963.)

THE RENEGADES

A *story based on Puerto Rican folklore by Ricardo
E. Alegría*

This happened many years ago, at a time, so they say, when God walked upon the earth.

The Maker had just created animals of every kind and he delighted in contemplating them all: in the air the ones that flew; on the land those that crept, ran and leaped; in the water, those that swam. But His happiness did not last long. Some animals were not satisfied with the form He had given them. The differences with which the Maker had endowed them to distinguish them from their fellows had begotten envy and dissatisfaction. This happened here, on the land.

One family of animals was envious of those that flew and wished to become like them. So they met with their fellows and expressed their intention of asking the Creator to change their form so that they could fly like the birds. But their fellows, who were proud to remain such as their Maker had wished them to be, refused to join in this petition. The ones who did not wish to be such as their Creator had made them were left alone and then, full of hate and rage because their fellows would not join them, they decided to take their case to God.

The Maker, saddened by what He already knew, expressed deep sorrow for the envy that led them to desire to change the form He had given them. And it was then, when the Creator refused to change their form, that they disowned their being, their fellows, and their Maker. That was the day when God, full of sorrow, left the Earth, and the Evil One, the Enemy, decided to use the passions of envy and covetousness to his own end.

The Evil One appeared before the Renegades and offered to grant them their wish, granting them what the Creator had refused. The Renegades, who in their envy and rage had forgotten that only God can create, accepted the Evil One's offer to give them wings to fly like the birds. But the Evil One could not create feathers such as the birds had. He could only stretch their skin to make wings, and, believing himself a Creator, change their body in his image.

The Renegades soon realized that their wish had been granted and that, thanks to the way the Enemy had changed their bodies, they could at last fly like birds. Full of hate, their first impulse was to go find their fellows, who had refused to change their form, and proudly display what they, with the help of the Enemy, had achieved. Great was their surprise on seeing that the others, their fellows, now fled in panic on seeing them in their new shape. No longer were they recognized as brothers and the new form with which they had been endowed by the Evil One caused only horror and disgust . . . as if the rest of the animals feared that they too might suffer such a change! At first, the Renegades were surprised at the behavior of those who had formerly been their fellows. But their arrogance, and the pride they felt in their new form, made them believe that now they were superior to the others and they decided to leave their former fellows forever and go live with the birds whom they so admired. So they took to the air. When the birds saw those featherless creatures that flew and who were made in the image of the Evil One, they forbade them to approach and refused to have anything to do with them.

Only then did truth dawn on the Renegades. They understood that they belonged to no family: that every animal, every single one, whether he ran or flew, despised and avoided them. They realized that in trying to undo, with the aid of the Evil One, what the Creator had made, they had only achieved a monstrosity from which all fled in horror.

They had gained their end but they had not fulfilled their ambition. Everyone knew of their treason and now they were ashamed and afraid. Perpetually fearful and humiliated, they hide from everyone.

That is why, even now, they only dare leave their hiding places when the sun sets and night falls; when the other animals are asleep; when darkness hides their shape, the outward sign of their treason to God and to their fellows.

Today, in our language, we call them . . . bats . . .

GUANINA

by Cayetano Coll y Toste

Afternoon fell, enveloped in a radiant red glow. Don Cristóbal de Sotomayor,[1] seated on a stool in the large room that he had had constructed in the Indian village of Agüeybana,[2] drowsily breathed in the amorous exhalations that the afternoon breeze brought to him from the immediate grove, as he thought melancholically of the Court in Valladolid and the Countess of Camiña, his dear mother, when with hurried step a beautiful Indian girl with bronze skin, expressive eyes, raised breast, soft contours, and abundant hair, half-gathered in braids in the old Castilian style, entered the room.

"What is the matter, Guanina, my dear, for you seem frightened and your large, beautiful eyes, always so lovely, are now filled with tears?"

"Flee, sir! Flee, my love! Your death has been decided upon by all the Borinquen chiefs. I know the most secret caves in our island and I will hide you carefully in one of them."

"You are delirious, Guanina! Your people have humbled themselves not to grow proud again," replied Don Cristó-bal, drawing toward himself the graceful Indian, kissing her on the forehead and trying to calm her.

"Do not believe, master, that my people are defeated. My good uncle Agüeybana's advice caused the Borinqueños to receive you with pleasure and in peace, and they enter-tained you well. They thought you were real *guaitiao*,[3] but the facts have come to prove, unfortunately, that you are not such friends and confederates, but that you aspire to be masters. Besides, some of your men have inconsiderately abused native generosity. And finally, the hard labor in the mines, in compact gangs, seeking those so-desired pieces of gold, that you value so highly, has driven them to despair, for, as you know, many kill themselves so they do not have to wash that wretched sand."

"I see you are also a rebel, Guanina," said Don Cristóbal, seating her at his side, and kissing her tenderly.

"I say what I feel, my love. And since your death is set by the chiefs, I want to save you. I come to warn you, because I do not want them to kill you," Guanina again exclaimed, with her eyes full of tears and tightly hugging the young nobleman, who held her in his arms with pleasure.

2

Suddenly Juan González,[4] the interpreter, entered the room, imprudently interrupting the amorous conversation of the young lovers.

"Don Cristóbal, there is no time to lose. The native rebellion will begin and it will be awesome. I have just witnessed an *areyto*, in which your own assistants, in singing and dancing, have sworn your death and that of all of us."

"You, too, good Juan, are easily impressed. I see with sorrow that these Indians' fears are beginning to stick to you. They are just servants giving vent to their feelings and nothing more."

Shrewd Juan replied: "For nights I have been seeing lights burning, and I have heard, in the silence of the night, the cry of alarm of the snail shell in the mountain, with the insistent call to arms. No doubt these are signs of courage, decision, already concerted. Soon the island will burn in terrible holocaust against us. Let us escape, sir, let us flee! I know all the shortcuts and paths that lead to Villa de Caparra. There is still time, Don Cristóbal."

"Me, Juan Cristóbal, flee!" he declared emphatically, with contained anger, rising furiously from the stool and letting go of the arms of Guanina, who laid her gentle head on the brave youth's shoulders; and he repeated:

"Me, Juan Cristóbal, flee! Do you not know that I am a Sotomayor, and that none of my family ever turned away from the enemy? I will leave here in the morning, in full sunlight, my visor high, my banner unfurled, followed by my friends and with my baggage on the shoulders of that rabble, who presently thunder in the *batey* with their clamor, and whom we shall soon punish. No more. Leave now."

While this dialogue took place between the two Christians, Guanina had withdrawn to the ledge of the window, and with sad eyes contemplated the darkness of the woods, as though seeking to peer into its secrets with her stare, the penetrating one of a wild creature; and machinelike, she finished braiding her abundant black hair, in the Spanish style, according to the lessons given her by the young Spanish nobleman, in his transports of love with the slender native girl.

"Come, Guanina, sit at my side. I am angry with your people, but not with you. Your love fills my soul. Kiss me, to make me forget with your caresses the sorrow that weighs upon me."

And the beautiful Indian embraced the young man's neck with her arms, and smiling, she kissed him, showing as she laughed her ivorylike teeth, which seemed like a row of fine pearls.

3

The morning was luminous, glowing. Quite early, good Juan González, the astute interpreter, called quietly at Don Cristóbal's door.

"Sir, sir, it is me, Juan González."

"Enter. What is the matter?"

"All night long we have been standing guard over your sleep. Let us leave, Don Cristóbal, let us leave."

"Call Guaybana, my assistant chieftain."

"I already called him, sir. He is below, at the door, awaiting your orders."

"Tell him to come in."

Juan González obeyed his captain's orders. And Guaybana, the main chieftain of Borinquen, entered the room.

Coldly he greeted Don Cristóbal, raising his right hand to his forehead, but maintaining his wrinkled brow. Guaybana was a robust, free and easy, proud youth. He had inherited the title from his uncle Agüeybana, and he hated the invaders with all his heart, to the death.

"I need you, Guaybana, to name a gang of your *naborias*, to take my luggage to Villa de Caparra. I am going on a trip and I want to leave immediately."

Juan González, the intermediary, interpreted for his captain.

"You will be obeyed," the chieftain answered dryly, withdrawing from the room without saluting, and with his brow wrinkled, as when he entered.

"Don Cristóbal, sir! What have you done? Why have you told Guaybana the route we are to follow?" exclaimed the interpreter, fearful of the imprudent frankness of Sotomayor, who gave little importance to the Borinqueños' rebellious movements.

"Juan, my good Juan, it's necessary for those scoundrels to know that we are not fleeing from them. Do not be apprehensive, my friend, for the God of victories is with us. No one can humble the Spanish flag. Ah, González, let us prepare for the trip!"

And the intrepid youth took down from the wall his Toledo sword, helmet, and buckler, placing them on the bed. Guanina, seeing what her love was doing, drew near him and whispered in his ear:

"Take me with you, my love! I do not want to remain here without your company. Take me! . . ."

"It is not possible now, Guanina. As soon as we leave this area, there will be a fierce *guasábara*, and I do not want an arrow to strike you or even wound or kill you. The slightest scratch to your skin would break my heart in two. I will come back for you, very soon. I promise you."

And embracing her in his arms he kissed her on the mouth with youthful ardor. Guanina began to weep sadly, the sobs welling up from her breast unable to change the arrogant noble youth's resolution.

The *naborias*, Indian servants, started to enter Don Cristóbal's room and divide up the baggage. The natives looked askance, with ill-disguised anger, at beautiful Guanina, whose eyelids were puffed from so much crying.

The procession was in the *batey*, awaiting the last orders. Don Cristóbal decided Juan González was to remain in the rear, with the baggage, and that his five friends would go with him at the front, on guard, to avoid any ambush. The leader, a good guide, would walk out in the open. As they were traveling on foot, they could not wear all their armor and hence only put on cotton breastplates, to deflect the blow of any arrow shot.

Once he put on his helmet of burnished steel, girded his sword, and took his buckler, Don Cristóbal hurriedly climbed the steps of the country house to kiss his beloved Guanina for the last time. They did not exchange a single word. They embraced and kissed again feverishly. As he came down the stairs, Don Cristóbal brought the pinky of his left hand to his cheek, to wipe away furtively two beautiful pearls that had sprung from his ardent eyes and that the brave youth did not want to be observed by his comrades at arms. It was the just tribute to the amorous reciprocity of the proud paladin to the enchanting native girl who had sacrificed, in the name of love, the sentiments of native patriotism, race, and family.

4

Don Cristóbal de Sotomayor's procession, taking advantage of the fresh air of the tropical morning, set out on the road that went toward Villa de Caparra. Soon the small party was lost from view. Then Guaybana gathered together three hundred Indians, his best warriors, and announced to them: "My friends, the hour of vengeance has sounded. Many moons have surprised me bewailing our misfortune. We have to destroy now all invaders or die for our country in the attempt. All our brothers from the other parts of the land are already prepared for the fight. The Cemi protector commands us to die killing. Today's sun will be favorable for us with its light. So it is necessary for you not to be inferior in valor to those brave warriors that Guarionex and Mabodomaca led. Fix your arrows' aim and fasten your club straps to your wrists. Forward! Forward!"

Guaybana displayed his multicolored plume of feathers, wearing around his neck the distinctive gold *guanín* of the chieftain and brandishing in his right hand the terrible quartz hatchet with which he struck down forests of cedar and combretaceous trees.

The resolute chieftain was followed by three hundred Indians, well armed, with their quivers on their shoulders and filled with arrows, bows in their left hands, and clubs in their right hands. They wore their hair gathered at the back of their heads with a cord of the century plant and their bodies daubed in stripes of the paste of the yellow annatto and the black juice of the inaja palm.

The Indians marched without order or formation along the road that shortly before Don Cristóbal had taken, and in whose pursuit they were advancing. All spoke or shouted, producing a devilish racket. They had lost completely their fear of foreigners.

5

The first one who felt the Borinqueños draw near, in a
hostile manner, was the interpreter Juan González, who was
bringing up the rear. The astute translator immediately gave
the order to the *naborias* to stop, in order to investigate
what that noise was. And as he realized that what he with
his good sense presumed to be was true, several Indians
leaped upon him. He received two blows from their clubs,
which broke his skull and splattered him with blood.
Fortunately he did not lose consciousness; and kneeling
before the proud chieftain Guaybana, whom he had just
bespied, asked him to spare his life and offered to serve him
forever.

"Leave that scoundrel alone, do not kill him!" Guaybana
shouted, and turning arrogantly toward his followers, declared:

"Advance in search of Don Cristóbal and his party!"

The armed Indian host obeyed and ran along the
shortcut, giving out furious war cries. The *naborias* sacked
the baggage, which shortly before they had carried on their
shoulders, and then scattered in different directions.

As Juan González saw himself alone, he thanked God for
saving his life, attended as well as he could his head wounds,
and climbed a luxuriant tree to wait for nightfall to be able
to flee toward Caparra with greater certainty of salvation.
The good translator preferred to be more a good Sancho
than a Don Quixote, saving his humble skin at the cost of
honor. In spite of his misfortune, he deeply regretted not
being able to warn his master what the avalanche of
enemies going to meet him was like.

6

Don Cristóbal and his five friends walked with great caution, on the constant alert. From time to time the breeze brought to them dissonant voices and strange sounds, coming from the woods. They crossed paths with utmost care. A puff of wind carried more intelligible words to them. They were native cries. Soon they realized the Indians were drawing near in hostile fashion, and that there would be a *guasábara*, a fight.

The leader, in spite of his being at the vanguard, stopped and gave the cry of alarm. Don Cristóbal shouted to halt, and all turned toward the dissonant voices, their bucklers well in hand, and their swords drawn. Soon the flow of arrows warned them that the enemy was numerous and that the fight would be fierce and bloody.

"My friends," declared noble Don Cristóbal, "prepare to stab well. Though we are few, we will triumph. We must not separate for an instant. Keep your eyes open, your feet firm, and your arms always on guard, and let your blows fall right so that they are fatal. Keep your dagger in your left hand. And may God protect us."

"Saint James and Sotomayor," his friends cried.

"Saint James and Sotomayor," they repeated.

Like an overflowing torrent that surges forth, fed by constant rains, so fell the horde of Indians on the small Castilian party. The first natives who drew near died immediately. They rushed so against the Christians that they were unable to use their bows and arrows, for they were fighting man to man. Human blood stained everything with its reddish color. Sharp, angry cries shattered the air. Don Cristóbal and his friends in turn shouted stentorian cries of encouragement to counterarrest those of their enemy, and with each sure thrust went a violent curse. The small force turned agilely, right and left. The natives attacked the Castilians on all flanks with terrible clubbing. Clubs, split in two by swooping sword thrusts flew through the air. Little by little the confused cries of battle fell silent and the breathing grew heavier. The ground was covered with bodies everywhere. The natives were able to replace their fallen numbers, but not the Spaniards. The last of them to fall was the noble and valiant Don Cristóbal, with his helmet smashed and his sword broken, but still facing his adversaries. He tried in vain to reach proud Guaybana, for when he finally saw him and ran toward the native, to run him through with his sword, he tripped on a bush rope, at the same time receiving a clout on the head, which deprived him of life, and likewise another formidable, glancing blow which broke his sword.

Guaybana and his warriors withdrew to a nearby hill to rest from the fatigue of combat, bury their dead, and orient themselves in the campaign they were going to undertake against the Christians. The first to speak was the proud chief of Guaynía.

"Great Zemí is with us! For in truth, my *guaitiao* Don Cristóbal was a valiant man. He did not take one step backward. If we had been Caribe Indians, we would have drunk his blood to infuse his great valor in us. We must pay him the honors of a great warrior and bury him with the pomp corresponding to his category of a Spanish chief. You, Naiboa, go to Guacarí, the head *bohique* and let my orders be carried out."

When the *nitayno*, or lieutenant Naiboa, went with twenty Indians to get the cadaver of the unfortunate son of the Countess of Camiña, they found Guanina, washing her love's face, and in her insane delirium, trying to give him back life with her passionate kisses. The native procession returned, bearing the sad news to Guaybana that his sister Guanina had not let them touch Don Cristóbal's body.

"All right, Naiboa. The guardian Zemí would have wanted it that way. Respect Guanina's sorrow, my friends. Tomorrow she will be sacrificed on her lover's tomb in order to accompany him in the other life."

And the triumphant chieftain added, in a doleful voice:

"You, Guacarí, the *bohique*, you will lead the bloody rite."

The witch doctor stood up and marched with the acolytes in pursuit of the disconsolate victim and the body of the Christian captain, with the purpose of preparing the funeral ceremony for the following day.

When they reached the site of the tragedy, they found Guanina dead, her head resting on the embloodied chest of the Spanish nobleman.

7

The bodies of Don Cristóbal and Guanina were buried together at the foot of a giant silk-cotton tree. And upon this humble tomb, red wild poppies and sweet-smelling white lilies sprouted spontaneously—Nature herself offering on the altar of simple love, soul of the world, mysterious breeze, divine breath and eternal joy of pure souls.

When at eventide the purple light reddens the west, as though bathing it in blood, and the shadow of the giant silk-cotton tree, ancient and worm-eaten, covers a great extense of land, neighborhood farmers believe they hear on that hill sweet songs of love, with the soft murmuring of the leaves. Aware of the tradition that valiant Don Cristóbal de Sotomayor and the beautiful maiden Guanina were buried there, they believe that it is the souls of the young lovers, faithful to their intense love, who leave the tomb to contemplate the evening star and to kiss each other in the moonlight.

Notes

1. Don Cristóbal de Sotomayor, native of Galicia, the son of the Count and Countess of Camiña, came to Puerto Rico, accompanied by his cousin Don Luis, "with the seal of vicinity for San Juan for both of them and an order to Ponce (Don Juan Ponce de León, governor of the island) to share with each of them one chieftain with the respective number of slaves." He was a Spanish noble of quality, who, according to the chronicler Ovando, had been secretary to King Philip the Fair. Proof of it is the distinction with which Ferdinand the Catholic king mentions him in the royal cedulas sent to the Governor of San Juan, where it was recommended to him "to help and maintain Don Cristóbal in the graces granted to him as well as to his brother Diego's son, who accompanied him." He was named principal justice by Ponce de León, having in his charge administration of justice in the colony.

Don Cristóbal de Sotomayor, with the authorization of Ponce de León, established a town in the neighborhood of the port of Guánica, and he was the initiator of horse breeding on our island. He carried out searches for gold throughout the region, toward present-day Mayagüez, whose plains were called Yagüeca. The residents of Guánica being plagued by the mosquitos emanating from the lagoon, Don Cristóbal de Sotomayor moved the town to the port of Aguada and gave it his name, that is, Sotomayor. Don Cristóbal de Sotomayor, along with Ponce de León, had well-deserved influence, he being the one who recommended imprisoning Juan Cerón and Miguel Díaz when they were named by Diego Columbus governor and chief justice, respectively, of the island, and came forth to take possession of their charges.

The event that the legend relates is rigorously historical. The chieftain Guaybana, in agreement with the other leaders of the island, initiated a general uprising against the Spaniards with the killing of Don Cristóbal de Sotomayor.

2. Name of the main chieftain of Puerto Rico, when Juan Ponce de León visited the island in 1508. The historian, Friar Iñigo Abbad, erroneously calls him "Agüeynaba." He was the uncle of another chieftain, Guaybana, named in the legend as Guanina's brother. The historians Oviedo and Herrera call these two chieftains brothers; and the famous Puerto Rican historian Don Salvador Brau calls them both by the name of Guaybana, an error that Dr. Cayetano Coll y Toste, author of the *Legends*, rectifies on page 100 of Volume IX of the *Historical Bulletin of Puerto Rico*.

3. In Indo-Antillean language this word means "friend" or "confederate."

4. This Spaniard, who served as interpreter for Don Cristóbal de Sotomayor, had familiarized himself with native life to the extreme that he painted himself as they did and partook in their festivities. He heard the plan for rebellion discussed and approved in a public assembly of the Indians, as well as the recommendation to Guarionex as chieftain of the Otoao (whence the present-day Utuado), with the phalanx of escapees that wandered through the northwest mountain range, to attack the town. In accordance with the story line of the legend, Salvador Brau recounts in his *History of the Colonization of Puerto Rico*, that when González, scurrying through the woods, took the path back to the farm, desirous of communicating to his chief the terrible news, the Indians had already reached the height of epileptic frenzy in the war dance with which they celebrated these functions.

III. THE EARTHLY PARADISE

"I am convinced this is the spot of the earthly paradise," Columbus wrote of the Caribbean. Of all the islands Borinquen "surpassed all others in beauty," thought the ship physician, Dr. Chanca, when the second expedition landed there, in 1493. Coming from the arid and stark hills of Spain, the lush greenery, flowering trees, and azure beaches seemed indeed a tropical paradise. For four centuries—the sixteenth, seventeenth, eighteenth, and nineteenth—the realistic fantasy beguiled priest, soldier, and poet alike, as these Romantic writings attest. Fray Damián López de Haro (1581–1648) was a bishop of Puerto Rico; his "Sonnet," in a letter to his friend Juan Díaz de la Calle, revealed another theme of fascination to the Spaniards—the easy and good-humored pace of life, so sweetly tropical. A soldier of fortune and adventurer, Juan Rodríguez Calderón (1775–1839), was exiled to the island, after deserting from the Spanish Army; his "To the Beautiful and Felicitous Island of San Juan de Puerto Rico" began a tradition of nature poetry— "Puerto Rico is eternal spring." The poet Santiago Vidarte (1827–1848), one of the early Romanticists of the nineteenth century, evolved these pastoral themes into patriotic ones, in his poems, included in *The Puerto Rican Album* and *The Song Book of Borinquen*, from which "Insomnio" has been taken. Luis Lloréns Torres (1878–1944), the bard of Modernism, revives the earthly paradise in his poetry, from which "Vida Criolla" is a selection. (Translated by José Nieto.)

SONNET

by Damián López de Haro
(Dedicated to a lady from Santo Domingo who wanted
to know about San Juan)

My Lady, this is a little island
lacking supplies and money,
the Blacks go about naked, as over there
and there are more people in the jail at Seville;

here are the scutcheons of Castille
in few houses, many cavaliers,
all dealers in ginger and hides,
the Mendozas, Guzmanes, and Padillas.

There is water in the cisterns if it has rained,
the Cathedral, few clergymen,
beautiful ladies lacking grace;

ambition and envy have been born here,
great heat and shade of the coconut trees,
and a little breeze is best of all.

TO THE BEAUTIFUL AND FELICITOUS ISLAND OF SAN JUAN de PUERTO RICO

by Juan Rodríguez Calderón

(*Selection*)

The most select coffee,
sugar, tobacco, and woods
of the most perfect texture,
the thrashing-floor always filled
with the most tasty rice,
the most beautiful corn,
this country offers the merchant
a well-known profit,
and the inhabitant enjoys
the reward of the work he has done.

Puerto Rico is
eternal spring, the climate you dispense;
and of the fierce season,
those dense snows—
those frigid ices—
that the heavens heap
on the land near the poles,
never were seen in You,
and thus your fields alone
deserved and merit
fame and glory.

In your land one sees no
fatal, death-bearing reptiles
whose poison contains
the saddest ills;

that on the continent
are the most imminent
danger to the peaceful ploughman,
who in all seasons
be it winter or summer
never can be wary enough.

All your inhabitants
that joy never abandons,
for the means and the ways
are daily more than enough
to make it never end;
they are of a mild temperament,
honorable and peaceful; inclined
to treat the foreigner well;
in them the defects
that cause such harm are not visible.

INSOMNIO

by Santiago Vidarte

(*Selection*)

Awake now, my love, time advances,
and as the sun's gold disk rises
you will see emerging in the distance
a green giant full of metals—

You will see a fantasy of flowers
at its base, prideful with blooms,
where rich with light, love, and life
April exhibits its beauties.

And you will see, when our boat
fleeting, draws near,
a whitish proud rock
dozing in the arms of the sea.

Ah, what pleasure we shall enjoy there!
Desire kills me; each hour is a century,
how long that sun delays! my beloved, let us row,
for the glimmer of dawn already dims.

Let us row, yes, how beautiful dawn is!
How beautiful, is the sea
with its limpid blue, oh! inspired
I sing a song to the Americas.

But, no, be still, . . . do you see the distant
yellow light, the burning globe,
rising from the sea in a thousand mirrors?
For . . . it is he that rises in the Orient.

It is he, yes, yes: that's it, my dove,
it is the Sun. Don't you see that shining giant
who luminously rises from the water?
That giant's name is—*Luquillo!*

And do you see there, beside its shadowy base
that fantastic garden rich in flora,
where April lives, my beloved siren?
For the garden is named—*Puerto Rico!*

The port is near. Do you see that rock
resting in the arms of the sea,
draped in castles, rich and beautiful? . . .
It is . . . Power of God, I am just dreaming! . . .

VIDA CRIOLLA

by Luis Lloréns Torres

Oh, how pretty looks my hovel
and how joyful my palm forest
how fresh the banana plants
on the little river brink.

How exquisite to feel cool
and to smoke a good cigar;
what happiness not to know
about letters and the stars,
and how delightful my woman
when she allows to be loved!

▼▲▼▲▼▲▼▲▼▲▼▲▼▲▼▲▼▲▼

IV. THE JÍBARO

In the mid-nineteenth century a cohesive national consciousness developed in the colony, which led to revolts and demands for independence from Spain. The *jíbaro*, the rural villager and country man, who was neither a peasant in the feudal sense nor landless in the modern sense, symbolized the emergence of "the most intimate, resistant and pure of Puerto Rican nationality," noted a contemporary writer. Pedreira, the critic, has said that the word *jíbaro* appeared in print for the first time in 1814. Then, in 1849, Manuel A. Alonso (1822–1889), born in San Juan, published, while a medical student in Barcelona, his book of sketches, *El Jíbaro*, "the first major effort by a Puerto Rican" (Wagenheim) to depict that national character. His poems "The Puerto Rican" and "A *Jíbaro* Wedding" reflect the "free and arrogant" nature of the *jíbaro*, "yearning for illusions," while remaining at the same time a realistic man of the earth.

THE PUERTO RICAN

by Manuel A. Alonso
(Sonnet—dedicated to my dear friend Don Pablo Sáez)

Dark in color, the forehead clear,
the glance languid, proud and penetrating,
the beard black, the face pale,
lean and austere, the nose well-proportioned,

medium build, rhythmic step,
the soul yearning for illusions,
sharp wit, free and arrogant,
preoccupied thought, fiery mind,

human, affable, just, generous,
in matters of love always variable,
ever seeking after glory and pleasure,

and in love for his country insuperable:
this is, without a doubt, a faithful portrait
to depict a good Puerto Rican.

A JÍBARO WEDDING

by Manuel A. Alonso

1

The gray kingbird was singing
in the top of a silk-cotton tree,
when some thirty persons
all of them dressed for the occasion
came. out of a house,
or rather, from under it.
All went on horseback
(or at least on an old mare).
The men wearing shoes
and almost all with jackets,
some wearing a handkerchief
tied on their heads,
and a hat of black nap,
woven cloth or braided palm leaves,
starched shirts,
taffeta trousers;
the women wore bonnets
of nap with black plumes,
gloves of woven cotton,
and some, silk shirts;
shoes of Morocco leather
and stunning finger rings,
those worth a few coppers
that shine like stones;

Small and large kerchiefs
of all sizes and shapes,

and little finger rings and earrings,
and gold necklaces and chains.
Every one to the last man
his animal well saddled,
some with silver bits
and bridles of different colors,
others with halters, and others
with their reins of leather straps.
Saddle-clothes, cushions,
harnesses, and baskets
were spanking new
and made for that fiesta,
which was the wedding of Pedro,
son of Guajón Iglesias,
to Gilia, the very well-kept
daughter of Tonio Rivera,
and on that day they were getting married
with the greatest of love.
The bride from time to time
saw the bridegroom in such wise
she said to him clearly:
Pedro, this jewel is yours.
And he let out a roar
of pleasure on seeing his woman,
for he would not have changed places
with the Sursum Corda even if such was
    requested;
the sun was already a yard
off the ground in the sky,
when through the midst of Barrero
they headed toward the church;

Having already dismounted
at the house of a relative.

They arrived, and the priest, who
was waiting for them at the door,
married them and said Mass,
altogether in a hurry;
but on leaving they found
the clothing shops and groceries
and taverns and huts all open,
and the lads, cigar smokers,
and youths and the old women.
The whole town waiting
for the newlyweds to come out.
Good God! What a hubbub
when they came out,
of wooden rattles and horns,
and with sticks and rocks
striking on the shop counters
or hitting the doors!
One cried out: "Get on,
ox, turn around and mosey on";
another: "Look, catch
that wild heifer."
And so quite harassed
they went to get the mounts
and left Barrero
on the road to Aguabuena.

2

There the guests
were more than sixty,
and the musicians, who as soon as
the newcomers had arrived
without waiting for formalities

and gifts to be exchanged,
grabbing their instruments
played some dances, called *caenas*
and the dancing lasted, hot
and furious, till lunchtime.
The in-laws and the godparents
sat down with the newlyweds
at the table; the rest of them
as best they could
squatting or in the hammocks.
Standing, and on the stairs.
The meat and rice dishes were not lacking.
With coconut and good milk,
nor were lacking yam crullers
nor candied orange preserve
nor rum and anisette,
nor wine and gin.
After filling their gizzards
the legs began to move again
till the hour for supper;
and once the supper was finished
with more desire than before
everyone danced and danced.
The sun found them dancing
without anyone giving up:
then they said good-bye
and here's where the fiesta ended.
Of what happened afterward
the newlyweds will give account.

▼A▼A▼A▼A▼A▼A▼A▼A▼A▼A▼A▼A▼A

V. EUGENIO MARÍA de HOSTOS: "CITIZEN OF AMERICA"

As a colony, Puerto Rico suffered two burdens of the declining Spanish Empire. It was the refuge for the monarchists and slave owners fleeing the armies of Bolívar, in the 1820s, and it was tortured by a succession of brutal and corrupt military governors, from Spain, who subjected the island to a century of repression, from the *Bando Negro* (Black Edict) to the *Ley de la Libreta* (Passbook Law). Eugenio María de Hostos (1839–1903) cajoled, lectured, and fought for half a century against these colonial regimes, and the slavery and repression they enforced. He was a philosopher and teacher, lawyer and writer, a man with "the face of an ascetic—sunken cheeks, swarthy skin, unfathomable gaze and Biblical beard," who toured America seeking to enlist the support of nations and heads of state, for Puerto Rico's independence. In exile, where he lived most of his adult life, he wrote endlessly on sociological and political themes. The Chekhovian essay, "On a Paper Boat," has the loving and haunting quality of patriotism he evoked, and which has endeared his writings to generations of Puerto Ricans, as is reflected in Margot Arce de Vázquez's (1904–) tribute to him, "Hostos, Exemplary Patriot" (*Impressions*, San Juan, 1950).

ON A PAPER BOAT

by Eugenio María de Hostos
(To Angela Rosa Silva, in repayment of an article of
hers that I inadvertently tore up)

1

On entering my house, to rest from my daily labor, I heard with a somewhat negligent ear they were recommending I read a literary article, "very well written," which they had expressly left on my reading table.

I had just sat down at it when the youngest victim of my fatherly extremities opened the door to my sitting room, sat on my lap, bribed me with a kiss, and asked for a paper boat.

I extended my arm, took the first printed paper I had at my reach, tore off a piece, took out a pair of scissors that, for this and other indulgent father's tasks, I always carry in my small pocket, and cut out as best I could a little square. I first folded it in a straight line; then at angles; then in very symmetrical borders; then the center to the edge; then from inside out; and taking it gloriously and showing it victoriously to the very attractive briber: "There," I declared, "a kiss or no boat!" She gave me the kiss, I gave her the boat.

2

And, what a boat! When we cast it into the sea in the washbasin filled with water and made waves with our fingers, you should have seen how the boat tossed: it luffed and sailed by; and now with the wind from our breath astern, now with a furious sea astern, which we produced by agitating the water, it rocked gallantly, or shook from stem to stern, or threatened to sink on us.

3

Not being enough to simulate so many things at the same time, winds from the four directions, shakings, waverings, oars, sails, captain, helmsman, and crew, we went out into the breeze on the balcony, which it occurred to her to open up, and set ourselves at a distance to view from afar our embarcation, bringing about the agreement of reality and fantasy (ah! the poor things . . . ! They live so disconnected in the world. . . .), the boat seen being reality, the tender farewells we directed to the imaginary crew the fantasy.

4

Already, without knowing it, we were many for the moment of farewell: first of all, the inseparable companion in roguery; then, hugging in continued embrace mother and favorite daughter; behind, pushing to get ahead, the two most devilish hot-livered individuals that the Antillean sea had injected into the hearts and minds of children. Only one person was missing: one who is on the road to the future, which is a very bitter road, very much uphill, without horizon, lightless especially in South America. And we sighed.

5

And there the boat sailed through the washbasin sea buffeted by the balcony winds, disappearing no doubt on the high sea because we hardly saw a part of it. A fixed point that is viewed is a magnet that is put at attention, sentiment, or desire. We hung from that point in such wise, that in effect we were witnessing the ever-growing distance of the boat.

"And where will it go?" there rose a voice.

"And what will it be called?" rose another.

"I want it to be called what it seems."

"And what is that?"

"A sea gull."

"Well, I want it to be called *Cuba Libre* (*Free Cuba*)."

"Silence! . . . The name of the victim is not uttered in the accomplices' house."

"True! 'Cuba Libre' sounds like 'Crete' in northern Europe."

It was already decided: it was called *The Seagull*, and it was sailing toward free Cuba.

There then arose a loud cry of joy that ended in a revel of enthusiasm. Everyone wanted to embark for Cuba.

The truth of the matter is that, in the distance as it was, and from the dark shadow, closed sky, icy atmosphere, desert solitude, from where we were watching it, the shining ship, completely bathed in sunlight, upheld on an open sea, sailing toward the light, was a temptation.

We were already almost on board when a slam of the door destroyed the sea, the boat, and our intentions of embarking.

Once, walking along one of those coasts, from afar we had seen something like a black skeleton abandoned on the shore of the sea. On drawing near, what a sad thing! We all felt sorry; it was the skeleton of a ship, it was the witness of a shipwreck.

The sadness of imagining the dire straits of the shipwrecked victims was no more intimate than that felt now, on seeing the wreck of the paper boat.

The first who arrived on the scene of the catastrophe read aloud *The Seagull.*

"What's that? It had the name on the gunwale, like real schooners?"

"I think not, because this seems, by the folds, that it was on the keel."

"Let's see! . . ."

And carefully placing the wet paper on the table, the speaker read, as though to herself: " 'The Seagull,' by Fer—"

And raising her head, concerned, she asked the little girl: "Where did you take this paper from?"

To which, shunning responsibility, the threatened girl replied: "It was Daddy."

And I, confused and frightened at the little one's fear, stammered an excuse: "I found it here."

"A fine thing you've done!"

And with a peal of laughter on seeing my face of an honorable delinquent, she exclaimed: "But, father, this was the literary article I recommended to you . . ."

" *'Et voilà comme / une femme abîme un homme,' "* I murmured, caressing my briber's hair, recalling a boulevard chanson in those times when Paris smiled at me.

"And what are we going to do?"

"What are we to do! Continue the trip," I declared with my honorable conviction, and defending the right that my accomplice had to continue the game.

"But if there is no more schooner . . ."

"But here is paper . . ."

Boy, was there a shout! I had no alternative but to drop the paper I had picked up, when I heard:

"No! No! That's the piece remaining of R's article!"

"Well, then."

And I found myself face to face with that intimate fool we all find in the first fold of our second frontal circumvolution each time we do not know what we are to do.

Against the disoriented one . . . (What is man but an intimate fool who goes around disoriented by the world?)

I was saying that against the sublime, the disoriented person there is nothing like the only oriented one in this world, the child, who always knows what she wants to do, and who, then, wanting a new boat, was looking at me with sparks in her eyes . . . (because it was she and he, the little ones). At a hundred sparks per eye, that was four hundred electric sparks, which would have been able to put into motion the whole East, let alone a disoriented man.

And when, the paper torn and another boat made and another sea emptied, we again sailed in the washbasin with our imagination, and the girl friend of the lady who wrote the article asked me: "And what are we going to do?"

"Tell her," I replied, "that just as there is no return to the homeland as that which is taken in an imaginary boat, in a paper boat, in a dream of people awake, with the sails of desire, with the steam of imagination, with the pumping of the heart, through the sea of hope, under the sky of charity, under the wing of innocence, thus there is no literary article or poetical composition or work of art that is not worth more in the region of the intangible than in the miserable region of the concrete."

HOSTOS, EXEMPLARY PATRIOT

by Margot Arce de Vázquez

The Atheneum of Puerto Rico tonight renders homage to Eugenio María de Hostos. In the series of acts organized with the motive of the centenary of the life of this patrician, spontaneous and free collaboration with youth has been lacking. But this absence is remedied today. In no moment has it seemed to me that the University Atheneum realized with greater fruition the goals for which it was created than in this moment of exaltation and respect for Hostos; on no occasion are students more worthy of bearing this name than on those occasions when they bow before the moral and intellectual superiority of a Puerto Rican patriot.

Don Fernando de los Ríos used to say that "one is not a student by the mere act of registering, nor by the act of attending a classroom, but by something more serious, more profound, and more personal: by a way of conduct before life." A way of conduct supposes, we add, an ideal; it supposes consciousness of one's own being, science, and responsibility. But no student, no man can reach this integration of his personality if he gets out of touch completely with his historical circumstances. One does not live on air; nor can one live, like Narcissus, feeding on his own image in an action that does not transcend the limits of the individual. Christian culture, which has formed all of us, is based on charity. Charity is first the love of God and then of mankind.

Each of us moves within historical circumstances to

which he is forced to pay attention. And the nearest and most demanding nucleus of each one's historical circumstances is the word. Before striking out toward the conquest of that which is international, universal, man must leave that piece of land where his life takes spacial and temporal reality. Charity begins at home, according to precise folk knowledge. Our first obligation is the knowledge and service of the homeland. But, first it is necessary to define what we understand by homeland. The word has been handled with much frivolity sometimes, with censurable bad intention other times, in unscrupulous oratory of party interests. The homeland is not an exclusively material object; nor is the sentiment of the homeland, that mawkish imitation which our blandness protests against when it is taken out of its daily routine, the comfortable posture of that which is familiar and known being forced to fit in a hostile atmosphere. If the homeland and the sentiment of the homeland were only that, it would be beneficial for the spirit to change homeland and shake up its indolence.

But the homeland is something more than the piece of land where one is born, and much more than the visible and tangible things that surround us from birth. The homeland is past, that is, tradition, patrimonial culture. The homeland is present, a work in evolution, a particular creation and collaboration of all its sons, rectification of the errors of the past, loving care of the received inheritance, active and constant enrichment of that heritage with the efforts of today. The homeland is also, and above all, future, aspiration toward a greater abundance, will power to transmit and perpetuate the inherited wealth, having increased it in the measure of our strength. Memories, traditions, experience, and customs of a human group, within a limited space of land, constitute the tangible wealth of a homeland. Its spiritual wealth is composed of the virtues that have characterized the social group as a tonic key of its collective moral conscience. The true homeland is above all this corpus of lasting values. We who think of it, feeling it, as an inescapable reality only desire that it persist adorned with those qualities. And when virtues are sullied or disappear, we deem it a categorical duty to work for its restoration or purification. No patriot would truly be one if he accepted a blemished homeland, if he remained indifferent before its degradation. The homeland, like a mother, must be loved pure, immaculate.

It is not enough to be a good patriot by following the law strictly, nor by establishing a family and procuring its spiritual and physical welfare. One must do more: one has to maintain those virtues alive, full of meaning; one must practice them and sharpen them with more and more delicate and exemplary shades of meaning. In every homeland, fortunately, there always live half a dozen men in whom those virtues are incarnate and produce rich fruit. These men become an example by their superior sensitivity and are recognized as guides and stimuli of action for their compatriots. These men are living symbols of the profound and eternal meaning of the homeland. It is the duty of the young, and especially of that perfect student, who according to Fernando de los Ríos, must possess a way of conduct before life, know, perpetuate, and emulate those moral heroes. Let his homage not be limited to words; let it be "an offering of labors and hopes," a hymn of love and work. In order to extol Don Fernando de los Ríos, the serious poet Antonio Machado commanded: "Sound, anvils; be still, bells; live, life goes on." And that continuity of fruitful life will always be the most beautiful crown on the tomb of a patriot.

Eugenio María de Hostos was a patriot, and also a symbol of the moral meaning of our homeland. Its most prominent virtues were incarnate in him, and in bringing them together he enriched them with his spiritual action and illuminated them with purer shades of light. Like a cutter, he knew how to cut the diamond's facets in order to achieve the greatest luminosity. The sentiment of the homeland was always the basis on which his acts were founded, acts that are, truly, love along with good reasons. In order to serve the homeland he formed himself in a severe discipline of science and conscience. And he devoted himself completely to the work of the moral expansion of Puerto Rico. This man, and so much a man, so conscious of human dignity, a man as strong as one of our ceibas, silk-cotton trees, as firm and passionate as the tropical winds, knew that the homeland, like men, can only be fulfilled in the tonic air of liberty. He lived and suffered calvary for the liberty of Puerto Rico. In no moment a vile consideration, a weakness of the flesh, a temptation of power and glory, separated him from his goal or weakened the intensity of his desires. On many occasions he went far from the homeland because they put obstacles before his actions or because he considered that he could carry them out more efficiently from afar. When he returned from forced or self-exile, faith in the reason of his yearning shone and cut like a sword. Constant sacrifice and self-abnegation lend austerity and genuine nobility to his moral figure. The name of Hostos is an emotion; it has the magic of shaking our spirit to its roots; his thought in constant creative acts, his deeds burning and clean as a mirror, his love for others, and his confidence in spiritual values constitute a valuable heritage for us Puerto Ricans.

Let Hostos be an example and mentor for university youth. The homeland was never so in need of the love of its sons, never were its virtues and its dignity more sullied. Let this youth rush to prompt remedy; let it imitate Hostos; let it devote itself like him to an impassioned labor; let it save Puerto Rico with deeds, without wasting itself on empty words; let it love liberty and exercise it with the dignity proper of men. Then and only then will it be worthy of pronouncing, without besmirching it, the prominent name of Eugenio María de Hostos.

VI. LA VIRGEN
de BORINQUEN

Dr. Ramón Emeterio Betances was the "Apostle of Puerto Rican Independence." He was the inspiration and foremost planner of the revolution of 1868 against Spain, at El Grito de Lares (The Cry of Lares), where the Republic of Puerto Rico was proclaimed. Betances was born in the rural town of Cabo Rojo, in 1827. He studied medicine in Toulouse and Paris, becoming one of the circle of Symbolist poets and bohemians that included Verlaine and Rimbaud. On returning to the island he became a national hero because of his selfless battle against the cholera epidemic of 1855. But he was exiled, soon after, because of his antislavery and nationalist ideas, and he died in exile in 1898.

While in Paris he became engaged to his young niece, María del Carmen Henri, daughter of his sister, Clara. One month before their wedding, on Good Friday, April 24, 1859, his beloved died in his arms, of typhus. *La Virgen de Borinquen* was his eulogy, not only to his love, but to his exiled self. In the hallucinations of this gothic romance, Betances was both "the doctor" and "the madman." (*La Virgen de Borinquen*, translated by Miquel Angel Santana, director of the French Department of the University of Puerto Rico, from the original French into Spanish; and translated from Spanish into English by Magali Soto and Stan Steiner.)

LA VIRGEN de BORINQUEN

by Ramón Emeterio Betances

We went then into a room where some men were sitting around a long table. Some rested their elbows on it and hid their foreheads and eyes behind their hands and their fingers twitched in their hair; others, looking at them, smiled mockingly; still others turned their backs to the table and mumbled between their teeth, without moving their lips, incomprehensible words. One of them, who was seated in the center of the assembly, suddenly got up. He was the true Christ figure with long hair. And extending his hands majestically, he said:

"This is my blood: Take it and drink it!"

"One of the most interesting of men is this man," said the doctor. "You will see, my countryman. If you question him skillfully he himself will tell you his story. Once I was his friend, but now he does not recognize me. At the same time he treats me with contempt, believing me incapable of helping him in his plans."

In one of the corners of the room, seated on the end of a bench, could be seen a thin man, tall, dark and austere, whose sunken eyes would just as soon flash a sinister glare, as reveal the most painful melancholy. Sometimes the end of his breathing was intertwined with a tearing sigh. He listened to himself as if hearing a strange voice. With his left hand, he convulsively squeezed his right arm above the wrist so strongly that, in spite of his bronzed skin, a white and red mark became easily visible on the squeezed flesh. He glanced about, and then fixed his sight on the floor.

When we approached him, he was sitting in this position. He stood up, abruptly, and facing me, stared into my eyes and began to question me, in an offhand manner.

"Are you Egyptian?"

"No," I answered, "but like yourself, I am a foreigner. What do you wish?"

"But surely you must come of the Egyptian race! What do you have to show me?"

"I come from the Antilles."

"Oh!" he exclaimed, taking a sweet and sad tone, "you undoubtedly have met her."

"Perhaps I will say yes, if you will be so kind as to describe her to me."

"Describe her to you? She had a good nature! . . . She was a gay young woman, loving and gentle, all bathed in modesty and ardent love, beautiful as the star and simple as the flower, sometimes thoughtful and serious. Cherished by infancy, loved by age, she possessed the joys of innocence and gave advice as if she were a wise person. Her words were treasures of an infinite goodness, and her deep, dazzling eyes revealed the thoughts of a great intelligence. Do you recognize her? Have you seen her?"

"She was," I answered respectfully, "Pure Reason and Reverent Love!"

"Yes," said the poor madman, deeply grieved.

"He was a sad and silent dreamer. He searched ardently, without rest, for her happiness. And he desired that the will of his betrothed be confused with his own; but he sought it too far from the country where love saw the light. He called her and she came to him smiling, in the lands where thick mists envelope the infinite splendors, and before he had ceased to call her 'Virgen de Borinquen.' One night, they found themselves together. As in a tomb!"

So poignantly did the madman say these melancholy words that I felt my eyes fill with tears. I turned my face. Until now he had spoken, always squeezing his right arm with his left hand, as if the hand and the arm had belonged to two separate bodies. At his last words, the hand and arm separated without any trembling. Then the man exclaimed:

"I have seen her cold like the water in the river! Green like the leaves on the edge! I felt the sigh of death! I lost my sad beloved virgin!"

At this moment he lifted his right hand to the sky. I saw the doctor grow pale, looking at his friend, without being able to understand what fear terrified him. Suddenly the madman stared at his hand; he saw it free, and smiling he hit the side of his heart and fell to the floor as if injured by lightning.

"He believes he has a dagger that strikes him irresistibly each time he frees it," the doctor said, his compassionate voice trembling. "I dread these strikes on his breast very much and would prefer that his right hand would waste away under the continuous pressure of his left hand."

At that moment he returned his hand to its habitual position. The madman, coming to, got up saying: "It is true! My work is not yet finished!"

"Listen," whispered the doctor; "he went mad after this."

"It is true," continued the madman, talking directly to me, undoubtedly amazed by my Creole appearance; "if it is

true that you are Egyptian, you will understand this story of
desolation and darkness and you will dedicate yourself as I
have to the study of the sciences that reveal the worlds
beyond."

An old woman with mummylike face had slipped into the
room and she sat before the madman. She laughed in a burst
of diabolic disbelief, then was instantly silent, glanced at the
Creole, impervious, and became immobile, as if nailed to
the spot, and her tiny eyes, denuded of lashes, gazed on
him, stilled.

"I found myself," he said, "in a room that measured
thirteen feet in all its dimensions. There were thirteen walls,
without any exits. And I found myself locked in this room by
that spirit—evil, blind, and destructive—who had killed my
betrothed with an evil eye and who was taking her to a
place where my thoughts were unable to reach. In that
room all was deep darkness, impenetrable and dismal night,
to the top of my longest hairs; gone was all bright light,
resplendent, luminous. In my prison of night, I was blinded
by the luminous atmosphere. Soaring birds, bats and crows,
dark like my prison, hovered over me; while on the white
ceiling horrible tarantulas pursued the black spiders, and
snakes, with round, immobile glassy eyes, and irresistibly
attracted the heavy and blind moles around which they
curled, and which hung down above me, with their infernal
hissing heads. In the darkness I could not see any part of my
body and if I lifted my hand to the light, the darkness rose
like a wave and covered even the tips of my extended
fingers. My efforts to escape this condition were in vain.
Later I felt the extension of my fingers shrivel, and they
sank into my hand and my hand vanished into my shortened
arm. In horror I turned my eyes away from these repugnant
things that I saw and turned my thoughts toward myself,
and looked inside of myself. Suddenly I felt myself seized by

an unyielding fear, a limitless cold took hold of me; my hairs curled on my head and waved as if they were in soapy water; I felt myself go backwards; and as I was sinking, the cold penetrated my body to a deeper and deeper degree; I suffocated it when it reached my heart. Oh, what anxiety! Then it rose toward my brain, which froze. So it was that I saw my skull bone unskinned; the vault of my cranium opened and closed with a loud noise, and the wind blew frighteningly, followed by the sound of dry leaves dragging their bodies on the dry earth. The wind blew upward and I saw an infinity of squares of white paper irregularly cut, each carrying an inscription, flutter among the frightening bats and crows. All my ideas had escaped from my brain, like birds from their nests! Each one of them was inscribed on one of the sheets of flying paper. I was stunned. . . . Little by little all became silent again and the white papers were saturated with strong vapors emitted by the darkness and again fell to the floor of my room. Then, the vertigo possessed me. I wished to gather up and bring together my ideas. As soon as each paper fell, I ran toward it; I searched for it groping on the floor, and if I found it I would take it between my hands, and my middle finger made the light. I wanted to reach each thought. The dark atmosphere enveloped my whole body, but the paper surpassed it and remained in the light. Once again I was about to take possession of my lost ideas, when a bat, passing, gave a sharp cry, touched the paper with its wing and made it fall. I went to pick it up, but a crow charged toward it with a tremendous croak and grabbed it from me with its beak. While a spider attached by an invisible thread fell as fast as a stone, and quickly ran over the dark floor, and took the paper, and ascending, tangled and wrinkled it between its legs, while a snake attached to the ceiling with the three points of its tongue, hung and balanced its body and twisted in the air, whipping its tail so terribly that the paper was stuck to it; and when, sometimes, the snake would touch my hand, I was left shivering from the cold. And yet I insistently went about my interminable task. My persistence in no way diminished the anger of my enemies. Their faces cold, insensitive, immutable, began to affect me. I felt myself bathed in cold sweat. My heart beat so quickly that I could not count its palpitations. I fell to the floor exhausted.

"The darkness and the day became one; the birds and the snakes threw themselves voraciously on the insects and moles and devoured them; then, throwing themselves against one another, they mangled each other, and from their wounds poured all their blood, and it was night; and as soon as the blood fell from them, drop by drop, it was transformed into the vapor of darkness, and vanished before my eyes; and my ideas were left in this chaos. So that, passing my hand before my eyes, I could distinguish nothing but a small, luminous spot and a still body, and I found myself beside the sacred corpse of my betrothed and a holy candle burned at the head of the Virgin of Borinquen.

"And it was she who had liberated me, and after my liberation, with her divine face hidden beneath a veil of tears, she disappeared . . . and I . . . I was left alone! Alone forever!"

I had listened to this account with all the interest inspired by a very deeply felt grief. The misfortune of the betrothed young woman about to enjoy so much love, and she herself loving with a sublime devotion; the emotion of the lover telling his dream, the death of these two spirits, were strong enough motives to arouse emotion in a sensitive heart. Along with this, there came another scene that left me in the deepest sadness.

"And now," the madman went on, tensely, "do you have something to teach me? This dagger that you see in my hand is ready. I would let it go, but I still have to find the world that She inhabits. If I let go of this hand, I will die without seeing the Spirit I seek, and to profoundly study these sciences that I cannot allow to remain chained. And so I ask all who pass: Do you have something to teach me? Let me drown in all your wisdom!

"And it has been said," he went on, "that other men have discovered impenetrable worlds and have communicated with powers possessed by all life and all science. I will do the same for her!" he said, as a proud lover.

"Lis-ten! Lis-ten!" murmured the old woman, pointing to the Creole as she withdrew. "Oh! Oh! Oh! Not everyone is permitted to go to Corinth."

The young man's eyes became fiery and he was imprisoned by a convulsive trembling and exclaimed: "Sibyl of desperation, be damned!" And he fell dead suddenly.

The Christ came to kneel near him, and praying, murmured: "It has come to pass because they loved each other greatly."

VII. THE CRY OF LARES

Lares is the *santuario de la patria* (sanctuary of the nation). It is, like the Bastille and Bunker Hill, a symbol of the fight for liberty—perhaps more intensely so, certainly more poignantly so, for it is the symbol of a revolution that was defeated. So, in each generation the poets and politicians have revived that symbol, using it to express their own ideas and hopes. Luis Lloréns Torres (1878–1944), essayist and poet, did so in his historical drama, *El Grito de Lares* (*The Cry of Lares*) (1914), evoking not only the revolutionaries' dreams, but his own concept of an Antillean Federation, "the union of America for the freedom of America." In political defeat, Lares lives forever as literature.

In his poem to Bolívar, the Liberator is exalted by Lloréns Torres as a symbol of the Latin American revolutions represented by the Lares uprising in the history of Puerto Rico. (The poem *Bolívar* has been translated by José Nieto.)

THE CRY OF LARES

by Luis Lloréns Torres

Scene VII

DON CHEO *and* DON AURELIO *are both sitting down.*

DON CHEO: So, once more.

DON AURELIO: Again. And what's new? How are things?

DON CHEO: Vegetating. We only vegetate. Before, at least, one conspired. . . . Today one emotion, to-morrow another. Now, the most unbearable monotony.

DON AURELIO: Are there no longer secret societies? Nothing is plotted?

DON CHEO: If there are, I'm not aware. You already know you never had full confidence in me. Who doesn't see that! My relationship with Frasquito. . . . And less now that he's married to Carmela. Haven't you seen any of those from the rebellion around here?

DON AURELIO: I did see Mediavilla and Camuñas.

DON CHEO: They're still together. Mediavilla thinks he's

still the mayor, and Camuñas hasn't been able
to forget the secretary's office.

Don Aurelio: They had a good fright that night.

Don Cheo: Of course, since you had them for a few hours
in the stocks.

Don Aurelio: I myself in person was the one who set
them free the next day. Not only them; all the
Spaniards who were captives. No one can deny
we behaved well. Of course, there was the
tumult and the damages that always happen
when the wave crest rises; but lives and
property were respected. . . .

Don Cheo: That was what was most influential afterwards
for the pardon.

Don Aurelio: I heard something there in Santo Domingo.

Don Cheo: And to what secret society did you belong?

Don Aurelio: The one in Pezuela district. The chief was
the Venezuelan Don Manuel Rojas.

Don Cheo: The one who led the uprising.

Don Aurelio: It was in his place that we met to fall upon
the town from there. There were many secret
societies conspiring on the whole island. And
the plan was the general uprising on the
twenty-ninth of September. I tell you that if
things hadn't gone awry on us, the island
would now be free.

Don Cheo: I'm aware of almost everything, but continue,
tell me; there's nobody better informed than
you.

Don Aurelio: On account of the jailing of one of the
conspirators we thought that everything had
been discovered; and on the twenty-second a
meeting was held in the house of the Yankee,
Mr. Brookman.

DON CHEO: Yes. . . . That Yankee!

DON AURELIO: At his farm it was decided to push things up, and from there many left who met at Rojas' farm on the twenty-third. The rest you already know as well as I. The rebellion failed after the Pepino skirmish.

DON CHEO: It failed for lack of organization.

DON AURELIO: More than that, the failure was due to the lack of response from the rest of the towns.

DON CHEO: That has to be understood, since the twenty-ninth had been decided upon . . .

DON AURELIO: In Ponce and Humacao, for example, they finally caught on when everything was already suffocated.

DON CHEO: It is useless. When things are going to turn out bad, there's no one who can straighten them out.

DON AURELIO: And what became of the Yankee? I read something about the rest of them in the papers regarding the trial.

DON CHEO: Don't recall the trial. It scares one. They brought court clerks from as far as Ponce. You only have to think of the numbers. More than five hundred persons indicted, and the transcripts more than ten thousand pages. Suffice it to say that they named the Biscayan Navascués chief judge. I've never seen a stupider lawyer. He mixed up and confused everything. A lunatic who saw a river where there was a mountain, and vice versa.

DON AURELIO: He probably confused everything.

DON CHEO: Even the government was finally convinced that he is slow-witted, and he is over there in

Spain, cast off in heaven knows what little town.

DON AURELIO: In what I read in the Santo Domingo papers no mention whatsoever was made of the leader Parrilla or of Mr. Brookman.

DON CHEO: You don't know what happened?

DON AURELIO: Not at all. That's why I'm asking.

DON CHEO: Once the rebellion failed and the leaders were discovered, the latter's only road open was to go into the woods, forming small bands that were dissolved little by little, pursued by the Spanish army. Only a picket of soldiers found Parrilla, and shouting at him to surrender, he answered them, "Parrilla isn't a man to surrender," and he died right there fighting against all of them. The Yankee Mr. Brookman was also very brave. He was sleeping one night in a shack, accompanied by the Dominican Baldomero Bauren, when they were surprised by the troops. Neither did they surrender. Both of them, the Yankee and the Dominican, grabbed their arms and alone fought against the picket of soldiers. And both died there. I could mention several other Puerto Ricans like them, who died in the same manner.

DON AURELIO: There's no doubt there were people with push at the head of that rebellion.

DON CHEO: The examples seen later confirmed it. They all behaved like brave patriots. The directors from the capital were the ones who gave no signs of life anywhere.

DON AURELIO: Hence their insistence on minimizing the importance of and even on ridiculing the patriotism of those men. "It was ridiculous," they declare. And they broadcast it so much that I fear those poor martyrs, the first and perhaps the last of our country, are going to pass into history as a bunch of fools. They, who gave all, the tranquility of their homes, the worldly wealth they possessed, and even their lives for the freedom of this land. They failed? What does failure matter?

DON CHEO: You speak like a patriot. The fact itself of having taken up arms to free the country, exposing themselves to what they did, shows that they loved this land above all else. And perhaps, as you think, the future will not do them justice. Always, in all epochs, there will be men incapable of doing what they did.

DON AURELIO: And to justify themselves they will say that they were lunatics. Heaven knows what will be said of them! There are martyrs who are martyrs even after death!

DON CHEO: All that means that we have no fatherland. The island, small; the peasant, ignorant. Patriot, but ignorant. Even more, innocent. And the men from above, the illustrious, the directors will always be what they are today: a group of shouters, clamorers, but not patriots. They'll grab hold of anything, this or that reform, any second-class ideal, to feign that they're doing something. But the essential, fundamental thing, trying to make a fatherland, like those from Lares tried to do, that . . . they'll never do. It's sad and discouraging; but it's the truth. There is no redemption! There will never be!

DON AURELIO: There's no redemption. That is the sentence. Look here now, Manolo el Leñero, that boy who waved a flag for the first time in our land and with his bloody arm continued waving it and crying "Long live liberty," who remembers that hero now? Perhaps some town rhymester. And isn't it sad that a man gives everything to his people, and that his people aren't even aware, because there are no patriots to erect his statue, nor historians to reveal his feat, nor poets to sing of his heroism? Where is this so-called Puerto Rican patriotism? for I do not find it.

DON CHEO: And the sad fact is, Don Aurelio, that so much misfortune does not depend nor will ever depend on us Puerto Ricans. If it were in our hands, don't you think there would be thousands of Puerto Ricans ready to forge the fatherland? Believe it. The same as you and I, Puerto Ricans think and feel; but neither we, nor anyone, do anything, nor will anything ever be done. Because we are convinced that it is all impossible. What a tragedy! To be strong and generous and brave, like the Cubans, Dominicans and Venezuelans; love our fatherland, as they love theirs; desire like them to have a homeland to defend and make it great . . . and being unable! Not being able! We have, like all men of the earth, a brain to think and a heart to love. But the rest of the men of the earth have a homeland; we Puerto Ricans do not have one, we'll never have one. . . . Don't you think this cruel impotence? . . . Don Aurelio, let's speak no more, for it's the only thing that moves me in life. Life! A clown, yes, but a clown who at times has grimaces and somersaults of tragedy.

DON AURELIO: And are you not consoled in thinking that the leaders of that movement were not only Puerto Ricans? A Venezuelan, a Yankee, and a Dominican died there, too.

DON CHEO: That may mean, perhaps, a lot more in the future.

DON AURELIO: It may symbolize, in the future, the union of America for the freedom of America.

DON CHEO: Such a symbol may console us. Because Puerto Rico is small; but . . . America is big.

DON AURELIO: And apart from that idea, the plan of the Puerto Rican rebels, Puerto Ricans, in accord with the Cubans and Dominicans, was the confederation of the three Antilles.

DON CHEO: Which would be one of the first-rate republics of America.

BOLÍVAR

by Luis Lloréns Torres

Politician, soldier, hero, orator, and poet.
Great in everything. Like the lands liberated by him.
By him, that was not born the son of any fatherland,
But many fatherlands were daughters born to him.

He had the courage of a sword bearer
He had the courtesy of a flower bearer
And entering the palaces, he threw away the sword,
And entering the battle, he threw away the flower.

The peaks of the Andes, in his eyes, were nothing more
    than exclamation marks of his audacity.
He was a soldier-poet. A poet-soldier.
And each liberated country
Was a heroic feat by the poet
And a poem by the soldier.

And he was crucified.

VIII. LA BORINQUEÑA

It was fitting that the revolutionary lyrics of the national anthem of Puerto Rico, *La Borinqueña*, be written by Lola Rodríguez de Tió (1843–1924). Ever since the days of the Indians, when a woman, Loísa, was *cacique* of the village that now bears her name, women have been among the leaders of most literary and political movements. Lola Rodríguez de Tió was a poetic and political revolutionary; a friend of Hostos, she, too, spent much of her life exiled from the island. Living in New York, she was honorary president of the political club Ruis Rivera, where she worked with José Martí in helping plan the Cuban revolution of 1895. Her books, *My Songs, Clarities and Mists, My Book of Cuba,* and *Return to My Hills,* from which poems like "The Song of Borinquen," and "To Blanca María" and the often quoted "Cuba and Puerto Rico" (translated by José Nieto) are taken, caused Rubén Darío to call her "Daughter of the Isles."

THE SONG OF BORINQUEN

by Lola Rodríguez de Tió

Awake, Borinqueños,
for they've given the signal!

Awake from your sleep
for it's time to fight!

Come! The sound of cannon
will be dear to us.

At that patriotic clamor
doesn't your heart burn?

Look! The Cuban will soon be free,
the machete will give him freedom.

The drum of war announces in its beating
that the thicket is the place, the meeting place!

Most beautiful Borinquen, we have to follow Cuba;
you have brave sons who want to fight!

Let us no more seem fearful!
Let us no more, timid, permit our enslavement!

We want to be free already
and our machete is well sharpened!

Why should we, then, remain so asleep
and deaf, asleep and deaf to that signal?

There's no need to fear, Ricans, the sound of cannon,
for saving the homeland is the duty of the heart!

We want no more despots! Let the tyrant fall!
Women, likewise wild, will know how to fight!

We want freedom and our machete will give it to us!

Let's go, Puerto Ricans, let's go already,
for LIBERTY is waiting, ever so anxious!

TO BLANCA MARÍA

by Lola Rodríguez de Tió

Do you know, Blanca María,
why we have no homeland,
and there are only sad memories
in our land in mourning?

Do you know why Borinquen
the new slave Poland
bends her head and hides
the deep pain that distresses her?

And why instead of inscriptions
of smiling hopes
she only displays epitaphs
and whited sepulchers?

Can you not guess? Well, listen
to what I write in this page
without dreaming like the poet
of stars and flames;

of banners that sustain
imaginary battles,
and continents and worlds
that neither begin nor end.

How is a country to be born
or a race to be raised
where hearts to give their sap
and blood are lacking?

How is the ideal of the homeland
to arise with life
on breathing the atmosphere
of an enslaved land?

Seeing her wandering children
resisting becoming outcasts,
watering with tears the road
of an unending exile!

You know now, Blanca María,
why we do not have a homeland
and why we called ourselves captives
of a hopeless pain.

Ay, the sad souls who dream,
after so long an exile,
of the river and the hills
where their childhood was spent!

Poor outcasts! In vain
they want to hang up their harps,
if the promised land
lies in the depths of the soul!

CUBA AND PUERTO RICO

by Lola Rodríguez de Tió

Cuba and Puerto Rico are
the two wings of a bird,
they receive flowers and bullets
on the very same heart.
What a lot if in the illusion
that glows red in a thousand tones,
Lola's muse dreams
with fervent fantasy
of making one single homeland
of this land and of mine.

THE HYMN OF PUERTO RICO

Notes by María Teresa Babín

The history of *La Borinqueña* is one of the most significant
aspects of the transformation that has taken place in the
inner life of Puerto Rican culture. Although, according to

the study published by Monserrate Deliz on the Puerto Rican anthem (*The Hymn of Puerto Rico*, Madrid, Grafispania, 1957), it is related to other songs of a similar rhythm in Peru, Brazil, Bolivia, Mexico, Cuba, and Haiti, *La Borinqueña* has always expressed the love for the homeland with a strong patriotic feeling. The melody of *La Bellísima Peruana* (*The Beautiful Peruvian*) and the Cuban song *Mi Amor* (*My Love*) are considered models for the Puerto Rican original version. The first lyrics, attributed to the Spanish tenor Félix Astol (1813–1901) and a guitarist, Francisco Ramírez (1844–1900), from the town of San Germán, were heard during the Christmas celebrations of the year 1867. These notable bohemian musicians popularized the first known version, called *La Almojábana:*

> Beautiful brunette,
> image of candor,
> from the Borinquen garden,
> pure and fragrant flower.

> Your presence enraptures
> every man who sees
> your gentle, friendly grace,
> your tiny and pretty foot.

> When you appear on your balcony
> the sunlight itself is eclipsed,
> the sunlight itself is eclipsed.

> Because your black eyes
> are two rays,
> and he who looks at them, beloved,
> feels his heart inflamed.

The birth of the song as national anthem came not long after. Lola Rodríguez de Tió wrote the poem for it, which became a cry for liberty in 1868 at the time of the revolution known in the history of Puerto Rico as the *Grito de Lares* (Cry of Lares) (see above, *The Song of Borinquen*, by Lola Rodríguez de Tió):

> Awake, Borinqueños,
> for they've given the signal!
>
> Awake from your sleep
> for it's time to fight!
>
> . . . . .

Thus the song of love became gradually a romantic chant to liberty and a symbol of patriotism. At a crucial moment of change, which came at the turn of the century—between 1898 and 1904—a third stage of the development of the lyrics was marked by a subtle, sentimental hymn written by Manuel Fernández Juncos (1846–1928). It has been perpetuated as *La Borinqueña*, known by all Puerto Ricans:

La tierra de Borinquen	The land of Borinquen,
donde he nacido yo	where I was born,
es un jardín florido	is a garden full of flowers
de mágico primor.	with magic charm.
Un cielo siempre nítido	A sky always blue
le sirve de dosel	is the canopy over it,
y dan arrullos plácidos	and sweet lullabies
las olas a sus pies.	sing the waves at its feet.
Cuando a sus playas llegó Colón	When on its shores Columbus arrived,
exclamó lleno de admiración:	he cried, seized with admiration:
¡Oh! ¡Oh! ¡Oh!	Oh! Oh! Oh!

Esta es la linda tierra
que busco yo;
es Borinquen la hija,
la hija del mar y el sol,
del mar y el sol.

This is the pretty land
I'm looking for;
Borinquen is the daughter,
born from the sea and the
sun,
the sea and the sun.

Poets and musicians have been inspired by the words and the rhythm of the original love song, and the voices of millions have been raised to honor the land of its birth with respect and devotion whenever *La Borinqueña*—considered a *danza* in traditional popular music—is played at public gatherings and official ceremonies. There are other lyrics of diverse character written by famous poets such as Luis Lloréns Torres and José de Diego. Francisco Amy (1837–1912), the author of *Bilingual Muse*, offered the following version in English, a very free interpretation of the same Fernández Juncos lyrics which had been included in the *Canciones Escolares* (*School Songs*; 1904):

How beautiful Borinquen,
my peerless native land,
thy verdant hills and valleys,
and palm encircled strand.

On thy fair bosom lovingly
the sun its radiance pours,
while murmuring waves with tenderness
caress thy sailing shore.

When thy rare beauty he first described,
with wonder thrilling, Columbus cried:
   Oh! Oh! Oh!
No land like thee, Borinquen,
the world does know;

I shall meet with no other,
no other wherever I go!

A melodic version by Ramón Collado, a "song without words," was adopted in 1952 as the official hymn of the "Estado Libre Asociado de Puerto Rico," known in English as the Commonwealth of Puerto Rico. Nevertheless, the persistence of patriotic sentiment attached to the other versions, and the popularity of the lyrics adopted at the beginning of the twentieth century, constitute the essence of the historical Puerto Rican national anthem.

▼▲▼▲▼▲▼▲▼▲▼▲

IX. THE ROMANTIC POETS

Romance is hope born of frustration, as love is the fulfillment of hope. So, in the mid-nineteenth century, the island's poets who were caught between the futile reality of colonialism and the futile hope of independence turned to Romanticism; influenced by the French pessimists (such as Baudelaire) and the American optimists (such as Whitman), they created an island idyll of love and death, the dichotomy of Romantic poetry, led by the exemplar of the mode, José Gautier Benítez (1851–1880)—who was paradoxically an infantry lieutenant in the Spanish Army. The quintessence of Puerto Rican lyrical poets, his Romanticism was the "most refined of the XIXth century," wrote one critic. From his single book, *Poesías*, the "Poem of Puerto Rico" and "Return" are taken. His contemporary, Francisco Álvarez Marrero (1847–1881), wrote of a more delicate, fragile, pastoral scene, as in "Madrigal," from his book *Flowers of a Broom Patch*. In the work of Pachín Marín (1863–1897), the lyrical and patriotic were strongly intertwined, ironically in "The Nightingale" and in "The Rag." José Mercado (1863–1911) died young, but unlike the others, Mercado, writing at the end of the Romantic era, when the political battles for independence were less symbolic and more actual, was a journalist and polemicist, as well; his "The Castilian Language" heralds the didactic "poetry of politics" that developed at the turn of the century with the invasion of the island by the United States Army. In Mercado, patriotism is not nostalgia, but reality.

POEM OF PUERTO RICO

by José Gautier Benítez

Borinquen! a name loving to the mind
as the memory of an intense love,
beautiful garden, flower of America,
America being the garden of the world.

A pearl the sea tears from its shell
in the graceful undulating waves,
heron asleep within the white foam
along the snowy edge of your shores.

You, who offer breezes to the seas,
in return for the kiss of the egret's
breath in your groves of palm trees.

You, who come to us amid the mists,
walking on extraordinary beaches
creating a fantasy city of foam
that the Undines sculpted, by chance.

. . . an enchanted garden
entranced by the waters of the tamed sea,
a swinging vase of flowers, between
the foam and coral, pearls and fragrance.
You, who in the afternoon lay down
upon the sea an ocean of color
of the setting sun, becoming
another ocean of floating fire.

You, who give breath to my life
and birth to spontaneous song
when inspiration in tumult
beats with feverish wings
upon the singer's forehead; hear my voice!

The sacred love within my breast
sketches a scene of pastoral peace;
for you, I cast love into the wind,
as your love enslaves the heart
of the Bard, so his heart is freed
by your love, that he returns to you.

In your fertile savanna is sugar,
a lake of honey waving in the wind,
the fragile foam of its stalks, swaying
like the white plumage of birds.

And the palm trembles in the air,
hiding in the dangling amphora
the pure water of its aerial fount.
And in the wide fold of your hills
where cedar and liana prevail,
the coffee tree is illuminated
by gentle garlands held in its limbed

crouch, bending to the ground
with carmine and emerald berries.

Yes! you have voluptuous nights
promising easy perfection of love
amid bowers of lilies and roses
where silver fountains murmur.

In the mountains turtle doves cry
with mimicry of plaintive sighs,
dove and troopials and mockingbirds
who nest in flowering lemon trees.

All is sensual and gentle in you,
sweet, peaceful, flattering, tender,
and your enchanted moral world
is born of the sweet influence
of your eternal island world.

No! you will be no prophetic ship
of war, armed, to defy the hurricane,
conquering the port, and dominating
waves and men, dauntless and brave;

but you will be a tranquil little boat
that at the nudge of perfumed breezes
rests in the ebb tide of the white shore:

for that, homeland, is your destiny,
to conquer liberty, science, and fortune,
not even a shred of your white clothes
left in the brambles beside the road.

If my name is to be wedded to your history,
to be the singer of your joy,

to be the herald of your glory;
may God permit me to see
fortune crown you with triumphs,
and may I have an unending life to love you!
and an immortal lyre to sing to you!

RETURN

by José Gautier Benítez

At last, heart, at last
come alive with hope,
for between carmine red clouds
the land may already be seen
upon the horizon.

Dawn in the east shines
breaking brown mists
and in the torrent-like light
stretches out along the wide forehead
of ever so green hills.

The thick fog slowly
clears from the sea;
the ship continues advancing,
and the land keeps rising
like Venus from the waves.

And there on the dark background
that its mountains give it,
under a beautiful, pure sky
enclosed in its white wall
my most lovely San Juan.

And though it be a beloved city
it encloses my affection,
with my exalted soul enthusiastic
I remember nothing
save seeing that land.

. . . . .

Homeland! garden of the sea,
pearl of the Antilles,
I feel like crying,
I feel like kissing
the sand of your shores!

Yours is the life that I breathe,
my inspiration is yours,
my thought is yours,
yours every sentiment
that is born in my heart.

No, luck matters not
if I must leave you,
for I aspire only to see you,
to the fortune of loving you
and the glory of singing your praise.

MADRIGAL

by Francisco Álvarez Marrero

Covetous Filena
of a snowy blossom, merrily
climbed a lemon tree,

when a licentious bee stung
the purest coral
of her bewitching lip.

In tears undone, after Lisardo,
who awaited her at the entrance of the wood,
ran the sad girl;
she showed the bulging lip to her love
and with graceful lament,
the unequaled Filena declared weeping,
"Ay, take out this dart!"

On the spot a kiss reverberated in the valley,
that Lisardo impressed on the injured lip
of his pure Filena:
prodigious remedy! for merrily,
with gracile frolic
I saw her quickly run with light foot
toward the shadowy wood,
and to the perceived enticement of her love
I heard her exclaim,
"Allow me to climb the lemon tree again!"

THE NIGHTINGALE

by Pachín Marín

1

I applaud the nightingale when at the hour
when dawn awakes lazily,
it pours out its trills, filled with mirth
like dawn its tears.

I applaud the nightingale at noon
for, from tree to tree when it jumps,
it burns, believing, on the altar of Phoebus
not incense, but wings. . . .

I applaud the nightingale, when in the evening
—its bride—it offers plaintive song,
and I applaud it also when at night
it intones a prayer. . . .

2

But if treacherous guest, through covetousness,
tears it from the woodland enclosure
to leave it a winged prisoner
within the hated cage;

the nightingale closes its bill,
sick, folds its dark wings,
and unable to break its chains,
dies in desperation. . . .

Then, oh! not only with applause
do I wave my hands,
but rather, I give form,
noble, unequaled, and proud, to this rash
    question:
"Why do not people enchained by tyranny
also learn to die of despair?"

THE RAG

by Pachín Marín

When a country does not have a flag,
a free flag to raise proudly,
pursuing its sovereign right
and patriotism, the gentle chimera,

if in the achievement of its entire glory it lacks
the strength of combat against the tyrant,
the proud dignity of the citizen,
or the instinctive bravery of the beast;

with enormous faith and singular bravery,
let it throw itself into the field of fecund honor,
take a rag, at random, pale or red,

and on staining it with blood the furious soul,
the miserable cloth will be seen transformed
into a rag that astonishes the whole world.

THE CASTILIAN LANGUAGE

by José Mercado

1

Virgin of Nazareth, sweet Mary,
Shelter the son of my love with your mercy.

Thus, with sad accent, that I still hear
vibrate in the depths of my soul,

holding me prisoner in her arms,
and my face bathed with her tears,
the unhappy martyr who gave me life
raised her prayer. And her beseeching
rose to heaven, draped in the apparel
of the harmonious Castilian tongue.

To civilize a new world,
Spain gave its blood and its culture.

Thus, with serious accent, which yet moves
my heart, sounded the words
of the noble old man who lent to my cradle
his decisive and caressing care,
and from the grave book of history
opened before me the immortal pages.
And that sentence the old man expressed
in the sonorous Castilian tongue.

2

Immortal tongue my grandparents spoke,
a sad bard sings of your beauty.

You remind me of the loving lullaby
of an unhappy mother; you evoke
the memory of my infancy; you revive
vague phantoms of my sunless childhood,
my hours of pleasure, which were short,
my hours of pain, which were long,
my titanic fight for life,
my brief triumphs, my vast defeats.

Immortal tongue, that my elders spoke,
there is no language as beautiful as you.

Through your energetic phrases I obtained
the beautiful concept of homeland,
and I know through you that God, supreme
     goodness,
pours his piety on men,
and on opening the immense book of history,
I learned that yours were the words
that Columbus pronounced, looking at the sky,
discovering the American lands.

Immortal tongue, language of Cervantes,
the native dweller of yesterday sings your glory.

You are an impetuous torrent. You plummet
and fall in a bedazzling cataract,
filling the space with sounds
and notes of fire, extinguished
with that vague mysterious rhythm
of a sigh of love. Sonorous and clear,
you express passion, and thought
through you takes on brilliant attire.

Immortal tongue, treasure of harmonies,
honor to you, sovereign of the world!

These are yours, the vibrant apostrophe
that wounds with the blade of sound,
and the sentence of celestial tenderness
with which the maiden forms her prayers,
and the melodic accent of the
beloved voice of the loved one,

she who carries sunlight in her eyes,
snow on her forehead, and scarlet on her lips.

Immortal tongue, my Borinquen land
is united forever to your existence.

The cannon roared, foreign soldiers
set here their bold foot,
and an inexorable law was fulfilled,
and Spain wept its great misfortune
with the same bitterness and sadness,
filled with bereavement and heartache,
that another great misfortune one day wept
the last Moorish king of Granada.

3

This knot, which force yesterday broke asunder,
tie it, my Castilian tongue.
Eternal messenger of harmony,
cross the immense sea that separates us
and carry from Latin America
to the nation that peoples our race
with the poor song of the sad bard
the fraternal kiss of our souls,
for a flag can be changed,
but never sentiments!

Ro...
"major... pragmatists ove...
pragmatists an...
ity? In those years... a prominent physician and... wrote a critic; Romanti...
tetralogy he titled *Chronicles of*... misery of rural...
novel, *La Charca* (*The Stagnant Pool*)... richness of (his) style...
he depicted the sloth and misery of... by Émile Zola; he attempted...
"naturalism à la Puerto Rico," ... of social ills in *Garduña* (*Mar*...
cism clothed by the "sensual richness... on a sugar plantation...
Zeno was inspired by Émile Zola; he attempted... dealing with comm...
portray a panorama of social ills in *Garduña* (*Mar*... and *Los Redentores* (*The Rede*...
(1896), dealing with life on a sugar plantation... the American reformers...
Negocio (*The Deal*) (1922), dealing with comm... this café scene has b...
life in the city; and *Los Redentores* (*The Rede*... no English translation...
(1925), dealing with the American reformers,
deemers, from which this café scene has b...
cerpted. There are no English translation...
monumental tetralogy.

THE REDEEMERS

by Manuel Zeno Gandía

The small café was aglow. The dense atmosphere, full of guffaws and wisecracks, was from time to time shaken by a whiplash of a piano that under the big hands of the player exhaled rhythms of popular *danzas* and popular songs. They supposed that was music. Frequently they played "La Borinqueña," a very melancholic sweet song that had taken root spiritually in the people of the colony. On other occasions they played roguish little airs that invited one to dance. That night they played one very frolicsome and rhythmical, while many present hummed the words that ran: "This little girl doesn't resign herself . . . resign . . ."

Some vulgar women, divided up in the corners, were flirting either with the already obtained clientele or with the newcomers. They were red with carmine, large painted eye sockets and lips of such a bright vermilion they seemed to bleed.

Pedro Piedra was playing orator. He took advantage of the opportunities to promulgate his ideas; the good doctrine, as he said. They always listened to him attentively; almost all those present showed signs of agreement with his conclusions, although later, in practice, they acted to the contrary.

Lucas and Sacristán were among his most convinced listeners. That evening Pedro was deploring the country's situation. What were the criollos? A country of hostages. Who dominated it? The law of force. And the saddest part of it was that the principal collaborators in that work were the very natives; yes, the little criollos. . . .

"Ah, political parties!" he would say. "They said of the Greeks that they had two doctrines: one for the Areopagus and one for their friends; and I have read this morning in the encyclopedia at the office that the Egyptians who worshiped ridiculous gods laughed at seeing monkeys and cats on their altars, but they prostrated themselves before them. Inspect these politics and these bad politicians: you will see them raving mad against foreigners but adoring them like idols and giving them banquets."

"If all were like me," adduced Antonio, "we would not have reached such extremes. The greatest responsibility for this situation is ours. The prevailing gesture is more or less the same as in the days of the Spanish government: sacrifice conscience and lie in order to be held as loyal. That vilifies and depresses the spirits. Before one could not say here that the conquest committed crimes in America, not even when one appealed to historical testimony; nor that the monarchy was ruining Spain; nor that favoritism rules the colonies; nor that the government was bad. To be a good Spaniard one had to flatter the Spaniards, flatter the monarchy, lie before history; while the true glories of the nation were unknown under servility. Although you were an exalted Republican, here you had to pretend to be a Carlist. A man of character could not make due criticism of the Spaniards without incurring anti-Spanish resentment. My father once had a serious row because he criticized a ballerina who some of his fellow countrymen called the glory of the homeland, just because she had been born in Spain."

"Many of us have been guilty of that intransigence," Lucas added. "Suspicion came between the closest friends."

"Well, we gained nothing after the war," Pedro affirmed. "The North Americans are carefree people and laugh at criticism; they listen to it before they reject it. But here some criollos and North Americans, to whose businesses the imposition of certain prejudices is often convenient, have repeated history. If you criticize the defects of these people and do not repeat that the first republic of the world is theirs, or that they are the depositaries of universal democracy, or that the rule they imposed upon us is paternal, or that this country is swimming in happiness and wealth, you will be anti-American. To be good it is necessary to flatter the North Americans and their colonial government."

"And our compatriots are the most demanding in that criticism. They postpone their right instead of exalting it; while reason is enough to make us know the rights of man that derive from this simple maxim; see how easy it is: between two sensitive beings, equal through nature, it is against justice that one makes his happiness at the expense of the other."

"You are right."

"Yes, very right."

There were then great cries. It was an uproar with whistling and laughing for a recent arrival. It was Guajana who had entered through one of the doors, dressed as a dandy, with a watch, gold chain, derby, and patent leather shoes.

"Leave me alone," he shouted. "Don't ask me anything. These damn shoes are killing my feet!"

And he fell into a chair under the cloak of general laughter.

Guajana made comments. How he prospered, eh? How good it was to find adequate protection! Some envied him. Others teased him. The profession he exercised in the University of Silence was no doubt productive.

At Lucas' table the topic was dropped. Antonio and Pedro continued their colonial idea; Lucas and Sacristán, quiet for a moment upon Guajana's arrival, gave themselves over to subdued buzzing.

"And evidently the affair continues, eh?"

"Indeed it does!"

"What a scandal! What nudity in a city that fits into the fist, where everyone knows his neighbor. They say it's the great restaurant; that the meals and drinks are the finest there are. Of course, everything costs an eyetooth. Only the rich can . . ."

Pedro, on the other hand, continued commenting on things with Antonio.

"And I repeat. They are abusing us. In the political history of the world this country is an interimship. It seems the Treaty of Paris is a perpetual code. It is not known on what laws, on what justice they are founded to keep us on one foot like cranes."

"That's why I don't agree with any political party. Only Hostos' Patriotic League. Independence . . . only independence! Reclaim that which is in our heart; fight for the only ideal that is in our conscience. Current politics is a pack of lies; those here and those on the mainland rival each other in mutual deceit."

"Oh, independence! A long time ago that ideal made its historic eruption in us. Here that is the only truth. All criollos carry it, more or less rooted, in the depths of their souls; and some North Americans would honor it also if it were not for the fact that it doesn't suit their interests."

"They think it is just to exploit their conquest."

"Yes, a conquered country. That is what we are."

"But we make progress, don't we?"

"That's what they say."

"Victor Hugo has said that conquest, guarantor of her sister swindling, is progress."

"Good money it cost us for the progress we were able to make!"

"Especially in the learning of English. What a lot of nonsense! To pretend that a people who speaks Castilian in its homes learn English in school! The work of the home unknown in school; the schoolwork undone at home! They spend our millions, so necessary for the fields and industries, in the teaching of a language that is for our people, in the conditions in which they pretend to teach it, a dead tongue. They seek that our language of the future be born from a cadaver."

"A waste of millions!"

"Yes, it's a shame."

"Never, among us, can our intimate thoughts be expressed in the English language."

"Never. . . ."

▼▲▼▲▼▲▼▲▼▲▼▲▼▲▼▲▼▲▼

XI. "WE ARE ALL MERCHANDISE"

The world of the *jíbaro*, of freely growing fruits and natural farming, died. Most of the richest land on the island was bought by American corporations to grow a single cash crop—sugar. Everything was valued in dollars and cents. "The world is a great grocery," says the character in Miguel Meléndez Muñoz's (1884–1966) story, "Two Letters"; "We are all merchandise." Meléndez Muñoz, whose novel *Yuyo* (1913) was in the Naturalist tradition begun by Zeno, became bitterly ironic, for, he said, the heroic drama had been replaced by a "common vulgar drama." So, too, José Padín (1886–1963), who became a commissioner of education, in his *Puerto Rican Sketches* (1967) years later, depicted, in "Military Justice," an earlier Spanish era with a caustic and cold eye.

TWO LETTERS

by Miguel Meléndez Muñoz
(Silver medal and diploma in the contest held on
August 9, 1908, in commemoration of the fourth an-
niversary of the Christian colonization of Puerto Rico)

"I can't stand this. Write to that damned guy, just
write. . . ."

"But, dad, I don't dare, because he left and we've heard
no more from him. . . . I work, I do whatever you want; but
don't make me write to him. . . ."

"Look, dammit! Write him right now, or I'll give you such
a beating you'll want to lick yourself with your tongue.
Why, that guy was able to do with you what he wanted, and
gone, and now . . . guess who did it to you? . . . Look,
Cachín, you don't seem like my daughter: the world is a
great grocery; some are clerks and others buyers, and we are
all merchandise; and the industry is for each one to know
how to appraise what he is worth. . . . That American
played a trick on you, in the shape of a red-faced baby . . .
there you have it. You didn't know how to appraise your
worth, and he made fun of you. . . ."

"Yes, dad; but I'm ashamed. . . ."

"Enough for you to die of hunger. . . . Don't make me

laugh, for my lip is split. Let's put quarrels aside, and go fetch paper from town, and write him right now, once and for all!"

A drama subject to infinite classifications. A common vulgar drama. But not because of that does it cease to be interesting at times, sometimes tragic and painful, others happy and frolicsome, and others comic and ridiculous, as will be observed by the reader of this fragment of my notes taken in my constant and frequent dealing with simple, rustic, ingenuous, and astute people in the mountains.

Don Gumersindo, ño Gume to his friends and neighbors, had suffered in the depths of his soul, as others suffered in their fortunes and ideas the consequences of the impulsive overwhelming leap of the new conquerors, who on July 25, 1898, disembarked in Guánica with the powerful energy of the young races that conquer lands and subjugate other races at a small price and with little risk.

Like the man who had his little shop, ño Gume had his little farm, and on it poorly settled, his family—his wife and his only daughter, Cachín.

Cachín was a solid girl with hard firm flesh, round breasts, blazing eyes, thick fleshy lips, which opened gracefully, showing her very white teeth of snowy enamel.

In the disorder that followed the invasion, a few gained a little, they rose, and others lost what they said was theirs.

No one was in agreement.

He who had attained his desires sought something else.

He who had lost it all was not consoled, and unceasingly clamored to the heavens for the Chinese, or Japanese, or any other barbaric people to displace the invaders.

What a new Babel was erected in Puerto Rico!

We had honorary cavalry colonels in the navy, great

captains who vaunted a fearless valor before descending from the invading ships, and who afterward were satisfied in waging bloody battles in cafés and public squares; interpreters who barked in English and roared in Spanish; patriots of all colors; farmers, ready to mortgage everything; and above all, the first clash of two civilizations.

Cachín, the provocative criolla, was overwhelmed by an American who, like the saints of France, "had clear eyes" but saw afar.

Poor Cachín resisted all she could; but the invasion was succeeding.

After the "me want very badly to marry you," came the cans of pears, plums, the little envelopes with the nice *Remember the Maine*, the corned beef, the tins of oxtail soup and all the food, that in that historic moment defeated more hearts and prepared with greater rapidity the assimilation than the famous Miles proclamation.

Cachín was resisting. She defended herself with tenacity and resolution; but the invader besieged her, and finally, she yielded. . . .

The lad was a passing bird, one of those God-forsaken birds that make their nest in no place. And thus, while Cachín lived more confident in the affection or in what she supposed was the blind love of her man, he, like the passing bird that he was, had already grown tired of the land and the nest improvised against his will, raised in flight . . . and left.

Don Gume denied Cachín, who felt moving in her womb the natural fruit of her love with the unfaithful blond. . . .

And while some lamented the depreciation of coffee, or tried attempts at cultivating pineapple and oranges, and others cast their glance, clouded with tears, toward Hawaii or Daiquirí, Cachín wept for the loss of her honor. And Don

Gume was ready to kill the first blond man he met in his path.

"There's no time to lose, daughter. Let's talk about the letter. You have to write him today."

"All right, father; but we have to send for Doña Andreíta."

"And why don't you saddle the animal so that woman can come?"

In the afternoon Doña Andreíta, awaited by Cachín, arrived at Don Gume's house.

She was a woman who, by her height, did not look as old as fifteen, but because of the wrinkles that creased her face and divided it, looked more than fifty.

She had, besides her wrinkles, facial excrescences and protuberances, very good penmanship and a good knowledge of rhetoric—epistolary rhetoric of her invention. And in the saying of the people, she was an expert in love letters, congratulatory, sympathy, and jilting letters, etc.

"Good day, Doña Andreíta, how are you?"

"Fine, just fine, my friends. Why do you want me?"

"Well, you can imagine . . ."

"We want you," Don Gume said, "with that good penmanship God gave you, and with all the sense you have, to write a letter to the American who left this girl . . . In the letter you have to tell him not to worry us, dammit, that he has a child here, and that if he doesn't want to come, don't come—for all he's needed here!—but to send money, for I'm old and can't support so many people; for there was a lawyer here and he told us we could put in a claim for rape, abuse, and abandonment of a child in the formative stage; but we don't want anything to do with federal or heavenly courts . . . because I believe a bad arrangement is better than a good court case. So you already know what's necessary to tell him. Gather the thread and write him a letter that strikes to the quick of that scoundrel."

"I understand, perfectly well."

Doña Andreíta sat before a table, took up her pen, unwrapped a roll of paper she had brought, and began to write with big strokes.

Don Gume smoothed his moustache and took big puffs on the cigar he held between his teeth.

Cachín, red and blushing, looked at the floor—and the pen continued scratching on the paper, guided as it was skillfully by Doña Andreíta.

Finally she stopped in her task, stuck the pen in her bun and exclaimed: "It's ready, I'm going to read it:

" 'Mr. Don Güiles Estante. . . .' "

"What? How's that?" Don Gume asked.

"Güili, Güeli. . . ."

"Okay. It's the same thing. . . . What a coincidence! . . . A *'güele'* face he had. . . . Continue, ma'am."

" 'My dear Güili. . . .' "

"That's English, right, ma'am? That's not bad, because that way he'll understand better."

"Yes, but I don't know English," Doña Andreíta replied, "and I've limited myself to writing in that language the heading and the *posdata.* . . ."

"And the what?" Don Gume inquired.

"The *posdata,* at the end," Doña Andreíta answered.

"That will be a buttercup for him to open up his wallet even wider," Don Gume concluded in turn.

"I continue," Doña Andreíta grumbled, "and I beg you not to interrupt me again. 'In this dark valley, where you abandoned me in a blind moment, I take pen in hand to write you with the blood of my heart. I remember those joyous days of love, when you came to see me and placed on my forehead, with your rosy lips, a perfumed kiss. . . .' "

"Look, Doña Andreíta, and forgive me for butting in the letter; I can't allow stories to be told in my presence even if they're written. Those days, as you say, may have been happy, but they cost Cachín enough tears: and that part about rosy lips and perfumed kisses, look, ma'am, those flourishes . . . are a little shameful, because that man drank whiskey and chewed tobacco, . . . but, I'm sorry, continue, 'cause that can't be erased. . . ."

Doña Andreíta continued: " 'Now weeping and pain have dried my poor defenseless soul. To get to the point, as your son and mine needs the means to survive the struggle for food, I beg you to make a sacrifice and provide him a pension of fifteen or twenty dollars. . . .' "

"Look, Doña Andreíta, write that to him in English," Don Gume urged, "for it's the most important. . . ."

" '. . . monthly, for I swear to you never again, never, will you hear the desperate cry of my pain, for it will not cross the seas and the blue mists to bother your ears. A negative response on your part will be the cause of my suicide, and I don't think the echo of my death, dragged across the seas, will reach your great country. Awaiting your hoped for reply as a worthy prize for my virtues and constancy in my love, I am always, forever and ever *faitfully*, and your *respertifuyi* . . . Posdata . . .' "

"Doña Andreíta," Don Gume corrected, "it's not *posdata* who signs it, it's Cachín, or Conserción, which is her Christian name. . . ."

"But, good heavens, don't interrupt me," Doña Andreíta reiterated. "Now comes the most important part." And she concluded: "A paragraph where the request is recalled. 'It is of the utmost necessity that you attend to my request, because I'm dying. Yours—Conserción.' "

. . .

Two weeks later Cachín received the awaited response. The fugitive made an effort, he recalled all the Spanish words he had learned here, and wrote her this letter:

Mis Cachín Perez

My dear Cachín:
Me received your letter. I am very well, and me *mucho contento* very [very glad] that you are well. When me leave Puerto Rico I buy in San Juan 15 mangoes and one dozen eggplants to eat in the steamer. In very short time very *malo* in the stomach. Cannot eat. Much revolution in the belly. Doctor say I die. I arrive New York very sick. I no work here. No money. Me *mucho bruja* [I bad off]. I cannot smoke cigarettes. I live in my brother's house, in Richmond.
The next year, if *Dios* willing, me send money for your *nena*.

Your obliging servant,
WILLIS STANT

MILITARY JUSTICE

by José Padín

That night was one of nightmares and frights. Tomorrow they were shooting the soldier who had killed his sergeant.

Mané, Aunt Baldomera, and I were sleeping in the room, each on a cot. Juan de la Cruz made himself comfortable in the attic, a kind of platform with a railing situated between the ground and the open sky, to which an inside stairway gave access. We slept with the light on because Aunt Baldomera had very definite ideas about the dark. It's true the gas lamp was controlled so that no one would remain awake, but the light was sufficient to reveal any intruding

spirit that would cross the threshold in spite of the lock and
bolt.

What a long night that was! Mané was snoring, Aunt
Baldomera was snoring, Juan de la Cruz was snoring on the
platform, sometimes alone, other times in a duet, often the
three of them in competition. The cats on the rooftops
meowed, tore around wildly, fought each other like devils,
ran again and meowed again, and after brief periods of rest
breathed contentedly. Juan de la Cruz's cot creaked as
though it couldn't endure the load.

In the early part of the night there was movement in the
Manila, the little corner café. There were no soldiers that
night. They were in the barracks because tomorrow they
were shooting the soldier who had killed his sergeant.
Women sang, accompanied by guitars. They sang without
enthusiasm, by habit. Ballajá was dressed in mourning, or it
was going to be. Some one began to hum the refrain of a
popular song, "Boy, what were you doing? . . ." and they
made him be quiet as though it were a question of sacrilege.
It was a song they didn't let me hum "because it was a bad
song."

My godmother Nicolasa was the cause of this situation.
The soldier who had killed his sergeant, and the sergeant
himself, fell in love with her. The former was a poor
fifth-rank private recently arrived from Spain, the latter, a
petty tyrant in charge of discipline and the training of
recruits. Nicolasa overwhelmed them. Shortly before the
tragedy they had gathered the Remingtons that the company used and had replaced them with Mausers. The
Mauser was a repeating rifle much harder to handle than
the Remington. The recruit wasn't able to load it and fire it
accurately, and the sergeant didn't waste the opportunity to
humiliate him. One afternoon the sergeant was in the

canteen having a few drinks when the recruit appeared with his Mauser.

"Sergeant!" the recruit cried.

As the sergeant turned his head, the recruit put a bullet between his eyes.

After a summary court-martial, the recruit was sentenced to be shot in El Morro fort.

Tomorrow they were shooting the soldier who had killed his sergeant.

At dawn, at the first cock crow, the San Cristóbal company passed on the way to El Morro through the Callejón de las Animas, marching to the sound of a drum roll. Tan, tan, tan! The whole company was going to be represented at the execution. Those from El Morro were the first to arrive. Then were added those of Ballajá and the Volunteers, the latter Spaniards of civil state who lent their services to the king to maintain in check the overseas anti-Spanish insurgents. A firing squad of twelve men was chosen by a sergeant from the four platoons. The soldier was placed back against the wall between the Santa Elena battery and the entrance to the cemetery, and the firing squad a certain distance from the soldier. At that moment Aunt Baldomera arrived, and grabbing me violently by the arm, took me from the crowd of young and old who were gathered to witness the execution. As we passed in front of the canteen, we heard a distant, hoarse voice shout: "Ready! Aim! Fire!" A volley sounded. Aunt Baldomera knelt on the sidewalk and after making the sign of the cross, said a prayer for the soldier's soul.

Years later, when I was no longer a child, we received the news of Nicolasa's death in Havana. She had died of love and a stab in the heart. Then Juan de la Cruz told me:

"Your adopted godmother just had to end up badly. There is no right to set women like that in the world, as though this roguish world weren't already the antechamber of hell. The Lord should not permit the devil to spread his agents over the land and make unfair competition for Him. Nicolasa was my niece, but on her left side she was Lucifer's relative. You must remember her. A redhead, with two eyes larger than a cistern's mouth. As green as the whirlpool at Peña Pará. She had the waist of a frivolous wasp. But the glory of her body was between her waist and her ankles. She didn't need filling. Many women had put on bustles to try to look like Nicolasa, who had brought hers into the world at birth. In Havana, when she put on her comb and Manila lace mantilla and went into the street, it was necessary to mobilize the police reserves in order to restore order. That's why the descendant of the Queen of Sheba had such a tragic end."

XII. THE SOCIAL CRITICS

The paradox of poverty in "the earthly paradise," of hunger on a lush, rural island, of industrial ugliness on "the pearl of the Antilles," soon enough produced a social satirist. Swiftian in his brutal, yet compassionate, wit was Nemesio R. Canales (1878–1923), lawyer, politician, journalist, and essayist. Canales's famous *Paliques* (1913) is a collection of articles, from which we have chosen "Riches and Poverty," in which he offers a sarcastic "modest proposal": "the killing of the poor," if only it were more economical.

Antonio S. Pedreira (1899–1939), the educator and scholar, was, perhaps, more subtle and in his best-known work, *Insularismo* (1934), he argued that the island was, by nature, "benign," "passive," and "feminine." These qualities were not weaknesses, but its strengths, wrote Pedreira. He urged, in "The Land and Its Meaning," excerpted from *Insularismo*, that the people seek the "essence," not the "presence" of *puertorriqueñismo*.

RICHES AND POVERTY

by Nemesio R. Canales

(*Selection*)

3

I was saying that our social organism has in its blood an infectious virus, the cause of ignorance, pestilence, and crimes.

Now then, this virus is none other than that of poverty. It suffices to stop to think just for an instant to be convinced of it. It is the poor, the sick with this terrible virus of misery who forever feed our hospitals and jails.

This being so, I want to be told if it is not a tremendous stupidity to think that it is only the poor who are affected by the problem of ceasing to be poor, that is to say, the problem of being the cause and root of all human afflictions, of all the evils that fill the world.

I say that it is the responsibility of the rich, the powerful, the privileged of all types, not for more or less nebulous philanthropic principles, but out of egotism, pure egotism, to seek to erase the horrible stain of misery from the land. What is the value of possessing a fortune, of having triumphed in the social fray, having scaled the summits of wealth or glory, if none of this frees us from living in a world that is a vast swamp, where we have to cover ourselves forcibly with mud up to our eyes? Why devote ourselves to the conquest of a redeeming million for life, if, as we accumulate more millions, we are more harassed, pursued by the sinister legion of the sick, the lepers, the ignorant, and criminals? Would not the rich sacrifice half their wealth in exchange for being able to enjoy in peace the other half in a world cured forever of the frightful cancer of ignorance, the mother of violence and grandmother of crime?

It is now time to declare that poverty is not combated with that plaintive pro forma charity that erects hospitals and asylums and from time to time makes a donation. One does not combat mange, smallpox, or leprosy by helping them to live with works of charity. They are combated by pursuing them and killing them.

Poverty is combated only by putting an end to the poor, and doing this is not accomplished by carrying them in bunches to hospitals and jails and helping them with ridiculous little gifts of charity to continue being poor.

If one could end poverty by killing the poor, in the style of Herod, I would not waver in advising that procedure as being more in harmony with the barbaric state of our present social condition, but besides the fact that the remedy would cure us only momentarily, for we would again fill ourselves with the poor, it is certain the rich, the rich themselves, would be the first who would combat tooth and nail against that Draconian massacre which would leave them deprived at one fell swoop of the arm of the poor, the sweat of the poor, that cheapest and most comfortable human machine of all.

We hold, hence, that we cannot kill the poor. And if we cannot kill the poor, what recourse, what remedy, what formula to utilize in order to free ourselves from poverty?

The remedy is quite simple.

In the same way as when we see an individual with symptoms of smallpox or yellow fever or bubonic plague, we consider it our business, and not his, to become alarmed and even go mad for fear of contagion, and we have him isolated and we find him an island or the most distant corner possible for the doctors to handle him or do away with him; and once he is dead, we continue to consider it our business—and not the dead man's family—to set fire to his house and clothes and even the memory of the deceased; in the same way that on similar occasions we consider it our business, our most pressing and respectable necessity to throw ourselves upon the diseased one and try through all the means at our disposal to combat the incipient infection in his person, I believe we must accustom ourselves to see in poverty an evil—not for the poor—but rather for all, the rich and the poor, an evil with which we would soon come to be convinced that the best business for the rich and healthy and powerful consists in permitting to no one the crime of being poor, as we permit to no one afflicted by smallpox, vomiting, leprosy, or rabies the crime of going freely in the street.

. . . . .

8

We agree that I was affirming that the state could prevent men from fighting each other for money.

How? Very simply: by becoming—the state, that is—the only capitalist. Instead of a capitalist here and another there who scoop up and monopolize all money, a single capital, one strongbox in the hands of the state, and all men becoming pension pupils of that state. Men, perpetually maintaining the state with their daily labor, a labor they would be required to lend to a determined age limit, and which, it is evident, would signify for each one only a daily sacrifice of two or three hours of their time. In exchange for that, the state, insuring him, guaranteeing to each man the full enjoyment of his life by means of a stipend paid daily in money which ought to be sufficient not only for the satisfaction of his basic or animal necessities, but also for those which are born of his nobler and more delicate sources.

In olden times, phlegmatic men broke out laughing when such a state was spoken of. Today trusts, those enormous omnipotent trusts, have come to prove the possibility and viability of the state in question. For if a corporation in which thousands of men are associated with a collective name for any given task is possible, there is no reason why all men of a country cannot unite to constitute in the name of the state, or any other, a formidable trust for the great task of socializing property and guaranteeing each man his share of life.

"But," it will be said to me, "if each man is assured a pension, very few would work." And I say that in the state I foresee, *based precisely on the work of all,* all would have to give his share of work in order to have the right to his share of life. The habitual bum—a candidate for pauper—would not be tolerated for an instant. In the same way that, without need of police or courts, we free ourselves today, through the immediate and instinctual alarm of the whole community, of the teeth of a rabid dog, in the new state the presence of a loafer—of a man ready to live a parasitical life in the style of today's wealthy individuals and bureaucrats, that is, consuming without producing—would be received with the same alarm as a case of rabies or other epidemic, and the loafer would run the same risk as the rabid dog. The motto of the new state would be precisely that: "neither loafers nor paupers."

"But," I will again be told, "if some, the most frugal, begin to keep a part of the pension received, soon they would begin to accumulate money, and we should return irremissibly to our old ways, that is, to the capitalism of today, with its natural sequel of ruin and poverty for the greatest number."

And I say that in the same manner that the community would shake off, through egotism, the loafer, fearful of his contagion, they would also react through instinctive alarm against a case of greed. And the man caught in the flagrante delicto of treason against the community for keeping for himself that part of his pension he refused to, or chose not to, spend, with the evil intent of grabbing it for himself from the resources of the state, would be treated with no respect, with the same implacable severity as the loafer and the rabid dog.

It is known that all that opposes tranquility, health, well-being, or prejudices of a collectivity in a fundamental way is indefectibly eliminated from the breast of the collectivity, without the need for police or judges. And a state can spend years and years promulgating laws, and if those laws do not take root at all in some corner of the collective soul, of the soul of the people, no one, neither judges nor jailers nor guards will spare them from being laughed at, trampled, and forgotten by everyone. On the other hand, when a law is based on a need or sentiment of the collectivity, each citizen, each man, each street, each house constitutes a jealous guardian of the aforesaid law.

Here is thus resolved the thorny problem of the cheapening of money. Here is money—which today is a curse—periodically visiting each man, shining like the sun for all and not for the few, coming like water to each house to sate the thirst for life of all men.   ·

There remains one other objection to make: the lack of impetus, the source from whence progress springs. "The ambition to accumulate money dead, human activity would also die, and there would be no progress," I hear someone say.

"Let's suppose," I answer, "that progress died. What does progress matter? Perhaps we have come into the world to serve progress? No; we have come to serve ourselves. Ourselves served and satisfied, progress can very well go to the devil."

I deny the fact that it is true that a man obeys no other stimulus to develop his activity than that of accumulating money.

Even more, for me the stimulus of money is purely artificial, and when removed, all the energies of the human machine would remain in perennial function.

If we fight each other today for a handful of coins, because unfortunately we have come to give more value to the symbol than to the thing, to the handful of coins than to man, tomorrow—the phantom of poverty dissipated forever—all the natural ambitions that today impel us would remain in force. Who dares deny what the ambition for knowledge, for love, for glory, strong, indestructible, and valuable springs in the human soul at all times, can do as a stimulus in man—even in the cheated man of today?

And as my paper is running out and I have reached the end, let it be stated that there is material for a million vignettes, and what I have expressed is, hence, a mere sketch and not a definitive and complete picture of a social reform.

Of a new, surging, and beautiful society that I already

feel advancing toward us with the velocity of the hurricane . . .

THE LAND AND ITS MEANING
by Antonio S. Pedreira

Our countryside possesses a measured meaning and harmonizes with the geography and ethnography. Nothing forceful, noisy, or extreme. The discreet decoration is in a minor key and lends itself, like our *danza*, to enjoyment and confidence. Its predominant note is lyrical: it is a tender, mild, soft, crystalline countryside. Samuel Gili Gaya aptly perceived it, when he said that "it is far from being imposing. Everything adopts a mild, flattering, likable, and profoundly feminine air. The mountains are only little hills dressed in bright green, the pastureland of cows that do not charge, an almost vegetable cow. The Asomante appears as though it wanted to grow furious but immediately repents from its killer gestures and bends very politely before the cobalt blue of the southern coast. We miss poisonous snakes, and we cannot believe in hurricanes or earthquakes that they say take place."

Nor do we find in our idiosyncrasy inaccessible peaks, nor burning deserts, nor deep precipices, nor roars, claws, or epic volume. We are a people alien to violence, and politely peaceful, as our countryside. Isolated in the rural zone, in eighty per cent of its population, it stretches its meekness to the point of indigence and multiplies its offspring at the edge of the law, aggravating more and more its perturbing socioeconomic problem. The forced exodus toward towns is depriving the Puerto Rican countryside of its fertile folkloric sense. The strong wave of the cane fields passed the limits of our plains and goes uphill, up the mountains, tearing down trees and leveling small vegetable farms, which offered the steady diet in poor country homes. Before its push, cottages keep disappearing, as did the swamps, farms, sugar plantations, woods, and the main road. In the present period of historical evolution in which we live, even the countryside varies its component elements, the same as history.

Thick columns of black smoke obscure, at certain distances, the blue clarity of the sky, and an admirable network of highways—white on green—tortures the muscles of the mountains, joining closely seventy-eight towns and more than forty sugar factories. From bend to bend a clamoring billboard, announcer of exotic products, casts its hawker's cry, perforating the mist of molasses and gasoline that frequently competes with that of hidden stills. The land is worked with forced enthusiasm and scarce benefit for the arm that milks it. Telephone and electric poles have lined the country like music sheets; technical progress has invaded rural zones in leaps and bounds, and towns grow outward, shortening the distances, already annihilated by our admirable means of communication. Our countryside has acquired an urbanity not suspected thirty years ago. The rural school, agricultural entities, irrigation, neighboring roads, radio, the car, etc., etc., have flatteringly changed the scenery. But the land continues in agony, sliding, accumulating social and economic evils, hard pressing, now as never before, the problem of our idiosyncrasy.

With the exception of England, Java, Belgium, and Holland, our country is the most populated in the world: 485 inhabitants per square mile. Japan and Germany follow her. If as one can see in the latest censuses its population doubles every forty-five years, and on top of this human excess there continue to gravitate the sanitary, social, and economic problems that beset us today, in the near future the tragedy will be frightening. Bald and bare of minerals, forests, and hydraulic energy to initiate permanent industries, the land will not be able to support on its agriculture alone the already perturbing superpopulation.

The first man who from Columbus' caravels spied for the first time the islands of the new world, pronounced in the seas the first Spanish word that America heard, and pointed out in advance a grave Puerto Rican problem: Land! From an ardent expression of joy it became, in time, a problem of painful anguish. The land, previously divided in small parcels, is today monopolized in the claws of great sugarcane landowners. Human competition sinks its teeth into our sick economy and lowers wages, carrying those who work toward indigence. Add to that the blows of nature, of uncinariasis, of one-crop farming and the dead season in which there is no harvest, and one will see that the land can no longer support the load.

Nowadays the measures of immigration or limitations on offspring, so contrary, apparently, to the Puerto Rican character, are not enough. Since we cannot reduce the number of births nor can we advance toward the sea to make territorial expansion, there is no other recourse except vertical expansion: up, up, in, down, in order to cultivate virile ideas and sentiments. If we do not increase ourselves culturally, we are condemned to the unpleasing condition of peons. Hence it is necessary to defend our spiritual subsoil and raise our eyes from the land—without ever forgetting it!—to assure for our people the air they breathe.

The geographic position of Puerto Rico determined the course of our history and our character. The point of view of Spanish sovereignty was commerce, and that of North America, strategy. Commerce and strategy intervene in the growth of our collective personality, as we shall see later. The height of despair was our fortune to fall isolated from the world and to be, among the Greater Antilles, the smallest one of them. This deprived us of the authority that great masses of people give to the demands of world respect. Our fatherland has always lamented nostalgically the lack of that mass of land so necessary to serve as a background.

In proportion to its size, its wealth is developed, and hence its culture, too. Being geographically the center of the two Americas, its lack of volume, its lack of ports and large-scale commerce make it a little corner. As a compressed center we only serve for strategy and for stopovers, and this belatedly and with such rapidity that the result does not upset determining factors in the environment. Being a strategic point does not benefit us very much; as a tourist point, our smallness seen in two days does not make up for the cost of the trip; and as an economic center the geographic extension permits only reduced business opportunities, in keeping with its size.

We bear the hindrance of territorial dimension. We are not continentals, nor even Antillean: we are simply islanders, which is like saying insulated in a narrow house. Crimped by the land, our gesture before the world has the same dimensions as our geography. Neither deserts, nor plains, nor vast valleys helps us to extend our vision, and we are accustomed to tripping on an immediate landscape that we almost touch on its four corners. That obstacle of proximity narrows our perspective and develops in us an ophthalmology that condemns us to a mere continental glimpse. We cut down great distances, and we atomize life with grave consequences for our destiny.

The land, hence, reduces the stage in which culture is to move. If our topography had been different, the course of our history would have been another. Ruiz-Belvis, Hostos, and Betances did not fit in it and fled to die, ostracized. Our

most prominent men, it is necessary to repeat, lack the mass
of land so propitious for making their figures clearer and
greater. This geological narrowness, linked with the difficult
geographic position, the debilitating climate, our biological
constitution, and the perpetual feudatory condition, oper-
ates on our collective psychology with a depressing, strictur-
ing effect. Lacking the right that force gives, that is, mass,
we have not been able to incorporate into our life the force
given by the law. Our country has always been unfortunate,
poor, and meager; we operate on a small scale. In exchange
for the vital defects that our civic action offers, we exhibit as
a substitute a trait we study in a separate chapter: rhetoric.

It is interesting to note that the economic aspect of the
land varies distinctly according to the three moments in
which we divide the course of our history. In the first, slow
and unitary, fief divisions and land tracts made of it a vast
farm half cultivated, with a considerable inactive sector of
woods, pastures, swamps, and unproductive land. In the
second, turbulent and decisive, it is fragmented in abundant
parcels in which the interest of the majority improves its
returns with small farms responsible for the greatest part of
our diet. And in the third, indefinite and problematic, the
land loses its small owners, and in spite of the law that limits
possession to five hundred acres, it returns to a larger
division, but this time under the superlative exploitation of
absentee corporations, responsible, among other things, for
their monopolizing dedication, for the dietary slavery in
which our people live today. Compare imports of the
nineteenth century to those of the twentieth century, and
the consequences of one-crop farming will be manifestly
seen.

The land, just yesterday, fell through our heart into the
lap of culture; today it falls from our hands in the
fluctuations of bargain and sale, altering its patriotic sense

into another exclusively economic. In the past, when the land was plural and obtained its best expression inside the parentheses that the farmer and the poet formed, it was not a motive for concern. Today that it is singular and has been made a bale of goods, not the individual man, but rather the group defines it: yesterday Gautier Benítez; today, the sugarcane factories. Observe in this isolated case the trajectory that our life is going to follow from the individual to the corporate. Mass production, two or three products in excess, scarcity of all the rest.

The land, hence, is in this painful process of transaction, which is like saying historico-economic transition. Where is the land going? No one will be able to say so long as it is not known what people are going to have the last word.

The home is the flower of the land. The straw and palm-bark hut, picturesque in the distance as a decorative element of the regional landscape but so miserable close up, is doomed to disappear because it does not bear the essential essences of tradition. There is no need to lament its absence, for the hut is but the expression of anguish and penury. If each peasant could have a comfortable, safe house of cement or lumber, with a metal roof and with all the sanitary advantages of modern life, it is better for it to be thus, and for the *bohío* to be sheltered in history, poetry, and folklore.

There is no right to defend presence when what must matter is essence. The image is an external thing. The *bohío* can only be defended from a purely economic plane: it is preferable for the peasant to possess his rustic dwelling than to become a mere tenant in modern buildings. His possession must be defended over the grave inconvenience of tenancy. But when that peasant can place his home at the level of those we possess in urban zones, no one ought to lament his changing his pigsty and the disappearance of that picturesque bit of local color from our landscape. The *barraca,* or storm shelter, seems more essential and necessary than a straw farmhouse.

The native *bohío,* besides, cannot be, because of its weakness and danger, the primary cell of our dwelling. This is constituted by the Spanish construction adapted to the exigencies of colonial need: walls of brick or cement, roofs of tile or brick, high, wide doors, and windows with blinds. The intense heat, the earth tremblings, and hurricanes determine the cause of our island architecture, which we have almost abandoned. The zinc and glass that today prevail in our homes are foreign elements superficially superimposed on the ancient cells. But imitation harms us, besides being inconvenient. The tropics demand a very special construction, very individual, strong, and lasting, to counteract the fierce attacks of its three natural enemies: hurricanes, earthquakes, and the destructive war of saltpeter and the moth.

If we had continued to develop our collective conscience without falling, perhaps we could have a regional architecture fully developed, without zinc and glass that are not produced here, and ending up with adobe. Since we possess that raw material the aforesaid architecture would in turn give rise to an autonomous and flourishing industry now completely disappeared: the production of tiles and bricks.

Inevitably we shall have to turn to it. The climate, the storms, the need and the national economy demand from us the creation of a house that would respond aptly to the demands of our territorial spirit. In order to reject or accept advantageously the path of the new civilization that today nurtures us, it is of utmost importance to recognize the orientation offered by the land and its meaning.

XIII. THE CULTURAL CRITICS

As the "green island" began to disappear beneath the black smog of factories and gray cement of highways, a chorus of writers began to lament its demise with joyous and reverent eulogies of its natural beauties. Lovingly, the literary essayist María Teresa Babín, (1910–), the author of *The Poetic World of García Lorca* (1954), *Panorama of the Culture of Puerto Rico* (1958), *The Puerto Ricans' Spirit* (1971), and *Fantasia Boricua* (1959), and other books, has evoked the "Symbols of Borinquen": in magic, in music, in life, in homage to "the sleeping Cemí (Indian) god that all of us Puerto Ricans bear within." The magic and myth in Puerto Rican culture is related to that of Latin America by the literary critic Concha Meléndez (1904–), whose early poetic vision in "The Mountains Know" has continued to animate her work as a literary critic and scholar. In his "Serenade of the *Coquí*," from his beautiful book *The Five Senses* (1955), the essayist Tomás Blanco (1897–) offers a hymn to the song of the *coquí*, as true a national symbol of the island as the eagle is to the United States. And in "'Puertoricanists' and 'Occidentalists,'" Nilita Vientós Gastón (1908–), the editor of *Asomante* and *Sin Nombre*, two leading literary magazines, searches for the "essence" of the "authentically national, as distinguished from nationalistic," returning to Pedreira's concept of "the Puerto Rican Soul."

SYMBOLS OF BORINQUEN

by María Teresa Babín

Magic Words

The inventory of the symbols of the culture of Puerto Rico could be attempted from many vantage points: the language, history, philosophy, art, poetry. A glossary of words from the letters A to Z could contribute light for a type of mythology of the Antillean land and man. Flora and fauna, the multiplicity of names with which we identify barrios and towns, mountains and plains, the customs and habits of the human being who inhabits our island, are saturated with its enchantment. Popular music, folklore, learned poetry, and cuisine of both rich and poor transmute the symbol into metaphor in order to praise the heart and please the body. It emanates from primitive springs and persists the same in the herbs of witch doctors as in the verses of Corretjer, the lullabies of Ester Feliciano, the lyric poetry of Lillianne Pérez Marchand, in the five senses of Tomás Blanco, in the bolero and the popular *plena* dance, in the journey of Juan Martínez Capó, in the flames and the labyrinth of Laguerre, in the masquerade of Arriví and the landscapes of Díaz Alfaro. So many others seek in different creative paths the essences and potent substances of the soul of our unique culture, for it is not possible to blind oneself and deny the magic and force of its spirit. Plastic arts will hear the call and will become enriched in forms and colors when they transform it into movement and visible space in sculpture and painting.

While studying and compiling data for a panorama of Puerto Rican culture, there arose in the path the poetic myths that lie in the subsoil of the creative life of my country. Discipline required casting them off and leaving them for a more propitious moment. I begin to take delight now in the treasure, having fulfilled the task of propounding and analyzing the vital facts I consider essential to assay as a whole the expression of Puerto Rican culture in the American atlas. In reliving and glossing these symbols, emotion is a fairy godmother who serves me as a guide, while the intellect yields so as not to obstruct the current of spontaneity and free will. I resort to prose because I find myself in its shade nearer to conversation and silence, overturning in the realm of evocation the magic of the symbols of the fatherland.

I invoke for this inventory four key concepts of language, in which the fruitful essence of myth beats. In sleeping eyes it awakens the warm image of an already hazy vision, spurring on fantasy to make itself plastic in word. *Casabe. Güiro. Bohío. Batey. . . . Batey. Bohío. Casabe. Güiro.* I begin to play solitaire, shuffling the mighty symbols with trembling and fear. I feel seized by a strange well-being. *Güiro. Batey. Casabe. Bohío.* They change place at will, varying the accent, amusing the pen in the clinking of each vowel, leaving the slight trace of its sonorous muteness in the roots of my race.

Other clear round names, bequeathed by the first man of

ancient latitudes and geographies, pile up in memory. Miners of the sixteenth century who extracted metals from my soil, washed the sands of my rivers, and brought the metals of my inheritance, changing gold for gold, transmuting saltpeter into fertile valleys, sowing sugarcane, coffee, and tobacco when the precious veins of the native arsenal were scarce. First Antillean greed, nurtured with ginger and roast bats, frightened with ants and animals the sun sustains in the air and swamp to defend the tropic's right with their arms.

The four cardinal points of this adventure remain safe from the tide: *Casabe. Güiro. Batey. Bohío.* What do they suggest across the centuries? Why do they sound so much mine in the full consciousness of the twentieth century, stirred by the thousand temptations and threats of the space lit by artificial lights? They sing to me and they weep in the still solitude of my unquiet life, plunging me into the discovery of Borinquen in myself.

Casabe (manioc-flour bread)

The trough covered with wide banana leaves hides the lost legend of the aborigines. In the hot fidgeting of the palm grove, it smells of wood, land crab fritters, stews with lard and annatto, and man's sweat. Mouths and eyes open and close with the slow rhythm of insatiable hunger. Without wanting to, the hands and feet of the mother, son, and father dance, anointed in their walking with the agile grace of the melting of three powerful races.

The trough. The trough. What does it keep under those withered green leaves whose century-old stain we Puerto Ricans will bear forever? Can it be *casabe* bread, bread kneaded with the calloused hand of time, the bread of the native yucca, which the other white bread has not been able to banish from our island? What can it taste like now? Can it be as good as the other? Isn't it adulterated? Could Doña Juana Ponce, the mother of Troche, have eaten it? Could Ayerra y Santa María have eaten it before going to the Mexican capital to write Gongoristic verses with Sister Juana Inés de la Cruz? Could Torres Varga have eaten it so as to feel more criollo than he was? Could Ponce de León have carried it in his saddlebag replete with hopes of finding the fountain of youth in Florida?

The banana leaves raise their skirts modestly, leaving the golden treasure in the open. Our eyes pop out and our hands leap from us. We touch the spherical loaf, we caress it before biting in, and we chew it with age-old fury to extract the juice from the dough in a desperate desire to nurture the body with the virgin sap of the yucca root. Guaybana's *casabe* from Coayuco, Guanina's *casabe*, who served it with coffee at daybreak to her lover Don Cristóbal, conquering the conqueror acclimated in the land of her elders.

How do you feel now, Don Casabe, among so many other exotic breads sliced in geometric series, hygienically wrapped in waxed paper? Did men and children of old gobble you up with the same desire as today's people eat other breads in a hurry? Doesn't it distress you to be relegated to folklore in your rough, honorable persistence, while those hodgepodges of spongy softness reign on the table?

Don Casabe speaks not, but stares, making his sporadic appearance in our appetite. He is hawked in San Juan by retailers from Loíza, he arises suddenly wrapped in the tumult smelling of gasoline, and continues on his path without losing form or taste. Who still prepares him? On what mysterious hearth is he prepared? My avid tongue savors him with amazement, as though the magic of a guardian god bore me to Coayuco and made me newborn in the year 1511.

Güiro (gourd musical instrument)

The dry marrow gourd, lined with parallel stripes, rests on the table, hangs from a nail on the wall, vibrates in the wrinkled hands of the blind beggar and the amused seer. Silent, it is like the smile of a wrinkled face in repose; speaking, it is like the indiscreet cackling of men in the wee drunken hours of confidences with dirty overtones. It offers itself simply to the touch and suggests forms of dances and hidden atavisms of other people. It isn't just a musical instrument, it's more than that: it is a work of art to be seen, without being heard, to be touched and handled with fingers and eyes. Sometimes it seems like a joker to me, butting in the popular *plena* dance, in the *seis chorreao*, the *danza*, and the *guateque* country dance. It excels as soon as it appears, sustaining the dialogue without surrendering, with the treble guitar, the Spanish guitar, and the accordion. Neither the maracas nor the drumsticks can choke it off. And it remains undaunted till dawn, stubborn and dry, like those ancient individuals who never yield in their persistence.

The poet has sung of it as if it were the fatherland, while it sings to the fatherland as though it were singing to a woman. In the evening noise in the mountain, its distinct penetration infiltrates the breeze and waters. Solitude feels bewitched by its monotonous well-tuned measure of waiting. The stick scratches it, beating with pleasure its strawlike body, enamored of its touch, both joining with the amorous sureness of a perfect marriage.

Can anyone tear sound from its body, make it vibrate and express happiness, sadness, disdain, tenderness, fury, or surrender? Ask the great witch doctor of spirited music. He will answer as he answered me, with the firm brow of his wisdom: "The *güiro* is supposed to be played with seriousness and love by he who knows its secrets, without losing the thread of music, with his senses concentrated on the stripes holding the stick firm, without frivolities or deviations. As long as we have the *güiro* we will have spirit."

Bohío (Puerto Rican peasant hut)

The wail of a newborn babe breaks the mist. The diffuse white sheets of fog softly clothe the frail, dark-brown *bohío*. The infant pouts and begins to sleep his only peaceful dream, already on the road toward the harsh, hard reality of his destiny. Absorbed in his thoughts, the man opens the door. The smoke redolent of coffee fills the early mountain morning, damp with wails and dew. The woman, strengthened by the birth, filters the coffee. The *bohío* seems to tremble and shrivel, as though it wished to protect in an embrace the tender innocence that lights up its misery.

Pulpy leaves of dry palm, rib bands of rough wood, pavement and roof are twisted with the trembling blush of fecund love. An *ay-ya-yay* song breaks the morning silence and a sunny hosanna filters through the cracks. The *bohío* has been transfigured: chickens come peeping, goats gambol, calves lull, and the balsam-apple opens for little birds. The mother rocks the cot, absorbed in the contemplation of the *bohío* son.

Batey (patiolike area in front of a peasant home)

Venus begins to appear in the sky, and on the ground the cactus flower opens. Disturbed *coquís* and feathered cane tassels tickle the tenuous evening breeze. From the four corners of the island surges in unison the song buried in the depths of the ancestral soul of our history.

Along the slopes of the mountains and the reefs of pirate coasts wander the truncated dreams of men in anguish, stuck to the earth with fingernails and teeth. At the invitation of the song all dreams stop the ear. They walk barefoot and hurriedly toward the destined *batey*, the *batey* swept and polished by centuries of waiting, open and bare, clean and warm for the dance.

The sleeping Cemí god that all of us Puerto Ricans bear within, the secret talisman Cemí, awakes from his lethargy in the hallowing solitude. And each one feels repeated in his neighbor, comrade, and companion with the renewed strength of hope. Venus shines like never before. The *batey* is flooded with light and the night is unable to obscure it. *Casabe* bread and the *güiro* bring supper and dance. The *bohío* is adorned as a feathered Cacique to receive the weary night watchers. The *batey* trembles with the weight of dreams at the hour of awakening.

At dawn, crouched in the cactus flower, erect in its green carapace, dreams look, undaunted, at the blue and white sky; secure and resting in the tranquil confidence of the thorny enclosure that protects them from evil, beating in the heart of the millennial Antillean plant.

    Casabe. Güiro. Bohío. Batey.
    Güiro. Batey. Casabe. Bohío.
    Casabe. Bohío. Batey. Güiro.
    Bohío. Casabe. Güiro. Batey.

THE MOUNTAINS KNOW

by Concha Meléndez

I love my country's lofty mountains!
Here, where all is soft and quiet,
They are untamed.
They are the symbol of a hidden power
That germinates through the ages.

Sometimes the storm bursts upon their summits;
Into their virgin bosom the dew shakes its tears;
The sun surrounds them with a thousand halos;
The mist offers them fantastic kisses;

But they lift their foreheads
Unmoved before the mysteries that life contains,
Before men's struggles and petty ambitions,
Which are nothing, if seen across unfathomable,
Infinite eternity.

The mountains, nearby, are like a glowing hope;
And from afar, like in a maiden's dream,
Floating in the blue distance.

Why do they rise thoughtful and serene?
Because they know many things unknown to us;
And in the nights full of blossoms,
The stars have told them the shining destinies
Of all the islands:
The great old past of the Isles of Greece,
The great new future that awaits the Antilles;
Of the genius of a victorious race,

The great deeds of Latin America,
The hymn of the peoples that are unfurling,
One and many at the same time,
The banner of Bolívar's dream!

The mountains know it,
The mountains lofty and unmoved!

SERENADE OF THE COQUÍ

by Tomás Blanco

In the capital of Puerto Rico, the day is usually noisy to the point of fatigue and exhaustion, to the very edge of neurosis; filled with yells, buzzing, and stridencies, thundering of planes; suffocated by loudspeakers and phonographs, deafened by nickelodeons, stabbed by car horns; wrenched by disturbances of spoiled dogs and stray children, vexed and harassed by insistent vociferations—mechanized and ambulatory—of politicians, announcers, speakers, charlatans, and propagandizers. . . .

Much of this urban but uncivil noise overflows to the advantage of the highways and radios, and inundates a good part of the rural zone. And as it still doesn't fit in the daylight hours, there always remains a residue that hides itself and stays in malicious lurking places to surge again, unexpectedly, with raucous bubbles or mechanical cries, from time to time during the night.

In the open countryside the night is sonorous, but of a sonority without abrupt sounds or alarms, rather tranquilizing and soporific for the person who is familiar with it. They are basic, natural, almost friendly sounds; in general, in a minor key, measured, without boasting. Except for the crowing of the cock, who is here not only the reveille of dawn and wakener of morning, but a repeating clock, sentinel of the night who, hour by hour, passes to his neighbor—and this one to another, and the other to another, till it is lost in the distance—his proud voice of alert. (If I do not announce in the tone of a challenge that I remain on guard—he seems to proclaim with his haughty "Here I am!"—I could proclaim the fact that someone dare to disturb the order of things and a catastrophe occur.)

In its sum total, nocturnal sonority spreads as in concentric circles toward the distance; and then murmurings and whisperings are heard, sounds the day's tumult and city traffic usually surpass and silence, but which, purified, are filtered through the distances of the tranquil night. Thus the sound of manly games of the sea on the shore and the fluctuations of the skirting, gentle brushing caused by the friskiness of the leaves with the wind reach the realm of the ear.

Perhaps, halfway in the distance, a wise-eyed owl pours the pitcher of its scolding voice on the oblique, unanimous, monotonous, and assiduous chorus of insects and batrachians. And from this minute and blinking acoustic multitude, which by dint of the invariable, unison reiteration results almost in lulling, the elf voice of the *coquí*—neat, clear, humid, liquid—is perceived and stands out; it is the most typical and characteristic sound of the Puerto Rican night.

The *coquí* is the herald of the nocturnal orchestra. It is the first to awake, when the sun has hardly set and twilight is not yet extinguished. From the mountains and savannas it reaches the towns; and it is not rare that it penetrate the most closely woven network of asphalted streets to the very heart of the cities, provided it find there a bit of garden or a little moist earth and some shrubs. Its ventriloquist notes acquire a curious tone of intimacy; and although it is outside the houses, shortly after it approaches them, it is listened to as though it were under the roof, sharing the very same room, and hidden, urging us, from the corners, to play hide and seek with it.

The onomatopoeia of its very name reproduces satisfactorily the theme of its song: an unending rhythmic repetition of the two syllables, *co-qui*, the latter more acute and crystalline and somewhat more prolonged, both very clear and precise, followed by a pause that lasts twice as long as that of the two notes together. The timbre is transparent, agreeable, quite similar to the human whistle, but a little hollow and somewhat xylophonic or aquatic; without great volume but very resonant. The tone is more tenorlike than baritone, like the call of a bird of medium size and excellent throat. It has the disturbing quality of fooling the ear as to the exact location of its origin. And it suggests a state of obsession, solitude, yearning. At times, now and then, it marks a variation in a brief series of notes—generally five—which are, perhaps, slightly more rapid and tenorlike, with the accent increased on the last: *co–qui–qui–qui*.

It is difficult for anyone to remain several days in Puerto Rico without hearing the *coqui*'s serenade. On the other hand, many have been born on the island and lived here all their lives without ever having seen it. Also, the person who doesn't know it and observes it for the first time in daylight will find it impossible to imagine that what he is looking at is the obstinate nocturnal singer. So much so, that I am in favor of believing the legend that my old nanny, María Antonia, an affectionate and magnificent Negress, of those who wore a Madras kerchief on her head, voluminous and banty-legged, and always smiling, clean, and starched, used to tell me. According to her the *coquí* must be a marvelous singing bird, beautiful as the hummingbird, which has been enchanted; a bewitched little bird, of spoiled character, playful and sociable, which—heaven knows for what self-devilishness or the envy of others—has been condemned to spend nights alone, completely isolated in the midst of life, calling and calling and calling in a vain attempt to obtain company, profoundly desolate, but without ever despairing. And if someone finally, after much searching, succeeds in seeing it, in that very instant it is transformed and disfigured in such a way that it is impossible to recognize in it the owner of the voice that invited the search for him.

But very scientific wise men—who almost always are right in a great part of what they say, although frequently they are as wrong as any neighbor's son, and at times they know nothing of the ultimate truths—affirm that this is not so, that it is all pure fantasy. Because the professional naturalists, especially the herpetologists, allege they have captured, dissected, studied and catalogued the *coquí*. And besides, they have photographed it for us, about to give its song to the wind, with its throat inflated like an enormous bagpipe.

The *coquí*, they say, is a minuscule animal, classified—perhaps somewhat arbitrarily, I say, for what will be seen later—among the amphibians, of the family of toads and frogs, but of a different zoological genre. The scientific name of its species is *Eleutherodactylus portoricencis*, which translated literally into Christian tongue means "the Puerto Rican with the free fingers."

So that the aspect of its digital freedom not be taken wrong, it must here be clarified that it is so called for not being palmiped like the common frog, and for not having either a remnant of natatory, or swimming, membrane between its toes or fingers. Hence it is not equipped to live in water. In compensation it has a type of disk stuck to the tip of each one of its toes, and it uses them to climb up plants, where it usually lives. For that reason I think it is quite arbitrary to classify it as an amphibian; for neither in its infancy nor young life was it a water tadpole. In fact, the Puerto Rican *coquí* is, in scientific literature, "really famous," as Karl P. Schmidt points out:

Because its eggs and embryos were the basis for the article by Peters, in which he described its direct development, with the suppression of the tadpole stage, a universal characteristic of the eleutherodactyl genus; and Peters' illustrations are still included in a great number of textbooks.

Apparently it is native to Puerto Rico, and is not found on any other island or the mainland. But in our island it abounds everywhere. It is found from Mayagüez to Humacao, from Ponce to Santurce, in El Yunque rain forest, at two thousand feet, and in Cataño, almost completely below sea level. It prefers to live in the midst of bromeliaceous and liliaceous plants or between the leaves of thickets of plantains and the guineo banana, but in cases of need it seeks shelter in any grass or shrub. Its size is very small: in general, the adult measures—from front to back—thirty-five or forty millimeters, approximately; the widest part of the body (some fifteen millimeters) is the head. The coloration is notable because of its many variations. The most frequent is that on its back it is dark, of different shades, between brown and grayish or dark honey, often reddish, often almost black, usually spotted or marked with lines or bands. Underneath, it is lighter, amber colored, yellowish or pale green; and the ventral surface or interior of the thighs is red or of an iron color or bright pink.

Such is the authentic genuine *coquí*, the Puerto Rican kind, the one which in singing says clearly, "Co-quí." Yet, it has a relative of its same genus though of a different species—*Eleutherodactylus antillensis*—which people also commonly call the *coquí*. But it is easy to distinguish one from the other. Visually they are differentiated mainly because the *antillensis*, or Antillean, is smaller, and features a reticulated dark drawing on the ventral surface of the thighs. The Antillean's song is less of a song than that of the true *coquí*; it is—in a manner of speaking—more multitudinous, less individual, and much less deliberate. Its timbre is rather more metallic. In reality, it never says, "Co-quí." It emits a frequent and relatively long series of uniform notes: "Ki-ki-ki-ki-ki-ki-ki . . ."; like a little bell a bit cracked. When occasionally it gives only two notes, it sounds something like *kri-i* and *tri-i-o*, perhaps *tro-i* and *to-i*.

The data of scientific nature that I have notated above were learned when my curiosity was spurred on to discover these things, quite some time ago. I do not know if from then to now the scientific criteria on our *coquí* has changed. Anything is possible, for they say being wise is to change opinions. And perhaps, nowadays, the most-documented naturalists would be in agreement with the hypothesis of María Antonia, my old nanny: that the *coquí* is, truly, a noctambulant sprite, a mysterious and rare enchanted little bird, which spends nights clamoring for company, without anyone's ever being able to discover it in its natural habitat. It wouldn't surprise me.

"PUERTORICANISTS" AND "OCCIDENTALISTS"

by Nilita Vientós Gastón

The dispute over universals and the battle between the ancients and the moderns are going to seem niceties compared to that which has risen in Puerto Rico between the "Puertoricanists" and the "Occidentalists." As in the great majority of polemics, neither side is completely right.

The Puertoricanists run the risk of becoming regionalists if they do not distinguish between what is national and what is nationalistic. The Occidentalists run the risk of becoming an imitation of the sophisticate, of he who belongs to no place. The first limit too much their field of vision. They approach what is ours so closely that they cannot see it clearly; they forget what there is beyond and all around. It is the vision of the myopic individual. The second extend their field of vision too much. They believe that what is ours is understood looking at the distant thing of which it is a part. It is the vision of the presbyopic person.

Puertoricanists as well as Occidentalists need corrective lenses. Because Puertoricanists have to be Occidental, or Western, and Occidentalists have to be Puerto Ricans.

To be Puerto Rican is by necessity to be Occidental. The fatherland and the cultural world to which the latter belongs are prior to any individual preference. They mark with certain characteristics the individual who is born and lives in them. This does not mean that he is to limit his spiritual world to that of the fatherland. Nor that what he believes he perceives of the rest of the world is to overpower his own.

He who wishes to see only his own country does not succeed in seeing even what happens there. He who insists on seeing that which is foreign and gives no importance to what is happening in his own country does not succeed in understanding anything. It is the knowledge of the one's own which leads to the knowledge of the universal; the understanding of what is one's own that leads to the understanding of what belongs to others. Provided the vision of the particular and individual is not deformed by chauvinism, prejudice, intolerance, or lack of compassion.

In that manner, what is authentically national—as distinguished from nationalistic—succeeds in attaining a universal category in art. Because what is national does not exclude what is universal, it is an aspect of the latter and as such understandable by men of other homelands.

This curious dispute is nothing more than another symptom of the spiritual confusion in which Puerto Ricans live because of the lack of confidence in their destiny as a people. Either they exaggerate their condition as a Puerto Rican or claim not to give it any importance.

How can a man who has two homelands, two flags, two constitutions, and two anthems feel integrated, whole? With the total of just one of each of these things, any man who thinks a little is preoccupied. With the total of two of each of them, what can be expected?

The Puerto Rican has to harmonize his intimate life to be able to face the world. As long as he does not know what he is, he lacks a point of reference to see what surrounds him, his own as well as that of others.

How much force the words Pedreira wrote in 1934 still have! "We honestly believe that the Puerto Rican soul exists disjoined, dispersed, in a luminously fragmented potency, like a painful puzzle that has never enjoyed its integrity."

▼▲▼▲▼▲▼▲▼▲▼▲▼▲▼▲▼▲▼▲

XIV. THE SONG OF THE BLACK DANCE

It seems that black slavery on the island never was as inhuman as elsewhere. The mountainous terrain did not encourage large slave plantations. Even in the early 1800s there were four "free people of color" to every slave, the only land in the Americas where this was true. In fact, the first slaves in Puerto Rico were "white Christians," and the first black man on the island, Juan Garrido, was a free, black conquistador, and friend of Ponce de León. So the literature of the African heritage tends to be one of joy and power, not horror and death, although the tragic memory of slavery does remain. In his world-acclaimed *Tun Tun de Pasa y Grifería* (1937), the poet Luis Palés Matos (1899–1959) celebrates the ancient rituals in Modernist forms. His "Black Dance" is renowned throughout Latin America. Although not a black, he was born and brought up in Guayama, a city of many descendants of slaves, and he evokes the love and mystery of this world, while he condemns the poverty and the tediousness of life in his hometown in "Pueblo"—"my poor town, where my poor people die of nothing." His "The Call" is inspired by the premonition of near-death. Of all Puerto Rican poets, Luis Palés Matos is the most quoted and most famous in Hispano-American literature.

BLACK DANCE

by Luis Palés Matos

Calabó[1] and bamboo,
bamboo and *calabó*.
The great Cocoroco[2] says: *tu-cu-tú*.
The great Cocoroca[3] says: *to-co-tó*.
It's the iron sun that burns in Timbuctu.
It's the Black dance of Fernando Poo.
The pig in the mud squeals: *pru-pru-prú*.
The toad in the pond dreams: *cro-cro-cró*.
Calabó and bamboo.
Bamboo and *calabó*.

The *junjunes*[4] break out in a furious *ú*.
The *gongos*[5] quiver with a profound *ó*.
It's the Black race that is undulating
with the thick rhythm of the *mariyandá*.[6]

The *botucos*[7] already arrive at the fiesta.
Dancing and dancing the Negress gives in.
Calabó and bamboo.
Bamboo and *calabó*.

The great Cocoroco says: *tu-cu-tú*.
The great Cocoroca says: *to-co-tó*.

Red islands pass, islands of shoeblack:
Haiti, Martinique, Congo, Camaroon;
The *papiamento*[8] Antilles of rum
and the patois islands of the volcano,
which in the grave sound
of song give in.

Calabó and bamboo.
Bamboo and *calabó*.
It's the iron sun that burns in Timbuctu.
It's the Black dance of Fernando Poo.
The African soul that is vibrating
in the thick rhythm of the *mariyandá*.

Calabó and bamboo.
Bamboo and *calabó*.
The great Cocoroco says: *tu-cu-tú*.
The great Cocoroca says: *to-co-tó*.

Notes

1. African wood for drums.
2. Main African tribal chief.
3. Cocoroco's wife.
4. Primitive violin.
5. Drums.
6. Black dance in Puerto Rico.
7. Minor chieftains.
8. Caribbean dialect of Curaçao.

PUEBLO

by Luis Palés Matos

Pity, Lord, pity on my poor town,
where my poor people will die of nothing!

That old notary who spends days
in his minimal and slow, ratlike job;
this adipose mayor with a big, empty belly
wallowing in his life, as though in a sauce;
that slow business the same as ten centuries ago;
these goats that frolic in the sun glare of the square;
some beggar; some horse that crosses,
sordid, gray, and skinny, these wide streets;
the cold atrophying Sunday drowsiness,
playing billiards and cards in the casino;
everything, the whole tedious flock of these lives
in the old town where nothing happens,
all this is dying, falling, crumbling
by dint of being comfortable and unrestricted.
Unleash some villain on these poor souls
to cast the redeeming stone of an extraordinary deed
against the dead water of their lives . . . ;
some thief to assault that bank at night;
some Don Juan to ravage that chaste damsel;
some professional gambler to get into the town
and stir up these honorable docile people. . . .

Pity, Lord, pity on my poor town;
where my poor people will die of nothing!

THE CALL

by *Luis Palés Matos*

They call me from afar . . .
long voice of dry leaf,
fleeting hand of cloud
that is dispersed in the autumn air.
Above, the call
pulls me with a fine thread of star;
below, the moving water,
with plaint of foam in the mist.
For some time I hear the voices
and I discover the signs.

Today I remember: it is a fortunate day
of clear sky and clear land;
erratic swallows
pluck the calm blue.
I am facing the sea and in the distance
the wing of a sail is disappearing;
farther and farther, fading away,
and I too am being erased in it.
And when I finally return
through a little chink of conscience
how far I already find me from myself!
What a strange world surrounds me!

Now, sleeping next to me, rests
my love on the grass.
The beating breast
rises and falls tranquilly in the tide

of the becalmed stimulus that dilutes
the ghostly indigo blue in her sockets.
I look at that fatigued sweet fabric,
a body of snare and prey
whose essential rhythm like playing
manufactures the aerial caress,
the narcotic lullaby and the kiss—
burning prelude of joyful complaint—
and I tell myself: It's all over.
But suddenly, she awakens,
and there in the black depths of her pupils
which are a farewell and an absence,
something invites me to her remote frontier
and takes me sweetly, unwilling.

They call me from afar . . .
My ship, prepared, is ready.
Around her, in clusters of silence,
shadows mutely coagulate.
An empty sea, without fish,
empty and black water,
without a vein of light to penetrate it,
nor footstep of breeze to disturb it.
Motionless background of shadow,
gray limit of stone. . . .
Oh, solitude, by dint of being alone
feels its own companion!

Solicitous emissary who comes
with occult message to my door,
I know what you intend
and your secret mission does not fool me;
they call me from afar,

but love asleep here in the grass
is still beautiful
and a joy of sun bathes the land;
may your implacable might grant me
an hour, another minute with her!

▼▲▼▲▼▲▼▲▼▲▼▲▼▲▼▲▼▲▼

XV. THE BLACK "DEVIL MASKS"

On the Fiesta de Santiago, July 25, the people of Loíza celebrate Santiago, or Saint James, the Spaniards' "Saint of Conquest," first in the wars against the Moors, and then in the conquest of the Indians of the Americas. And the villagers of Loíza are almost all descendants of African slaves and Borinquen Indians. The fiesta is a celebration of complex paradoxes, in which the masked dancers taunt and mock those to whom they pay homage. In his drama *Masquerade: Devil Masks*, the playwright Francisco Arriví (1915–) captures the duality of the revelry and the rapine, the ecstatic and the ordinary, by humanizing the holy symbols of the religious ceremony, which is both sacred and profane. (Translated by Dr. R. E. Coulthard.)

A darker footnote to this "superstition of sex and violence" in America appears in José A. Balseiro's (1900–) "The Black Trumpet" from *Eve of Shadow* (1959). Written while the poet lived in the United States, it is a poem of "pain and mystery" of "the oppressed dream of the race struggles"—as is the Fiesta de Santiago.

MASQUERADE: DEVIL MASKS

by Francisco Arriví

Characters (in Act I):

Toña	A young girl
Benedicto	Toña's seducer and keeper

Carnival maskers and drummers on the feast of Santiago in Loíza

Bathers on the beach of Luquillo

Act I

Before the curtain rises, there is the beating of drums, which increases in intensity. The chorus of drummers sings incessantly over and over again the same line:

> Joyalito, ay, Joyalito
> Joyalito, ay, Joyalito
> Te olvidaron en el puente.

The lights come up on a warm tropical afternoon. First is seen the floating flame of the flamboyant, then the straw peasant huts against a background of coconut trees. The singing continues. The drummers come forward, twisting their bodies. They are dressed in the style of the first decade of the twentieth century: bright colored handkerchiefs on their heads, shirts and pants of white drill. Every now and then they become possessed, shake spasmodically, and stamp their feet in the sand.

TOÑA, a young brown girl of slender firm body bursts on to the center of the stage and laughs excitedly. Her face sparkles with grace and animal health. She is wearing a tight skirt, flared around the bottom. Her head is covered with a bright handkerchief. The singing continues loudly. TOÑA waves her hand. She looks around as the drummers sing enthusiastically. TOÑA goes toward the left, playfully suspicious. Suddenly she runs off toward the right, laughing. She disappears as the CARNIVAL MASK appears from the left. He stands in the middle of the stage and looks around. He is staggering like a person who is drunk. He glimpses TOÑA among the palm trees and runs off after the girl, whose laughter can be heard all the time. Drumming continues loud and intense. TOÑA again bursts onto the stage, this time to the right, followed closely by the CARNIVAL MASK. She laughs with affected fear as the monster describes circles around her. She disappears off to the left with the CARNIVAL MASK at her heels. Drumming and singing continue. TOÑA runs quickly on from behind the peasant huts and stops, looking at the palm trees. The CARNIVAL MASK sneaks up unperceived behind TOÑA. He stands there staggering, looking from behind the flamboyant trees on the right. He constantly shifts his balance in order not to lose sight of the girl's physical splendor. TOÑA turns around, and her eyes meet the monster's; he bursts into loud laughter. The girl

*also laughs, joyfully, with the lustiness of a young healthy
animal. An old drummer stands up "possessed by the saint,"
and the rest of the drummers stop singing.*

DRUMMER: (*Over the beating drums*) Dance the *bomba,*
black girl!

CHORUS: Dance, black girl!

TOÑA *has her eyes riveted on the* CARNIVAL MASK, *who
invites her to come to him with a simultaneous gesture of
both his gloved hands.*

DRUMMER: (*Moving his body to the beating of the drums*)
Dance the *bomba,* Toñita!

TOÑITA *faces the drummers.*

CHORUS: Dance, black girl, dance!

Without facing the CARNIVAL MASK, TOÑA *looks at him
with a side glance and begins to mark the rhythm of the
drums with head movements.*

CHORUS: Dance, black girl, dance!

TOÑA *gathers up the two ends of her flared skirt, and with a
rhythmic shake of her body greets the* PAMPERED ONE, *then
the* SPOILED ONE, *and finally the* CARNIVAL MASK, *abandoning
herself to the frenzy of the* bomba *dance as the
drummers begin to sing again. The* CARNIVAL MASK *contorts
grotesquely, trying to imitate the muscular agility of* TOÑA.
*The girl, in a crescendo of rhythmic compulsion, dances
close to the* CARNIVAL MASK, *facing him with the voluptuous
insinuation of the different sequences of the* bomba. *The*
CARNIVAL MASK, *his senses aroused, moves about frantically
as if under a wild spell. As* TOÑA *repeats one of the flashing
sequences of the dance several times, the monster snatches
off his horned mask, revealing the ruddy, moustached face*

of BENEDICTO, *a Spaniard in his prime, who is obviously
excited by overdrinking.*

BENEDICTO: (*Concentrating on* TOÑA's *waist*) Dance, black
            girl, dance!
TOÑA: (*Her back to the mask*) Dance, Spaniard,
            dance!
BENEDICTO: (*Trying to seize her*) For Santiago and Spain!
TOÑA: (*Setting herself free with a dance step*) Dance,
            Spaniard, dance!

The MASK *tries awkwardly to keep up with the dance, and*
TOÑA *shows her amusement in side glances.*

BENEDICTO: (*With another lewd advance*) For Santiago and
            Spain!
TOÑA: (*Freeing herself again*) Dance, Spaniard,
            dance!

*Shrill voices in obvious falsetto are heard offstage, and a
group of* CRAZY MASKS *rush in—men dressed in women's
clothes with sooted faces, another feature of the traditional
revelry of the feast day of Santiago. They surround* TOÑA
and BENEDICTO, *laugh with parrotlike hollowness, make
high-pitched comments about the pair, and end up dancing
gleefully and chattering at the same time.* TOÑA *weaves to
and fro among the* MASKS *with supreme grace and agility.*
BENEDICTO *pursues her tenaciously, stumbling and bumping
against the* CRAZY MASKS, *who, with shrill protests, pretend
to be angered. The* CARNIVAL MASK *tries to seize* TOÑA
*several times, in vain. Then he decides to dance in the
middle of the* MASKS, *and pretends he is taking no notice of*
TOÑA. TOÑA *comes very close to him and gives him a push.
Then, in her overconfidence she gets too close, and the*
CARNIVAL MASK *manages to seize her. They struggle;* TOÑA
gets away, and with a push knocks the CARNIVAL MASK *over*

*on his face. She takes advantage of the following noise and
laughter of the* Masks *to run out of the dance and disappear
among the palm trees to the left. The* Carnival Mask *gets
up. He looks for* Toña *among the* Masks; *when he can't find
her, he separates himself from the group. Several of the*
Masks *seize hold of him and make him dance against his
will. In one of the turns, he sees* Toña *amidst the palm trees.*

Benedicto: Toña! Come here! Don't refuse me your sweetness.

The Carnival Mask *gets away from the others, who laugh
and screech in falsetto, and he runs stumbling after the girl.
The* Masks *move to the left to see what is going on;
commentaries are made in excited, parrotlike voices. The
drummers, completely possessed by the music, are slapping
the leather of their drums violently and singing out their
song with great enthusiasm.*

First Mask:(*Looking toward the palm grove*) He can't
catch her.
Second Mask: He'll catch her.
First Mask:He'll lose her in the bush.
Second Mask: He'll catch her.
First Mask:(*Pushing the other* Mask *jokingly*) Why do you
think he is going to catch her?
Second Mask: Because Toña wants to be caught.
First Mask:Why do you think Toña wants to be caught?
Second Mask: Because she likes the Spaniard.
First Mask:Don't be foolish! She doesn't pay him any
mind!
Second Mask: Maybe she only says that, you understand?
First Mask:'Course I understand. Maybe that's not what
she means. (*He laughs.*)

SECOND MASK: (*In a natural voice*) The Spaniard has been
             after Toña for days.

FIRST MASK: Heavens, ·Mask! Don't speak in that man's
             voice! You frighten me.

SECOND MASK: (*In a natural voice*) She's got a devil in her
             today, and he'll catch her in the bushes.

FIRST MASK: (*Putting his fingers into his ears*) Let me cover
             up my ears.

SECOND MASK: (*In a natural voice*) Those Spaniards always
             take off the prettiest dark girl.

FIRST MASK: (*Taking one finger out of his ear*) What did you
             say?

SECOND MASK: (*Raising his voice*) The Spaniards always
             carry off the prettiest brown girls.

FIRST MASK: What are you worrying about? We all know
             that the brown girls love the Spaniards. Let's
             go and dance.

*The revelers start to dance with great energy and noise,
moving slowly off right. The* SECOND MASK *stays motionless,
looking into the palm grove. The lights dissolve into
twilight—a silhouette of the hut, the palm trees, and the
fringe of violent sea. All one can see is the flame of the
poinsettia, a motionless fire in the darkness. The singing and
the beating of the drums can be heard away in the distance.
The silvery light of the moon comes up to attenuate the red
of the flamboyant.* TOÑA *and the* SPANIARD *become visible.*
TOÑA *is seated on the sand. She is leaning on her left arm,
wearily. The kerchief that covered her hair, now disheveled,
is hanging down over one shoulder, and her dress and her
skirt are rumpled. She is staring fixedly at the sand in front
of her. The* SPANIARD, *wearing a shirt and pants, is putting
on his beret. The remnants of his drunkenness make his
movements clumsy, but he is now looking at* TOÑA *without*

desire. He picks up his gloves, his costume, and his carnival mask, which are scattered on the sand around the girl, shakes off the sand, and then glances at TOÑA.

BENEDICTO: There is nothing to worry about. These things can easily be fixed.

TOÑA *remains silent.*

BENEDICTO: (*Raising his voice*) I told you that these things can be fixed. Tomorrow I shall speak to your father.

TOÑA *raises her head slowly, looks at him with slight hope.*

BENEDICTO: (*Emphatically, trying to impress her*) First thing in the morning!

TOÑA: (*In a weak voice, afraid to express what she really feels*) I can't go home.

BENEDICTO: Of course you can go home.

TOÑA: You know my father? He is capable of cutting me with a machete!

BENEDICTO: I'll say I know him. I have bought thousands of coconuts for my shop from him. He usually splits them with one blow of his machete.

TOÑA: He'll do the same with me.

BENEDICTO: Well, just think of it. If you lose your head and do anything foolish, both of us will be buried. And all that just for a piece of foolishness between a man and a woman. Half this village was born in the same way.

TOÑA: What am I going to do?

BENEDICTO: (*Silent for a few moments; then he makes a decision and kneels down next to* TOÑA.) Listen carefully to what I am going to tell you and don't argue.

Toña *looks at him suspiciously.*

BENEDICTO: Cheer up, girl! There is nothing to worry about. You'll easily get out of this business.

Toña *is silent, waiting.*

BENEDICTO: In the first place, you had better fix your hair and your dress, okay?

Toña *is silent.*

BENEDICTO: What's happened to your tongue, girl? Have you swallowed it?

Toña: (*Expressionless*) I'll fix myself.

BENEDICTO: That's fine. Now in the second place, you go back to the dance, as though nothing had happened. Tell the people that I couldn't catch you. Understand?

Toña: (*Beginning to understand what the Spaniard means*) I see.

BENEDICTO: What do you see?

Toña: (*With a shrug of her shoulders*) Nothing.

BENEDICTO: Cheer up, I say. (*After a moment's hesitation*) All right, you dance for a while, then you go back home. As usual you ask for your parents' blessing, and you say good night to them and you go to bed.

Toña: (*Mechanically*) To bed?

BENEDICTO: (*Getting up*) Of course! And you have my absolute promise that you will see me first thing tomorrow morning. First thing.

Toña: Thanks.

BENEDICTO: If you take my advice everything will work out all right.

TOÑA: (*In a hopeless voice*) What are you going to say to my father?

BENEDICTO: To your father? (*He stands up and looks at her for a few moments.*) Now, you must make an effort not to get annoyed. Right now you need all your presence of mind. No nerves. If any indiscretion of yours makes your father suspect what has happened, it will be good-bye to your head and good-bye to mine. I am as sure of that as I am sure that Alfonso XIII reigns over Spain and the Americans stole Puerto Rico from us ten years ago.

TOÑA: (*In a hard voice, trying to hurt him*) And what are you going to say to him?

The SPANIARD *remains silent.*

TOÑA: (*Trying not to cry*) What!

BENEDICTO: (*After a pause; lowering his voice*) Would you like to wash my clothes, cook my food for me?

TOÑA: (*Hurt*) That?

BENEDICTO: (*Stretching out a hand*) Don't take it that way. There are reasons for my making this suggestion.

TOÑA *starts to cry.*

BENEDICTO: Come now! None of the women think with their head. Whether black or white. (*In a conciliating tone*) What are you crying for, if I am going to fix everything?

TOÑA *turns round and weeps with her back toward the* SPANIARD.

BENEDICTO: You shouldn't let what happened worry you

like this. How many girls in the village started out this way? And today are selling themselves on the streets of San Juan.

Toña *lets herself drop to the ground and weeps.*

BENEDICTO: (*Kneeling down again*) There is a little wooden house behind my shop. You could have it for as long as you want.

Toña *shakes her head.*

BENEDICTO: Be calm. It's just for the time being. Soon I shall be able to look after you in a better way. My brother is well established in San Juan, and if he knew anything about this he'd cause me a lot of trouble. People back home in Spain want to marry me off to a girl from my village. I don't want to upset them. (*He gestures with both his hands.*) They don't understand that a man may fall in love in the West Indies. They say that African blood should stay overseas.

Toña: (*Sits up and looks at him proudly, although still weeping*) You needn't bother about me. You sound as if you are talking about an animal rather than a woman.

BENEDICTO: (*In a firm voice*) Ah! Peace and love! Don't lose the only way that can keep us together. It is true that I shall ask your father to let you work for me as a servant. There is nothing else we can do. But in the shop, when I have closed up everything for the day, then we shall be alone together. Toña will be for me the prettiest brown girl and the best rhumba dancer in the whole island.

Toña: (*Scornfully*) You pig!

The SPANIARD *laughs.*

TOÑA: (*Angrily*) And what if there is a child?
BENEDICTO: We will speak of that in due course.
TOÑA: Tell me, what are you going to do if a child is
             born?
BENEDICTO: (*After a pause*) I'll dress him and feed him.

He takes her in his arms and tries to kiss her. TOÑA *struggles.
Men's voices are heard approaching. The* SPANIARD *looks to
the left and stands up.*

BENEDICTO: (*After listening to the voices*) Well, you know
             what to do. Tomorrow morning. No foolish-
             ness, no nerves. You will be my servant in the
             daytime but at night you will be my queen. As
             time goes by and things change, who knows,
             we may be able to fix things better.

He runs off into the darkness to the right. TOÑA *looks
vacantly for a few moments, then turns her head and looks
after the* SPANIARD. *More* MASKS *come in from the left. The
disguises, which are adorned with sequins and multicolored
ribbons, shine fantastically in the light of the moon.*

MASKS: (*All shouting together*) Toña!

TOÑA *turns around and looks at them.*

FIRST MASK: What are you doing here?
TOÑA: Nothing. I went to sleep in the moonlight.
SECOND MASK: Ha! The same tricky girl as always.
TOÑA: It's nice to be kissed by the light of the moon.
             It tastes like the foam of the sea.
SECOND MASK: It would be better if you were kissed by a
             man. (*He laughs.*)
TOÑA: I'll think about it. There are so many pigs in

	this village. But nothing could make me dream as I've dreamed tonight.
First Mask:	And what did you dream about?
Toña:	That my body was changed into a ripe naseberry.
First Mask:	Hmm. You must be in love.
Toña:	A knife of fire opened the naseberry in two.
First Mask:	I see. You must have gone to sleep looking at the flamboyant. They say that flamboyants fall in love when they're in flower. And that they need to kiss and kiss until they cover their last branch with flowers.
Toña:	That is what people say.
First Mask:	What else did you dream about?
Toña:	I dreamed that out of the sweetness was born a child whiter than myself.
Second Mask:	That is the dream of all brown girls. White children. They say the Spaniard Benedicto ran after you in the palm grove.
Toña:	For a while.
Second Mask:	Where is he now?
Toña:	(*Pointing toward the back of the stage*) I left him caught up on a bush in there. (*Brushing the sand off her dress*) You should have seen how he was kicking and shaking his horns.

All the Masks *laugh.*

Toña:	(*Taking up her multicolored handkerchief from the bush*) He looked like a devil caught by the hand of God.
Second Mask:	If he troubles you, just let me know. I've promised him a beating if he goes too far.
Toña:	(*Straightening her dress*) Oh, I let him chase after me, but I don't like him. He has got a face

like a rotten tomato and has more whiskers
than ten cats together.

SECOND MASK: Those Spaniards like us only from the
outside. They give their souls to possess our
women.

TOÑA: Let's dance, boys. Let's go on with the dance.

FIRST MASK: Who could refuse Toña? Prettiest brown girl in
the village.

TOÑA: (*Clapping her hands*) Well, let's all go and
dance out the night of the Feast of Santiago.

The MASKS *begin to beat out the rhythm of the song with
their hands.* TOÑA *takes up her dress, bows to each* MASK,
and then starts to dance herself. The CRAZY MASKS *come in
dancing from every side. They surround* TOÑA *and the
others.*

CRAZY MASKS: Toña, Toña, Toña, Toña.

Drumming and singing continue off in crescendo. TOÑA
sings one chorus in solo.

TOÑA: Long live Santiago! (*She remains motionless.*)

The MASKS *stop and look at* TOÑA.

TOÑA: (*After looking around her*) Good night. (*And
she goes off toward the left.*)

FIRST MASK: Don't go, Toña.

TOÑA: (*From the left side of the stage*) I have to go to
bed early.

FIRST MASK: But you always dance the whole night. The
light of day finds you under the flamboyants.

TOÑA: I can't keep my eyes open tonight.

SECOND MASK: (*In a natural voice, coming up to* TOÑA)
You look very tired, Toña.

TOÑA: The flamboyants are responsible for it. They
have been kissing me too much.

The MASKS *laugh.* TOÑA *disappears.*

FIRST MASK: She doesn't fool me. She isn't the same Toña.

SECOND MASK: (*In a natural voice*) I knew that the Spaniard . . .

FIRST MASK: She loves him?

SECOND MASK: (*In a natural voice*) She would die for him.

FIRST MASK: In that case, what can we do about it?

SECOND MASK: She'll soon leave the village.

FIRST MASK: You think so?

SECOND MASK: Very soon. Didn't you see the look in her eye?

FIRST MASK: Looks as if she had been crying.

SECOND MASK: The Carnival Mask has got into her soul.

FIRST MASK: (*In a falsetto*) Let's dance, boys.

The SECOND MASK, *dancing grotesquely, screams in a falsetto voice the song that has been sung throughout the play. All except the* FIRST *and* SECOND MASKS, *who remain still looking after* TOÑA, *throw themselves into the singing and dancing. The curtain comes down on the scene of the flame of the flamboyant. In the distance, during the interlude, comes faintly the beating of drums.*

THE BLACK TRUMPET

by José A. Balseiro

In New Orleans the black trumpet cried.
In Saint Louis the black trumpet cried.

The air is filled
with smells of starch and watermelon;
but there is a more pungent smell that escapes
from the burning coal of the armpit.

The trumpet scratched the last scale
looking for sharps from lost regions.

The roots of Africa are twisted
in the fury of the black trumpet.
The atavism of the centuries bites
superstition of sex and violence.

The oppressed dream of the race struggles
to express its pain and mystery
of words bewitched by the moon.
Along the arabesques
of improbable rhythm overflowed
there are confessions of new sadness
which dissolve the ice of the whites.

In New Orleans the black trumpet cried.
In Saint Louis the black trumpet cried.
And its cry is blue, like the illusion
of velvet
in the eyes of the blacks.
And its cry is blue, like the sorrows
that are dissolved
from the depths of the chest
in the tumult of dislocated jungles.

There are flashes of lightning
in the volcano of the black trumpet.
The shadow of the fingers
on the silver keys invents
broken boasts of old outcries
to conquer with its distant complaints.

Tears without weeping flow
over cloths of frustrated torsos.

The cabaret squeezes its throat.
The whip of hate
no longer strikes.
It only listens, only listens to
the black trumpet
with its suffering of sorrows and absences,
   the black trumpet,
      the black trumpet . . .

▼▲▼▲▼▲▼▲▼▲▼▲▼▲▼▲▼▲▼▲▼

XVI. THE MUÑOZ DREAM: FATHER AND SON

In February, 1898, Spain granted Puerto Rico autonomy. The island had more political freedom than it ever had, before or since. Luis Muñoz Rivera (1859–1916) became the "Prime Minister of Puerto Rico" in the short-lived autonomous government of which he was the foremost architect. He sought to define his tactics of statesmanship, achieving "compatibility between my political dreams and patriotic duties," in the fragment, "What I Have Been, What I Am, What I Shall Be." Barely five months after Spain granted autonomy, the United States invaded and colonialized the island again. For years Muñoz Rivera sought to gain the autonomy Puerto Rico had won, and lost, from its new conquerors. When during World War I, in May 1916, the Congress declared Puerto Ricans citizens of the United States, without their wish or consent (the Jones Act), Muñoz Rivera, as Resident Commissioner in Washington, D.C., made a bitterly ironic and angry speech to the House denouncing the arbitrary act ("Give Us Our Independence," speech by Luis Muñoz Rivera to the U.S. House of Representatives, May 15, 1916. *Hearings of the United States–Puerto Rico Commission*, 89th Cong. 2nd Sess., Document 108, 1965).

In 1898, Muñoz Rivera's son, Luis Muñoz Marín, was born. He was to become the first elected Puerto Rican governor of the island, in 1948. But Don Luis was a "man between two worlds": a bohemian poet, in Greenwich Village; El Vate, the Bard, who industrialized the island; a former *independentista* and Socialist, who encouraged the Americanization of the island, through the investments of American corporations. In his youth he envisioned his dream, and his achievement of "the Puerto Rican miracle," in a prophetic poem, "Pamphlet" (*An Anthology of Contemporary Latin American Poetry*, edited by Dudley Fitts, New York, New Directions, 1947). As governor of Puerto Rico, he created the concept of the free associated state. One of his famous speeches, dated January 19, 1960, is representative of his prose style and his dream of a good civilization.

WHAT I HAVE BEEN, WHAT I AM, WHAT I SHALL BE

by Luis Muñoz Rivera

(Fragment)

Between the redeeming republic and the redeeming monarchy, how to vacillate? I would have chosen the republic. Only the republic in Spain did not rise, it does not rise. And I was not sacrificing Puerto Rico to my preferences, my ideals, my theories. In my heart, in my will, Puerto Rico comes before Spain, before the United States, before

Europe, and before America. And when Puerto Rico needed to or needs to save itself, I went to Spain, I will go to the United States; I don't stop with the advice of my *amour propre*. Up with the interest of my island and down with the beauties I learned in my books, the illusions on which my soul was nurtured; if it were necessary, down with popularity, laboriously achieved in thirty years of effort and sacrifice.

Now, there is no danger in being a republican. I am one. This compatibility between my political dreams and my patriotic duties pleases me; but if another monarchy arrived triumphant at the doors of Washington, like Cataline at the doors of Rome; if a Theodore Roosevelt created the American empire as did Isabel with the Spanish empire; if there were reproduced the circumstances in which *I served not the monarchy but rather I managed to put the monarchy in the service of my homeland*, I would accept from Theodore Roosevelt as I accepted from Christine of Hapsburg, the salvation, the redemption of Puerto Rico.

This I was; this I am and this I will be till I fall into the silence and the repose of the tomb. This I understand that the good and perspicacious compatriots of mine ought to be. And for this reason I champion for the Union and *I remove obstacles for the union*, and thus have to embrace my ill-mannered adversaries and forgive my ill-mannered enemies, and forget that one day the pickax destroyed my shops, and demagogy threatened my home; and the reaction brought me to the prisoner's bench. That is naught; it is less than naught, for that is my anguish, my pain, because that, if I felt differently, could be my shame or my pride.

And the rest . . .

And the rest is my homeland.

GIVE US OUR INDEPENDENCE
by Luis Muñoz Rivera
(Speech given to the U.S. House of Representatives)

Mr. Speaker, I want to state, in the first place, that I have taken great pleasure in the declaration of the gentleman from Virginia, Mr. Jones, the other day, and also in the declaration of the gentleman from Iowa, Mr. Towner, this morning. Both gentlemen are doing justice to my country. Both have endeavored to make this bill, which I consider a general proposition, a democratic measure, acceptable to all of my countrymen in Porto Rico.

On the 18th day of October 1898, when the flag of this great Republic was unfurled over the fortresses of San Juan, if anyone had said to my countrymen that the United States, the land of liberty, was going to deny their right to form a government of the people, by the people, and for the people of Porto Rico, my countrymen would have refused to believe such a prophecy, considering it sheer madness. The Porto Ricans were living at that time under a regime of ample self-government, discussed and voted by the Spanish Cortes, on the basis of the parliamentary system in use among all the nations of Europe. Spain sent to the islands a Governor, whose power, strictly limited by law, made him the equivalent of those constitutional sovereigns who reign but do not govern. The members of the Cabinet, without whose signature no executive order was valid, were natives of the island; the representatives in the Senate and in the House were natives of the island; and the administration in its entirety was in the hands of natives of the island. The Spanish Cortes, it is true, retained the power to make statutory laws for Porto Rico, but in the Cortes were 16 Porto Rican representatives and 3 Porto Rican senators having voice and vote. And all the insular laws were made by the insular parliament.

Two years later, in 1900, after a long period of military rule, the Congress of the United States approved the Foraker Act. Under this act, all of the 11 members of the executive council were appointed by the President of the United States; 6 of them were the heads of departments; 5 exercised legislative functions only. And this executive council, or, in practice, the bureaucratic majority of the council, was, and is in reality, with the Governor, the supreme arbiter of the island and of its interests. It represents the most absolute contradiction of republican principles.

For 16 years we have endured this system of government, protesting and struggling against it, with energy and without result. We did not lose hope, because if one national party, the Republican, was forcibly enforcing this system upon us, the other national party, the Democratic, was encouraging us by its declarations in the platforms of Kansas City, St. Louis, and Denver. Porto Rico waited, election after election, for the Democratic Party to triumph at the polls and fulfill its promises. At last the Democratic Party did triumph. It is here. It has a controlling majority at this end of the Capitol and at the other end: it is in possession of the White House. On the Democratic Party rests the sole and undivided responsibility for the progress of events at this juncture. It can, by a legislative act, keep alive the hopes for the people of Porto Rico or it can deal these hopes their death blow.

The Republican Party decreed independence for Cuba and thereby covered itself with glory; the Democratic Party is bound by the principles written into its platforms and by the recorded speeches of its leaders to decree liberty for Porto Rico. The legislation you are about to enact will prove whether the platforms of the Democratic Party are more than useless paper, whether the words of its leaders are more than soap bubbles, dissolved by the breath of triumph. Here is the dilemma with its two unescapable horns: You must proceed in accordance with the fundamental principles of your party or you must be untrue to them. The monarchies of the Old World, envious of American success and the republics of the New World, anxious to see clearly the direction in which the American initiative is tending, are watching and studying the Democratic administration. Something more is at stake than the fate of Porto Rico— poor, isolated, and defenseless as she is—the prestige and the good name of the United States are at stake. England learned the hard lessons of Saratoga and Yorktown in the 18th century. And in the 19th century she established self-government, complete, sincere, and honorable in Canada, Australia, and New Zealand. Then in the 20th century, immediately after the Anglo-Boer War, she established self-government, complete, sincere, and honorable, for the Orange Free State and the Transvaal, her enemies of the day before. She turned over the reins of power to insurgents who were still wearing uniforms stained with British blood.

In Porto Rico no blood will be shed. Such a thing is impossible in an island of 3,600 square miles. Its narrow confines never permitted and never will permit armed resistance. For this very reason Porto Rico is a field of experiment unique on the globe. And if Spain, the reactionary monarchy, gave Porto Rico the home rule which she was enjoying in 1898, what should the United States, the progressive Republic, grant her? This is the mute question which Europe and America are writing today in the solitudes of the Atlantic and on the waters of the Panama Canal. The reply is the bill which is now under discussion. This bill cannot meet the earnest aspirations of my country. It is not a measure of self-government ample enough to solve definitely our political problem or to match your national reputation, established by a successful championship for liberty and justice throughout the world since the very beginning of your national life. But, meager and conservative as the bill appears when we look at its provisions from our own point of view, we sincerely recognize its noble purposes and willingly accept it as a step in the right direction and as a reform paving the way for others more acceptable and satisfactory which shall come a little later, provided that my countrymen will be able to demonstrate their capacity, the capacity they possess, to govern themselves. In regard to such capacity, it is my duty, no doubt a pleasant duty, to assure Congress that the Porto Ricans will endeavor to prove their intelligence, their patriotism, and their full preparation to enjoy and to exercise a democratic regime.

Our behavior during the past is a sufficient guarantee for our behavior in the future. Never a revolution there, in spite of our Latin blood; never an attempt to commercialize our political influence; never an attack against the majesty of law. The ever-reigning peace was not at any time disturbed by the illiterate masses, which bear their suffering with such stoic fortitude and only seek comfort in their bitter servitude, confiding in the supreme protection of God.

There is no reason which justifies American statesmen in denying self-government to my country and erasing from their programs the principles of popular sovereignty. Is illiteracy the reason? Because if in Porto Rico 60 percent of the electorate cannot read, in the United States in the early days of the Republic, 80 percent of the population were unable to read; and even today there are 20 Republics and 20 monarchies which acknowledge a higher percentage of illiteracy than Porto Rico. It is not the coexistence of two races on the island, because here in North America more than 10 States show a higher proportion of Negro population than Porto Rico and the District of Columbia has precisely the same proportion, 67 white to 33 percent colored. It is not our small territorial extent, because two States have a smaller area than Porto Rico. It is not a question of population, for by the last census there were 18 States with a smaller population than Porto Rico. Nor is it a matter of real and personal property, for the taxable property in New Mexico is only one-third that of Porto Rico. There is a reason and only one reason—the same sad reason of war and conquest which let loose over the South after the fall of Richmond thousands and thousands of office seekers, hungry for power and authority, and determined to report to their superiors that the rebels of the South were unprepared for self-government. We are the southerners of the 20th century.

The House of Representatives has never been influenced by this class of motive. The House of Representatives has very high motives, and, if they are studied thoroughly, very grave reasons, for redeeming my country from bureaucratic greed and confiding to it at once the responsibility for its own destinies and the power to fix and determine them. They are reasons of an international character which affect the policy of the United States in the rest of America; Porto Rico, the only one of the former colonies of Spain in this hemisphere, which does not fly its own flag or figure in the family of nations, is being closely observed with assiduous vigilance by the Republics of the Caribbean Sea and the Gulf of Mexico. Cuba, Santo Domingo, Venezuela, Colombia, Costa Rica, Honduras, Nicaragua, Salvador, Guatemala maintain with us a constant interchange of ideas and never lose sight of the experiment in the colonial government which is being carried on in Porto Rico. If they see that the Porto Ricans are living happily, that they are not treated with disdain, that their aspirations are being fulfilled, that their character is respected, that they are not being subjected to an imperialistic tutelage, and that the right to govern their own country is not being usurped, these nations will recognize the superiority of American methods and will feel the influence of the American government. This will smooth the way to the moral hegemony which you are called by your greatness, by your wealth, by your traditions, and your institutions to exercise in the New World. On the other hand, if these communities, Latin— like Porto Rico—speaking the same language as Porto Rico, branches of the same ancestral trunk that produced Porto Rico, bound to Porto Rico by so many roots striking deep in a common past, if these communities observe that your insular experiment is a failure and that you have not been able to keep the affections of a people who awaited from you their redemption and their happiness, they will be convinced that they must look, not to Washington but to London, Paris, or Berlin when they seek markets for their products, sympathy in their misfortunes, and guarantees for their liberty.

What do you gain along with the discontent of my countrymen? You as Members of Congress? Nothing. And the Nation loses a part of its prestige, difficulties are created in the path of its policies, its democratic ideals are violated, and it must abdicate its position as leader in every progressive movement on the planet. Therefore if you undertake a reform, do it sincerely. A policy of subterfuge and shadows might be expected in the Italy of the Medicis, in the France of the Valois, in the England of the Stuarts, or the Spain of the Bourbons, but it is hard to explain in the United States of Cleveland, McKinley, Roosevelt, and Wilson.

This bill I am commenting on provides for a full elective legislature. Well, that is a splendid concession you will make to your own principles and to our own rights. But now, after such a magnificent advance, do not permit, gentlemen, do not permit the local powers of the legislature to be diminished in matters so important for us as the education of the children. We are citizens jealous of this dignity; we are fathers anxious to foster our sons toward the future, teaching them how to struggle for life and how to reach the highest standard of honesty, intelligence, and energy. We accept one of your compatriots, a capable American, as head of the department of education, though we have in the island many men capable of filling this high office with distinction. We welcomed his appointment by the President of the United States. In this way the island will have the guarantee to find such a man as Dr. Brumbaugh, the first commissioner of education who went to Porto Rico, or as Dr. Miller, the present commissioner, who deserves all our confidence. But let the legislature regulate the courses of study, cooperating in that manner with the general development of educational work throughout our native country.

I come now to treat of a problem which is really not a problem for Porto Rico, as my constituents look at it, because it has been solved already in the Foraker Act. The Foraker Act recognizes the Porto Rican citizenship of the inhabitants of Porto Rico. We are satisfied with this

citizenship and desire to prolong and maintain it—our
natural citizenship, founded not on the conventionalism of
law but on the fact that we were born on an island and love
that island above all else, and would not exchange our
country for any other country, though it were one as great
and as free as the United States. If Porto Rico were to
disappear in a geological catastrophe and there survived a
thousand or 10,000 or a hundred thousand Porto Ricans,
and they were given their choice of all citizenships of the
world, they would choose without a moment's hesitation
that of the United States. But so long as Porto Rico exists on
the surface of the ocean, poor and small as she is, and even
if she were poorer and smaller, Porto Ricans will always
choose Porto Rican citizenship. And the Congress of the
United States will have performed an indefensible act if it
tries to destroy so legitimate a sentiment and to annul
through a law of its own making a law of the oldest and
wisest legislators of all time—a law of nature.

It is true that my countrymen have asked many times,
unanimously, for American citizenship. They asked for it
when through the promise of General Miles on his disem-
barkation in Ponce, and through the promises of the
Democratic Party when it adopted the Kansas City platform—they believed it not only possible but probable, not
only probable but certain, that American citizenship was
the door by which to enter, not after a period of 100 years
nor of 10, but immediately into the fellowship of the
American people as a State of the Union. Today they no
longer believe it. From this floor the most eminent statesmen have made it clear to them that they must not believe
it. And my countrymen, who, precisely the same as yours,
have their dignity and self-respect to maintain, refuse to
accept a citizenship of an inferior order, a citizenship of the
second class, which does not permit them to dispose of their

own resources nor to live their own lives nor to send to this Capitol their proportional representation. To obtain benefits of such magnitude they were disposed to sacrifice their sentiments of filial love for the motherland. These advantages have vanished, and the people of Porto Rico have decided to continue to be Porto Ricans; to be so each day with increasing enthusiasm, to retain their own name, claiming for it the same consideration, the same respect, which they accord to the names of other countries, above all to the name of the United States. Give us statehood and your glorious citizenship will be welcome to us and to our children. If you deny us statehood, we decline your citizenship, frankly, proudly, as befits a people who can be deprived of their civil liberties but who, although deprived of their civil liberties, will preserve their conception of honor, which none can take from them because they bear it in their souls, a moral heritage from their forefathers.

This bill which I am speaking of grants American citizenship to all my compatriots. It authorizes those who do not accept American citizenship to so declare before a court of justice, and thus retain their Porto Rican citizenship. It provides that—

"No person shall be allowed to register as a voter in Porto Rico who is not a citizen of the United States."

My compatriots are generously permitted to be citizens of the only country they possess, but they are eliminated from the body politic; the exercise of political rights is forbidden them and by a single stroke of the pen they are converted into pariahs and there is established in America, on American soil, protected by the Monroe Doctrine, a division into castes like the Brahmans and Sudras of India. The Democratic platform of Kansas City declared 14 years ago, "A nation can not long endure half empire and half republic," and "Imperialism abroad will lead rapidly and

irreparably to despotism at home." These are not Porto
Rican phrases reflecting our Latin impressionability; they
are American phrases, reflecting the Anglo-Saxon spirit,
calm in its attitude and jealous—very jealous—of its
privileges.

We have a profound consideration for your national
ideas; you must treat our local ideas with a similar
consideration. As the representative of Porto Rico I propose
that you convoke the people of the island to express
themselves in full plebiscite on the question of citizenship
and that you permit the people of Porto Rico to decide by
their votes whether they wish the citizenship of the United
States or whether they prefer their own natural citizenship.
It would be strange, if, having refused it so long as the
majority of people asked for it, you should decide to impose
it by force now that the majority of the people decline it.

Someone recently stated that we desire the benefits but
shirk the responsibilities and burdens of citizenship. I affirm
in reply that we were never consulted as to our status, and
that in the Treaty of Paris the people of Porto Rico were
disposed of as were the serfs of ancient times, fixtures of the
land, who were transferred by force to the service of new
masters and subject to new servitudes. The fault is not ours,
though ours are the grief and humiliation; the fault lies with
our bitter destiny which made us weak and left us an easy
prey between the warring interests of mighty powers. If we
had our choice, we would be a free and isolated people in
the liberty and solitude of the seas, without other advantages than those won by our exertions in industry and in
peace, without other responsibilities and burdens than those
of our own conduct and our duty toward one another and
toward the civilization which surrounds us.

The bill under consideration, liberal and generous in
some of its sections—as those creating an elective insular

Senate; a Cabinet, the majority of whose members shall be confirmed by the Senate; and a public-service commission, two members of which shall be elected by the people—is exceedingly conservative in other sections, most of all in that which restricts the popular vote, enjoining that the right of registering as electors be limited to those who are able to read and write or who pay taxes to the Porto Rican treasury. By means of this restriction 165,000 citizens who vote at present and who have been voting since the Spanish days would be barred from the polls.

Here are the facts: There exist at present 250,000 registered electors. Seventy percent of the electoral population is illiterate. There will remain, then, 75,000 registered electors. Adding 10,000 illiterate taxpayers, there will be a total of 85,000 citizens within the electoral register and 165,000 outside of it. I cannot figure out, hard as I have tried, how those 165,000 Porto Ricans are considered incapable of participating in the elections of their representatives in the legislature and municipalities, while on the other hand they are judged perfectly capable of possessing with dignity American citizenship. This is an inconsistency which I cannot explain, unless the principle is upheld that he who incurs the greatest misfortune—not by his own fault—of living in the shadow of ignorance is not worthy of the honor of being an American citizen. In the case of this being the principle on which the clause is based, it would seem necessary to uphold such principle by depriving 3 million Americans of their citizenship, for this is the number of illiterates in the United States according to the census of 1910. There is no reason that justifies this measure, anyway. Since civil government was established in Porto Rico, superseding military government—that is, 16 years ago— eight general elections have been staged. Eight times the people with a most ample suffrage law, have elected their legislative bodies, their municipal councils, their municipal courts, and school boards. These various bodies have cooperated to the betterment and progress of the country, which gives evidence that they were prudently chosen.

Perhaps one or a hundred or a thousand electors tried to commercialize their votes, selling them to the bidders.

For the sake of argument I will accept that hypothesis, though it was never proved. But even supposing that we had not to do with a presumption, but with an accomplished fact, I ask: Were there not and are there not in the rest of this Nation those who negotiate their constitutional rights? Did not the courts of a great State—the State of Massachusetts—convict four or five thousand men of that offense? Was there not a case in which the majority of a legislature promised to elect and did elect a high Federal officer for a few dollars? I do not think that these infractions of the law and breaches of honor reflect the least discredit on the clean name of the American people. I do not think that such isolated crimes can lead in any State to the restriction of the vote. They are exceptional cases, which cannot be helped. The courts of justice punish the guilty ones and the social organization continues its march. In Porto Rico, if such cases occur, they should have and do have the same consequences. But it would be a sad and unjust condition of affairs if, through the fault of one, 1,000 men were to be deprived of their privileges; or, to speak in proportion, if, through the fault of 160 electors, 160,000 were to be deprived of their privileges.

The aforesaid motives are fundamental ones that require careful attention from the House. But there are deeper motives yet, those that refer to the history of the United States and of the American Congress. Never was there a single law passed under the dome of the Capitol restrictive of individual rights, of the rights of humanity. Quite the contrary, Congress, even going to the extreme of amending the Constitution, restrained the initiative of the States for the purpose of making them respect the exercise of those rights without marring it with the least drawback. There is the 14th amendment. Congress could not hinder States from making their electoral laws, but it could decree and did decree that in the event of any State decreasing its number of electors it would, ipso facto, decrease its number of Representatives in this House. The United States always gave to the world examples of a profound respect for the ideal of a sincere democracy.

I feel at ease when I think of the future of my country. I read a solemn declaration of the five American commissioners that signed, in 1898, the Treaty of Paris. When the five Spanish delegates, no less distinguished than the Americans, asked for a guarantee as to the future of Porto Rico, your compatriots answered thus:

"The Congress of a country which never enacted laws to oppress or abridge the rights of residents within its domains, and whose laws permit the largest liberty consistent with the preservation of order and the protection of property, may safely be trusted not to depart from its well-settled practice in dealing with the inhabitants of these islands."

Congress needs not be reminded of its sacred obligations, the obligations which those words impose upon it. Porto Rico had nothing to do with the declaration of war. The Cubans were assured of their national independence. The Porto Ricans were acquired for $20 million, and my country, innocent and blameless, paid with its territory the expenses of the campaign.

The Treaty of Paris says:

"As compensation for the losses and expenses occasioned the United States by the war and for the claims of its citizens by reason of the injuries and damages they may have suffered in their persons and property during the last insurrection of Cuba, Her Catholic Majesty, in the name and representation of Spain, and thereunto constitutionally authorized by the Cortes of the Kingdom, cedes to the United States of America, and the latter accept for themselves, the island of Porto Rico and the other islands now under Spanish sovereignty in the West Indies, as also the island of Guam, in the Mariannas or Ladrones Archipelago, which island was selected by the United States of America in virtue of the provisions of article 11 of the protocol signed in Washington on August 12 last."

You, citizens of a free fatherland, with its own laws, its own institutions, and its own flag, can appreciate the unhappiness of the small and solitary people that must await its laws from your authority, that lacks institutions created by their will, and who does not feel the pride of having the colors of a national emblem to cover the homes of its families and the tombs of its ancestors.

Give us now the field of experiment which we ask of you, that we may show that it is easy for us to constitute a stable republican government with all possible guarantees for all possible interests. And afterward, when you acquire the certainty that you can find in Porto Rico a republic like that founded in Cuba and Panama, like the one that you will find at some future day in the Philippines, give us our independence and you will stand before humanity as the greatest of the great; that which neither Greece nor Rome nor England ever were, a great creator of new nationalities and a great liberator of oppressed peoples.

THE PAMPHLET

by Luis Muñoz Marín

I have broken the rainbow
against my heart
as one breaks a useless sword against a knee.
I have blown the clouds of rose color and blood color
beyond the farthest horizons.
I have drowned my dreams
in order to glut the dreams that sleep for me in the veins
of men who sweated and wept and raged
to season my coffee . . .

The dream that sleeps in breasts stifled by tuberculosis
  (A little air, a little sunshine!);
the dream that dreams in stomachs strangled by hunger
  (A bit of bread, a bit of white bread!);
the dream of bare feet
  (Fewer stones on the road, Lord, fewer broken bottles!);
the dream of calloused hands
  (Moss . . . clean cambric . . . things smooth, soft,
  soothing!);
  (Love . . . Life . . . Life! . . .)
I am the pamphleteer of God,
God's agitator,
and I go with the mob of stars and hungry men
toward the great dawn . . .

A GOOD CIVILIZATION

by Luis Muñoz Marín

January 19, 1960

Honorable Members of the
Legislative Assembly:

We are now starting a new decade. We must surely
maintain and hasten the integral development of Puerto
Rico in all its phases. But something more deserves our
fundamental attention, our finest dedication, in this new
period.

We devoted the decade that started in 1940 to beginning
the struggle to abolish poverty. To do that we set aside
political status as an issue. During the decade that started in
1950 we directed our energy especially toward the creation
of a new political status vitally adapted to the economic
needs of Puerto Rico. During the decade that is now
starting I propose that we devote special attention to what
kind of civilization, what kind of culture, what deep and
good manner of living the people of Puerto Rico want to
make for themselves on the basis of their increasing
economic prosperity.

This is the true ideal of a people, their real aim. And this
is the true ideal and the real aim of the people of Puerto
Rico: what kind of community and what goals of individual
moral and spiritual realization, within this community, are
worthy of respect in the heart of Puerto Ricans.

Decade for Education

Economic development is not an end in itself but a basis for
a good civilization. Political status is not an end in itself but

a means of attaining economic development and the creation of a good civilization. If a good civilization is the final goal, and if we are to devote to it the larger part of this new decade, we must set above all other duties the duty of education—education in the school and out of the school: the improvement of all means of communication, such as schools, universities, radio, television, and the press. We must do this by government action where it is legitimate, and by citizens' action where the responsibility belongs to them.

Let us start by raising the teacher to the position of prestige that is fitting to his task. Let us resolve that before the end of this decade education in Puerto Rico, in all its aspects, shall have reached a level comparable with that of the states and countries best served by education. Teachers' compensation is an integral part of the great reform. Let us therefore determine—beginning right now!—to have this recognition we owe our teachers reach the levels prevailing in the United States before this decade ends.

Growth of the Economy

Before I go on considering the challenges presented by the agenda of the future, I must now fulfill my constitutional duty to inform you of the state of the country and submit to your consideration several recommendations for legislative action.

The economy of Puerto Rico is in the full throes of expansion.

Puerto Rico weathered very well the economic recession in the United States, which ended by the middle of 1958. It continued growing in spite of that recession, although at a somewhat slower pace.

When the recession ended, the economy of Puerto Rico started again to climb rapidly. During the fiscal year

1958–59 net income increased by 7½ per cent. This is the greatest increase of past years. The income of the United States is increasing at a rate of only 3 per cent. The total net income of Puerto Rico in 1958–59 reached one billion 148 million dollars. These figures represent an increase of 78 million dollars over last year's income.

One hundred eleven (111) new factories started to operate, a record under the Industrial Development Program.

In agriculture, there were increases in the sugar and dairy industries that more than offset a decrease in coffee production. (1958–59 was the low point in the biennial cycle of coffee production.) The net result was an increase of 4 per cent in agricultural income.

Income derived from the activities of the Commonwealth and municipal governments increased by 13 per cent, while income derived from Federal Government activities remained at the level of the previous year.

Income from the remaining sector of the economy, such as commerce, transportation, and services, registered an aggregate increase of nine per cent—a little higher than the general average of the economy.

Exports increased by 9 per cent. The products of the new factories were the principal factor in this increase. These products, which were not made in Puerto Rico before 1950, now represent more than 50 per cent of the total export value.

Imports registered an even greater proportional increase. However, capital goods, including raw materials for production, were the principal items in this increase. Consumer goods increased by only 5 per cent. Tourism had a very active year.

Higher paying jobs in industry, building, and services

continue to replace the decrease in the marginal sectors of the economy.

Fixed capital investment, mainly in factories and machinery, reached 292 million dollars. For the third consecutive year investment represented 21 per cent of the country's total production.

Preliminary estimates indicate that the economy continues to grow at an accelerated pace, driven mainly by the large investments made in Puerto Rico for the past three years, and stimulated by economic recovery in the United States.

At this time it can be predicted that net income in Puerto Rico will increase during the fiscal year 1959–60 by almost 100 million dollars, that is, by $8\frac{1}{2}$ per cent, to reach a level of one billion 250 million dollars.

It is estimated that capital investment will reach 318 million dollars. These figures will again total 21 per cent of the value of total production.

Barring adverse climatic conditions, the value of agricultural production at farm level should reach 254 million dollars, an increase of 11 per cent over last year's figures. The reason for this is that the high phase in the biennial cycle of the coffee industry will coincide with recovery in the sugar industry and with the normal increase in the dairy products industry. The value of manufactured goods is expected to increase by 14 per cent to reach a total of 276 million dollars.

Government economists give the following reasons for their prediction that the economy will increase by $8\frac{1}{2}$ per cent this year:

The sugar industry payroll in the past few months has been from 20 to 30 per cent higher than last year's payroll for the same period.

Employment in factories established under the Industrial Development Program surpasses the level of 45,000, that is, 9,000 more than last year's level on this date.

Many of the large industrial plants, such as Grace, Union Carbide, and the Commonwealth Refinery at Guayanilla, began to operate at full capacity for the first time.

Tax receipts of the General Fund during the first five months of the fiscal year have been 9 per cent higher than those for the same period of the previous year.

As to fiscal year 1960–61, for which I already submitted to you my budget recommendations, the prospects are just as good. The total income of the economy will probably reach one billion 350 million dollars.

The high demand for the products of Puerto Rican industry in the U.S. market is expected to continue.

It is hoped that agricultural activity will continue to increase in Puerto Rico. Such an increase has been observed during the present year.

A larger number of hotel rooms, together with faster air transportation service, will increase the flow of tourists.

A gradual increase in employment is expected as the decrease in marginal industries reach their limit.

Education

Whether the kind of education given to children and young people is adequate for a free world is open to question not only in Puerto Rico but also in the United States and many other parts of the world. Public schools in Puerto Rico have performed a highly commendable function in aiding the creation of a democratic way of life and of respect for the dignity of man. For sixty years they have performed their task amid great difficulties under a highly centralized system administered until a few years ago under a colonial administration, with appointments originating outside Puerto Rico.

Changes in method and attitude were frequent, often capricious, during the stage of colonial administration of public education. Teachers' salaries were low, and at one time they were reduced twice in a few years.

In the past teachers have enjoyed well-deserved prestige in the community. They continue to deserve that prestige; but a certain superficial trend in the scale of values of Puerto Rico has raised the prestige of the mere possession of a multiplicity of objects. The result is that the function and merit of the teacher is unfairly regarded as having relatively less importance in the community. Our society, in its endeavor to improve spiritually, to enlighten its understanding, to understand itself better, must restore to the teacher his legitimate position. It can do this not only by paying him a proper salary as rapidly as possible, but also by creating, with the help of the teachers themselves, a more balanced vision, a vision less superficial in the Puerto Rican scales of values.

Compensation in terms of money for the teachers is only one part—although important—of the entire educational reform that will be under your consideration. You will have at your disposal not only the studies commissioned by this Legislature, but also those conducted by the Department of Education, those that the universities may submit, and the study I shall submit to you, to bring new light to the consideration of our problem, on the basis of recommendations by the European scholars I invited here from European democracies that are prominent in education.

We must, as I said before, work out a plan of gradual but steady improvement in the salaries of Puerto Rican teachers to bring them to the level of those in the federated States of the Union. Even before that, we must try to effect an immediate salary increase. In a special message I shall discuss the educational system in greater detail, including the enabling acts for the University and for the system of public education in Puerto Rico.

Cultural Development

A mere enumeration of the cultural activities developed in Puerto Rico with the stimulus and help of this Legislative Assembly would fill several pages. Under the direction of the Institute of Puerto Rican Culture alone, numerous programs are being carried out that help Puerto Ricans to know themselves better by understanding the positive values of their heritage.

What has been done in Puerto Rico in the field of music, from the modest but excellent Free Schools of Music to the Casals Festival, the Symphony Orchestra, and the Conservatory (which has just opened its doors) should make Puerto Rico feel very proud. The Casals Festival alone brings to our country each year outstanding interpreters and lovers of music, including distinguished Puerto Rican musicians. This has been made possible in our time by the presence among us of a man we can regard as a spiritual fellow countryman, a man eminent in music, eminent in human virtues, eminent in liberty. Of all his qualities the least is music—and he is one of the great musicians of the world: Maestro Pablo Casals!

Social Compensations

I propose that the Unemployment Compensation Program in the sugar industry be modified to stimulate additional employment, provide a higher income for the worker and accelerate production to complete and surpass the sugar quota assigned to us. During the weeks now prescribed by law, the Compensation Fund should pay the laborers wages for one out of each two days covered by the employer at the minimum salary rate prevailing for general farm work. This plan would benefit the farmer by giving him two mandays of work for the wages of one day, and would benefit the worker by more than doubling his income. At the minimum rate indicated, this would be seven dollars, instead of the three dollars he receives now. The aggregate income of unemployed workers would be increased from two million dollars to more than four million. This would help to retain a larger number of workers necessary for the efficient improvement of our agriculture.

Three years ago we created in Puerto Rico the Unemployment Insurance Plan providing benefit payments for industrial workers who involuntarily lose their jobs due to the normal fluctuations of the economic life of the country. This program not only provides the worker and his family relief from the economic problems of unemployment; it also maintains the purchasing power in the working group, a factor in reducing the economic consequences of unemployment both for the workers and for commerce and general community life.

There are now more than 221,000 workers insured against these risks. Taking into account both experience and the financial situation of the Reserve Fund of the program, I recommend an amendment to the act, to increase substantially the maximum general payments that the workers may receive, as well as in the number of weeks for which payments may be received. This increase should not be accompanied by increased contributions to the fund.

Changes increasing the number of workers eligible to receive the benefits of this law should also be considered.

The Minimum Wage Law of the Commonwealth provides that the Minimum Wage Board shall periodically revise wages in all industries and activities, but it does not empower the Board to fix a minimum wage above one dollar an hour. Of course the workers may, by collective bargaining—a right guaranteed by the Constitution of Puerto Rico—obtain higher wages than one dollar an hour. But the Minimum Wage Board cannot fix salaries above that limit. This provision has been in force since June, 1956. From that date until the present time, the Board has approved 37 mandatory decrees covering approximately 196,000 workers, increasing their income by approximately fourteen million dollars. In October, 1956, the average wage per hour of production workers in manufacturing industries was 66 cents an hour; in October, 1959, this average wage had increased to 86 cents an hour. To date there are 36 industries and divisions of industries having a minimum wage of one dollar an hour fixed by federal law and by the Minimum Wage Board of the Commonwealth. These industries provide employment for approximately 38,000 workers.

I believe the time has come to raise the level of minimum wages prescribed by Puerto Rican law. The Board should be empowered to fix minimum wages, in cases where it seems advisable, up to one dollar and 25 cents an hour.

Following the recommendation I made last year, an organization was created in the Employment Security Division of the Department of Labor with responsibility for finding social remedies to the unemployment produced by progress in technology. This task could have started earlier if the economist, Dr. Isadore Lubin, whom the Secretary of Labor had invited to perform it, had not been forced to decline our invitation for health reasons.

I hope that during this legislative session I shall be able to make specific recommendations on this project. Progress in technology is necessary for the economic development of our country in the direction of higher and higher levels that will benefit all Puerto Ricans. But to find relief for the human suffering temporarily caused by this very progress is a necessary duty. Later on in my message I shall make a recommendation on this.

As part of our effort to lessen the differences between the standards of living of the rural and urban zones, it is necessary to continue strengthening public services in the rural areas. By public services I mean schools, student transportation, school lunchrooms, electric power, aqueducts, roads and paths, rural medical centers, recreation services, promotion of factories in the rural zone, distribution in rural communities of parcels of land in permanent usufruct to all those who wish to stop being landless users, and rural housing constructed on a mutual help basis with government cooperation. Later in my message I will also make a recommendation partly related to this.

Sugar Industry

In my Budget Message I recommended the appropriation of $1,050,000 to continue, during the coming year, to help and encourage the sugar industry to make new plantings so that Puerto Rico might sooner reach and surpass its quota. I further suggest that the possibility of exempting from land tax those farmers who achieve a production of more than four and a half tons of sugar per *cuerda* be carefully studied. The purpose is good, but let me point out that it needs a more careful study than it has so far been possible to carry out.

I believe it is important to provide the means of financing the acquisition of agricultural machinery and equipment, in addition to the already existing facilities, to help sugar cane planters to attain the optimum efficiency in production. These methods, however, should go hand in hand with measures to provide social remedies for unemployment caused, as we have already seen, by technological progress. For such unemployment we are in duty bound to compensate.

I also suggest that the collection of the tax to finance compensatory remedies related to shipments of sugar in bulk be postponed until January 1, 1963. The workers, of course, should continue benefiting by the remedies already provided by law.

In the past the sugar industry dominated the country's economy. Many of us Puerto Ricans had the conviction that it thus improperly exercised a large measure of the political power that in a democracy belongs properly to the people. This situation, as we all know, has changed altogether. The sugar industry exercises its economic function of helping the country's production, like many other industries that are helped by the government as part of its public policy of stimulating economic progress for the benefit of all Puerto Ricans. However, the industry still faces certain hostile attitudes created by its already extinct political power. These are mere historical vestiges that should disappear. In considering legislation presented on the subject, we should regard it very objectively, in the light of the economic realities of today, and not of the political and economic realities of yesterday. . . .

Coffee, Tobacco, and Dairy Industries

The unified coffee program, especially the program to stabilize the price for coffee paid to the farmer, whose continuance I recommend, is making an important contribution to the improvement of our coffee industry. The program is costly, but the government has considered it advisable to maintain the price of coffee at rates noticeably higher than those prevailing in the world market, so that farmers may continue improving their farms and paying higher salaries to the workers.

The tobacco problem, as we all know, is very difficult. If we try to solve it by manipulating the market, we may lose a large part of the market. The road to improvement is the continuing development of a better quality through the seed distribution program already in operation and the improvement of tobacco sheds. These programs, together with credit improvement and increasingly better supervision of tobacco grading, should be continued and intensified.

Progress in the dairy industry has been outstanding during the past years. It is already our second rural industry.

During my visits to various municipalities of Puerto Rico, to make on-the-spot observations of their problems and discuss them with the citizens, I have frequently encountered the paradox of a great number of idle hands near an extension of uncultivated land. How can we put those hands to work this land? It seems to me that for this purpose the citizens and the government could profitably cooperate in each municipality. Later on during the session I propose to submit to your consideration alternate plans to attain this goal. . . .

Institutions for Children

With the appropriation made last year by the Legislature, a study of institutions for children is being made and will soon be finished. During this session I hope to be able to inform you of the findings and recommendations of this study. In this connection I believe that when changes in the educational system are considered, a special study should be made regarding the creation of public kindergartens for pre-school age children between 3 and 5. This is a very important recommendation made by the European educators I invited two years ago to advise our government on educational problems.

Traffic and Safety Problems

The progress that is effectively solving so many of our economic problems is also creating others. The increase in the income of Puerto Ricans during the past years has produced a large increase in the number of motor vehicles. Due in part to this, traffic accidents have become a very serious problem in Puerto Rico. However, there are other factors that contribute to this situation. They have to do with the attitude of many drivers and pedestrians. Many roads have been constructed. The number of kilometers of roads has increased by one hundred per cent. Road design and quality has improved in a way that is obvious to all. On the other hand, the number of vehicles has increased by five hundred per cent since 1940. I believe it imperative to have, rather than amendments to the traffic law, a completely new traffic law adapted to the specific problems we face and to the economic development we are proposing for the future.

The rapid industrialization of Puerto Rico, with the resulting growth of cities, has intensified public safety problems. Last year I recommended that the police force be increased by 300 members. This year it should be increased by 350 more. The force should continue increasing at a similar rate from year to year. As a matter of justice, and in order to attract more recruits, I recommended in my budget message the appropriation of a sum to increase the salary of the police, especially in the lower ranks. Besides, the Police Superintendent is constantly exploring new methods to make more efficient use of the force and equipment available to him. The establishment of the mounted police for patrolling our beaches has already shown positive results.

Tax Reduction

In my message last year I recommended a study of ways to reduce taxes on houses. Later on that year the House of Representatives asked the Executive Branch to study how to implement this recommendation.

In accordance with the recommendations made to me by the Department of the Treasury, I submit the following plan to your consideration:

All houses valued at less than $20,000 should be granted a reduction of 20 points in the property tax; that is, approximately ten per cent. All houses whose value is between $6,000 and $10,000 shall be granted an additional reduction of another 20 points; that is, of approximately 20 per cent of the tax. Houses valued at less than $6,000 should have, in addition to these two reductions, a further reduction of 20 points; that is, a total reduction of approximately 30 per cent of the tax. This tax relief would be in addition to the discount of 10 per cent prescribed by law last year for taxpayers who pay their tax on time. This benefit is received by most of those who own their houses on a basis of FHA and bank transactions.

Houses valued at less than $3,000, which under the present law are totally tax-exempt, will continue enjoying that right.

One of the greatest obstacles to public policy and to the desire of every family in Puerto Rico to own a home, is the ever increasing value of land available for development and the high prices charged by banking institutions for home financing transactions. If a way could be found to prevent fraud, a progressive tax could be levied, to be collected at the time of the sale of land for development. This tax would ultimately be passed on to the eventual purchaser of a home on such lands. The community would thus participate in the benefits of the increase in land value, which is not brought about by any individual, but by the community itself. The increase would be devoted to the social purpose of making it easier for all families in Puerto Rico to acquire homes at a lower price. This deserves very careful study and the most rapid action compatible with the care it requires.

Another possibility, though not an easy one, is for each municipality to acquire the lands it may need for development purposes in the coming ten or twenty years. In some cases the Commonwealth government might offer aid. The municipality could then sell them at cost to those who want to buy them in good faith for building homes of their own, even if the sales were made in future years when the value could have greatly increased. This would involve a large investment of money, recoverable in the long run by the Public Treasury.

As to our semi-rural developments, I want to inform you that we have already found a way to finance the sale of these houses to the present tenants with either the complete parcel of land or a renovated lot. The sale price will be the amount still owed, which is considerably lower than the actual value of the properties. This sale and renovation project will start within the next few months.

The sales plan will be within the means of every family living in these developments. Most families will continue paying the monthly rent they are now paying. Those paying a higher rent may acquire the properties with reductions in their monthly payments. A small number of families may acquire the properties with a slight increase in their monthly payments. In all cases the properties shall be tax exempt for 10 years.

The high cost of many medicines is among the factors

that raise the cost of living of the middle class and that part of the working class whose income is too high to allow them to qualify for free medicine. Both this problem and the problem of reduction of the cost of health services deserve the preferential attention of the Legislative Assembly and the Executive.

The Medical Association is working out a plan on this subject. The Government of the Commonwealth of Puerto Rico will receive, through its Department of Health, a report requested some time ago from Columbia University, on the best way to provide medical services for all the population as efficiently and cheaply as possible. In due time I shall transmit, together with my recommendations, the Columbia report.

Preservation of Our Natural Heritage

Places of great beauty in Puerto Rico are a heritage of the people of Puerto Rico. They are to be used for the public benefit. There are two ways of using them for this purpose. One way is to establish hotels and great tourist attractions, which, as part of the economic development of the country, attract capital, provide employment, put money in circulation. The other is to provide easy access to these places for the people in general, whether their economic means are plentiful or scarce. I think that the public policy should be to accept both ways of using our natural heritage: that of stimulating economic progress and that of providing beauty, pleasure, serenity, and equality in the enjoyment of beauty regardless of differences in economic position.

The Planning Board is making a census of places of exceptional beauty, in order to determine which should be available for one or the other use. The Board is also surveying sites for inexpensive facilities for local tourists and tourists from the United States and other countries. Of course, in accordance with law, the great tourist installations are open to all citizens, to all inhabitants of Puerto Rico; but the prices they have to charge, due to the large investments they involve, put them out of reach of a large number of Puerto Ricans and potential visitors.

Juridical Branch

Justice in Puerto Rico is slow. Slow justice, it has been said, does not have the integral quality of justice.

I recommend that the Legislative Assembly study what facilities should be provided by legislation or what appropriations should be given to the judicial branch to put an end to this situation. I am sure that the judicial branch, on being consulted by you, will cooperate fully.

Our conscience rejects the spectacle of women, old people, and children being used by big racketeers in the numbers racket. But it is even more repulsive to observe that democracy, precisely because of its principles of human freedom, frequently finds itself in the position of jailing poor people who are not morally perverse, while letting go free the big corruptors, the big racketeers, the big criminals of the numbers racket. Democracy should assiduously search for a way to prevent this. Its great respect for human freedom must not be used as a tool to guarantee impunity to these racketeers and criminals.

I suggest the creation of a special commission, consisting of private citizens and officials of the judicial and executive branches, to find the way to put an end to such a despicable spectacle.

Civil Rights

The Government of Puerto Rico took an initiative two years ago that, we are proud to say, is the first of its kind:

With the advice of the eminent defender of civil rights,

Mr. Roger Baldwin, who is connected with the United Nations in this respect, a committee of distinguished citizens from all political parties was appointed to inquire into the state of civil rights in Puerto Rico. The committee, advised by a competent staff of University professors, submitted its report a few months ago. Referring to the basic rights of citizens it says:

In general terms the status of civil rights is satisfactory. There are deficiencies in some areas, such as: the protection of political minority groups (this refers mainly to Nationalists and Communists), the excessive discipline and the serious limitations to internal democracy in the parties. Likewise, there are grave problems as to the quality of the press; the objectivity that should characterize a free press is absent.

On the positive side, we may point out the efforts of the government and the people to improve their economic levels and guarantee the right to education. Freedom of thought and expression do not present grave problems as regards protection against government restrictions. The press has no limitations other than its own; there is freedom of worship; there is freedom of discussion, and no serious problems as to the right to assemble; universal suffrage without coercion is guaranteed and elections are peaceful, orderly, honest, and free.

However, the committee unanimously made a great number of recommendations that, in its judgment, would improve civil rights in Puerto Rico.

My Cabinet is studying the recommendations requiring legislative and executive action. Although the study has not been completed, I can already recommend to you the following measures proposed by the Committee on Civil Rights:

Shortening of the probationary period of teachers in the University of Puerto Rico.

Elimination of the law against participation of teachers in political activities during their free time.

Regulation of the use of loud-speakers.

Establishment of a municipal civil service.

Extension of the law punishing racial discrimination in the sale, distribution, or leasing of houses.

Representation for minorities in the municipal assemblies.

Elimination of delays in the transactions of the Planning Board.

Establishment of an agency to plan remedies for unemployment problems.

Provision of auditing services free of charge to unions that cannot afford them.

The Legislative Assembly has taken or is taking action on some of these recommendations. I urge action on the others. As the study of the report progresses, I shall make other recommendations based on it to the Legislative Assembly.

The judicial branch, of course, will take such action as it may consider appropriate on the recommendations falling under its jurisdiction.

Uses of Increased Income

This year the factories established at the beginning of the Industrial Development Program will start paying taxes. During the past ten years, these factories have been making an important contribution to the economic growth of Puerto Rico. From now on they will also contribute to the financing of government services. Although the sum received in taxes from them will be small this year, it is estimated that by the time the effects of the tax exemption law terminate in 1975 these new taxes will yield two hundred seventy million dollars to the general fund of the Treasury. In this estimate, allowance has been made for the number of factories that may discontinue their operations.

Although I am not proposing the creation of special funds, I do propose that this new source of income be used to strengthen three basic purposes of our government:

(1) educational reform;

(2) to guarantee that such regions as have not yet sufficiently participated in Puerto Rico's general progress—like the *Barrio* Doña Elena in Comerío—shall henceforth enjoy a greater share of it; and,

(3) to help finance compensation payments for those who are temporarily unemployed as a result of Puerto Rico's technological progress.

The problems of *Barrio* Doña Elena in Comerío are at present the subject of an excellent research and experimental project carried out by a group under a great woman who serves Puerto Rico generously and beyond the call of duty, Dr. Lydia Roberts of the University of Puerto Rico. This study will orient us as to what can be done in other communities having similar problems.

Nothing could be more just than to use this new source of income to finance our educational reform and to improve the conditions of people living in those regions that so far have not felt the full impact of Puerto Rico's great economic progress of these years.

Political Status

The history of Puerto Rico in the past decades has been that of two drives seeking to merge into one: the drive to abolish poverty and the drive of the people toward the ideal image of themselves. This image was once confused with the concept of political status, a grave error. The people's image of themselves is not based on their political status. From 1940 to 1948 a political movement of deep spiritual meaning—including justice, hope, respect for human dignity, the will to overcome obstacles—existed. All are qualities of the spirit. Yet this movement did not include the concept of political status.

In many former colonial countries these two drives coincided. In Puerto Rico they did not, and could not, coincide so long as political status was conceived as the ideal image, the goal, and so long as the only two alternatives to colonialism were independence and federated statehood, both of them economically inconsistent with the abolition of poverty. The objective is, I repeat, a good civilization based on the abolition of poverty.

A political status that puts obstacles in the path of that ideal cannot be, so long as it creates obstacles, the status that gives real freedom to the people of Puerto Rico. It is inconceivable that an enlightened people should seek to nullify the possibility of attaining their own high ends with the very means that should serve to fulfill them.

Commonwealth status provides us with a means adapted to the high end of creating an excellent civilization here in Puerto Rico.

There is talk as to whether the Commonwealth status is or is not permanent. Strictly speaking, nothing in the world is permanent; but, accepting this as a relative term, I will say that the Commonwealth status shall be as permanent as the people of Puerto Rico may desire. It is fruit of our people's freedom of thought, and its permanence or impermanence should be the fruit of our people's continuing freedom to make decisions.

When the economic development of Puerto Rico reaches a point where any other political status may be consistent with a prosperous life and a good civilization, the people of Puerto Rico may then take up the question of political status. For they will then be free, truly free, of the coercion of destructive and inexorable economic realities, to decide whether they wish to continue using Commonwealth as a means toward the ideal of the good life, or whether they prefer to use any other status as a means to this end. What I am saying is that a political status should not be a straitjacket, a fetish, an unreasoned prejudice, but a great means toward much deeper and more significant ends.

A government is not an end in itself. It is a means for the appropriate organization of a political community. Neither is a political status—for the same reason—an end in itself. Does one, in any sense, live for a political status? Is it not perhaps truer to say that the purpose of a political status is to enable us to live in terms of a good culture, spiritual well-being, and a good economy? I repeat, the best political status for a country has the consent of its people and helps, or at least does not greatly hinder, the growth of its economy. It participates in the development of what is good in its culture—the culture that the people desire for themselves—on the basis of this economy.

I believe that if Puerto Rico had been a federated state of the Union in, say, 1945, at the end of World War II, it would never have been able to attain the economic development, with its consequent social progress, which has been observed and admired by the whole world all these years.

If Puerto Rico had had to pay direct income taxes to the Federal Treasury during these years, it would have been impossible to provide the incentives to industrialization that have produced so rich a harvest of economic development, employment opportunities, ever-increasing wages, and ever-expanding circulation of wealth for the whole Puerto Rican community. Our Legislature would have been empowered to exempt new industries from state taxes but powerless to exempt them from the high federal taxes. Puerto Rico, as a federated state, would inevitably have had to pay these taxes by mandate of the Constitution of the United States, uniformly applicable to federated states, but currently applied in a different way to Puerto Rico. Regarding indirect federal taxes on such articles and services as public shows, gasoline, etc., the poor among Puerto Rican consumers would have had their standard of living lowered in proportion to these indirect federal taxes that they do not have to pay now. Furthermore, since the Puerto Rican taxpayer could not have afforded paying both kinds of taxes—federal and state—our people would have been deprived of a large proportion of the schools, roads and other public works and services that have contributed so much to the noteworthy progress of these years.

With these impediments, could Puerto Rico have experienced the tremendous upsurge of its standards of living that it has experienced during these years? Would we have today an income of one billion 150 million dollars for the life of our entire people—almost three times the 450 million dollars (in term of dollars adjusted to actual purchasing power), which the people of Puerto Rico had in 1940? Obviously not. Without these impediments, progress has not been easy. With these impediments, it would have been impossible.

In order to observe on the spot the achievements of the people of Puerto Rico, more than 10,000 persons, mostly young people, have come from one hundred and seven countries. Notwithstanding the progress indicated by this, the distance to be covered is even longer than the distance we have already covered. It is evident that we must continue to progress as rapidly as possible, not to flatter our vanity by comparing ourselves with other countries, but because it is necessary and fair, for the sake of all Puerto Ricans, that this progress continue.

The Agenda for the Future

What is the prospect before us for the economic development of Puerto Rico in the years ahead? Economists have worked out projections covering not only this coming decade but the whole period ending in 1975. This is the economic agenda of the future. It expresses not simply a wish. It is the result of research and computation based on the observation of the factors contributing to the ease or difficulty of Puerto Rican development in recent years. The projections are the following:

The net income of the Puerto Rican community is today, I have said, one billion 150 million dollars a year. It will be approximately three billion 500 million dollars by 1975. Puerto Rico's income will have tripled. The population will have increased, by a relatively small percentage, possibly by five or six per cent, as against a 300 per cent increase in income. This means that the average individual and family income will have increased enormously. The distribution of this great wealth—the way in which it is apportioned to profits, wages, and professional salaries, education, health, continuing economic development, social security, recreation, housing, communications—is extremely important. A just government, deeply concerned with the welfare of our entire people, should continue the equitable distribution that has so far prevailed in the process of great economic development taking place in Puerto Rico from the end of World War II in 1945 to the present. I propose that economic justice be maintained or improved as part of the agenda of the future.

I will give two examples of this:

In the two decades since 1940 the percentage of profits within the total income decreased from 41 to 29 per cent, while that of salaries increased from 56 per cent to 67 per cent. In the past ten years an average of 12,000 families each year have attained or surpassed the level of $2,000 annual income.

Another example:

At the beginning of the 1940 decade, income taxes, from which practically all families with a modest income are exempt, yielded to the Treasury of Puerto Rico one dollar for every seven dollars of consumption taxes paid by all. At the beginning of the 1960 decade, this proportion is only one dollar of income tax for each $1.20 of consumption taxes. These are two examples of economic justice, of the way in which the benefits of the great increase in production that has taken place in Puerto Rico have been distributed among Puerto Ricans. It is, I think, beyond dispute that our people wish these principles of justice to prevail throughout the decade that is now starting, indeed throughout the fifteen years covered by the projections I speak of.

We have seen that Puerto Rico could not have reached its present levels if it had been a federated state since 1945, with the great and inescapable economic burdens that this status would have imposed. I now ask: Could Puerto Rico attain the levels indicated by its agenda of the future if now, or in the near future, these burdens were to fall upon its shoulders? The honest answer must be: Obviously not.

The federal tax burden, in addition to state tax, would have been 188 million dollars by 1959, according to the Federal Bureau of the Budget. This federal organization cannot be presumed to have any interest in a political debate in Puerto Rico.

When I mention these figures, I am speaking of much more than dollars and cents. I am speaking of liberty and justice. I am speaking of the need of the people of Puerto Rico of every social class to have these projections for the years ahead come true. We must not put obstacles in the path of their realization. We must stimulate and facilitate this realization. It is not merely 188 million dollar bills and coins counted out as a miser would, or written down in account books, as in a bank. It is 188 million dollars' worth of liberty for the Puerto Rican people, of individual freedom for every Puerto Rican. It is 188 million dollars in the hands of those who receive them for their work, for their contribution to the economy, to be used by them as each one of them freely decides for the education of their children, for health, security in old age, a life easier than at present, for housing, travel, recreation, study—study for the pleasure of knowledge, for the freedom that knowledge gives. It is 188 million dollars' worth of personal liberty that I speak of. It is the personal liberty of each and every Puerto Rican, because federal taxes include not only income taxes, which some pay and others do not, but also consumption taxes, which everyone has to pay.

It should be clear that when I use the word "liberty" here, I do not refer to any political status. Political liberty—under any political status—is in itself only one of the many expressions of human liberty. And it is of every *other* expression of political liberty that I speak now. The man who knows something today that he did not know yesterday is today, in that degree, a freer man than he was yesterday, because ignorance is servitude and knowledge is freedom. Parents who know today that they can provide their children with an adequate education are much freer than they were yesterday, if yesterday they lived in uncertainty as to whether or not they could educate their children. If a family knows it can move from a slum to a public housing development and later, as its economic condition improves, to a home of its own, it has greater freedom of spirit than one that despairs of ever being able to improve its lot. (I say this fully aware of the disadvantages of some public housing regulations.) In a rapidly growing economic system such as Puerto Rico has and should continue to have, with increasing opportunities for greater economic well-being, all who now have hope, rather than despair, are freer because of this hope. It is all this that I am speaking of when I talk about 188 million dollars. My friends of the Legislative Assembly, it is *this* I speak of, and not of dollars and cents.

The political status that facilitates this personal freedom of Puerto Ricans, that facilitates the carrying out of the agenda of the future, that provides the style of life that the Puerto Rican desires to have, *that* is the political status Puerto Rico needs, call it what you will. If in the future another political status, because of our economic development, should make possible these same liberties, this same style of life, there is no reason why our people should not, at that time, give such status their most careful consideration and freely reach the decision to which their spirit guides their will.

Our Final Goal: A Good Civilization

Once more I will speak of a good civilization, our true final goal. When our income is three and a half billion dollars, we should not desire merely to possess or consume three times as much as at present. That would not be a good civilization. It would be relative economic abundance ill-spent by a bad civilization. A good civilization, it seems to me, is one which continues to work energetically to create more wealth, but directs this wealth toward the fulfillment of deeper values. Once certain basic needs are satisfied and certain basic comforts are available to all, it turns its attention to the attainment of more meaningful and lasting satisfactions than the mere possession and consumption of merchandise. It is not within anyone's competence, nor is it in anyone's power, to give an exact prescription for a good civilization. But I believe that some broad propositions worthy of general acceptance may be made and that these propositions help to shape what the political philosophy of the Puerto Rican people might be, giving unity and a firm sense of self to this good human community. Many elements of this public philosophy already exist in Puerto Rico: the democratic spirit, the religious spirit that exists even in those who do not practice any specific religion, the love of peace, the respect for human dignity, the feeling of friendliness toward other peoples, the pride of serving—in all modesty—other peoples in their techniques of development and their explorations of democracy, the willingness to see the world through the mirror of two great languages, the adherence to federalist rather than to isolationist principles.

To all this I would add the need to understand clearly that, once the basic needs and comforts are provided for, this growing economic energy should be used to create more personal freedom in all its multiple aspects. We have already pointed out what these are: more universities, more museums, more laboratories and libraries, more opportunities for adults to continue their education beyond the mere attainments of techniques for earning a living, more individuality in decisions, better neighborly feeling, better neighborhoods, greater appreciation of, rather than imitation of, the neighbor—in short, more serenity.

Preeminent among these is the freedom that education gives. Our public philosophy is a sort of consensus of what Puerto Ricans think of themselves, of what they are and what they wish to be. This is to be understood not in a merely juridical sense, but in a human sense, in the sense of human personality, under any economic changes and any political status. The public philosophy of our people should be much more than their political status; much more than their technology and their economy. It is—or should be—the deepest expression of their unity and their soul. Economy and politics are there to serve the public philosophy of the people of Puerto Rico. As to the part that education must play in all this, let us dedicate this new decade to the grand enterprise of a great education for Puerto Rico. Let's get busy!

▼▲▼▲▼▲▼▲▼▲▼▲▼▲▼▲▼▲▼▲

XVII. THE KNIGHT OF THE RACE: JOSÉ de DIEGO

One of the brightest representatives of the generation that experienced the transfer of Puerto Rico from Spain to the U.S.A. was the statesman, poet, and political philosopher José de Diego (1866–1918), who became president of the House of Delegates of Puerto Rico. In his terse essay, "No," de Diego declared this to be "the only saving word of the freedom and dignity of enslaved people." Though a leading statesman of his time, serving as a cabinet member in both the autonomous government under Spain and the colonial government established by the United States, de Diego became known as "the Knight of the Race," because of his brilliant oratory and patriotic poetry, as in his books *Songs of Rebellion* (1916) and *Jovillos* (1911). His sonnets "In the Breach" and "Ultima Actio" are typical of the fiery declamations of this free spirit.

NO

by José de Diego

Brief, solid, affirmative as a hammer blow, this is the virile word, which must enflame lips and save the honor of our people, in these unfortunate days of anachronistic imperialism.

Two or three years ago Doctor Coll y Toste wrote some brilliant paragraphs to demonstrate that Puerto Ricans do not know and ought to know the protest of an energetic affirmation. The knowledgeable doctor was wrong: our greatest moral affliction is an atavistic predisposition to the irreflexive concession and to weakness of will, which bend lovingly, like a rose bush to the sighs of the wind.

In truth, the affirmation has impelled and resolved great undertakings in science, in art, in philosophy, in religious sentiment: all the miracles of faith and love; the death of Christ and the life of Columbus; saintly wonders of affirmations, which were raised to the glorious summits of the rising spirit, to divine light.

In political evolution, in the struggle for freedom, the affirmative adverb is almost always useless and always disastrous, so soft in all languages, so sweet in the Romance tongues, superior in this sense to the mother Latin tongue.

Certe, quidem do not have the brevity and the harmony of the Spanish, Italian, and Portuguese *sí* and the French *si*, when the latter substitutes for *oui* in the most expressive sentences; *si* in singing, a musical note (B), an arpeggio of the flute, a bird's trill, noble and good for melody, for rhythm, for dreaming, for love: more for the protest and impetus, for the paroxysm, for wrath, for anathema, for dry fulminating hate, like the scratching of a ray of light, the *no* is far better, the rude, bitter *O* vast, like a roar, round and ardent like a chaos producer of life through the conflagration of all the forces of the abyss.

From the almost prehistoric uprisings of savage tribes against chieftains of Asiatic empires, the negative to submission, the protest against the tyrant, the *no* of the oppressed has been the word, the genesis of the emancipation of peoples: and even when the impotency of the means and the efficacy of the goals, as in our homeland, separate the revolutionary fire from the vision of the ideal, the *no* must be and is the only saving word of the freedom and dignity of enslaved people.

We do not know how to say "no," and we are attracted, unconsciously, like a hypnotic suggestion, by the predominant *sí* of the word on thought, of the form on essence—artists and weak and kindly, as we have been made by the beauty and generosity of our land. Never, in general terms, does a Puerto Rican say, nor does he know how to say "no": "We'll see," "I'll study the matter," "I'll decide later"; when a Puerto Rican uses these expressions, it must be understood that he does not want to; at most, he joins the *sí* with the *no* and with the affirmative and negative adverbs makes a conditional conjunction, ambiguous, nebulous, in which the will fluctuates in the air, like a little bird aimless and shelterless on the flatness of a desert. . . .

We have to learn to say "no," raise our lips, unburden our

chest, put in tension all our vocal muscles and all our will power to fire this *o* of *no*, which will resound perhaps in America and the world, and will resound in the heavens with more efficacy than the rolling of cannons.

IN THE BREACH

by José de Diego

Oh unfortunate one, if pain overwhelms you,
if fatigue numbs your members;
do as the dry tree: grow green again;
and as the buried seed: beat.

Resurge, breathe, cry, walk, fight,
vibrate, undulate, thunder, shine. . . .
Do as the river with the rain: grow!
and as the sea against the rock: strike!

From the storm to the irate push,
you are not to bleat, like the sad lamb,
but roar, like the wild beast roars.

Rise! Gather resolve! Resist!
Do as the corralled bull: bellow!
Or as the bull that bellows not: charge!

ULTIMA ACTIO

by José de Diego

Hang on my breast, after I die,
my green shield in a reliquary;

cover me completely with the shroud,
with the three-colored shroud of my flag.

Seated and sad there will be a Chimera,
on my funeral stone. . . .
It will be a solitary spirit
in a long vigil, in a long vigil, in a long vigil. . . .

A tumultuous day will arrive
and the Chimera, erect on the
sepulcher, will utter a cry. . . .

Then I will seek my reliquary among my bones!
I will arise then with the banner of my shroud
to unfurl it o'er the worlds from the peaks of
    infinity!

XVIII. INDEPENDENCE: "A REVOLUTION OF OUR PEOPLE"

In the years after World War II, the followers of independence began to leave the Popular Party. Commonwealth, an idea of "perfected union" with the United States, had become Muñoz Marín's official policy. In 1946, led by a gracious and respected lawyer, Gilberto Concepción de Gracia (1909–1968), the believers in independence established the Puerto Rican Independence Party. Frustrated at the polls, when the majority of the voters voted for the Commonwealth, a group of Nationalists rose in armed revolt in October 1950. Concepción de Gracia, in seeking to explain the uprising, also delineated his own belief in independence ("A Revolution of Our People," speech by Gilberto Concepción de Gracia, November 1950).

This was the time of the Korean War overseas and the McCarthy era in the U.S.A., and it was also the time of "sacrifice and courage," said Pedro Albizu Campos (1891–1965) the Harvard-educated lawyer who led the Nationalist Party, a mystic and deeply religious Catholic whose political ideas had been influenced by the Irish Revolution. "Everybody is quiet but the Nationalist Party," he said; they were "the conscience of the people." On September 23, 1950, he stood in the Plaza of Lares and declared, "The day of Lares must be the day of Lares, the day of the Puerto Rican Revolution" (*Habla Albizu Campos. The Historic Speech of Pedro Albizu Campos, September 23, 1950, Commemorating the Rising at Lares.*

New York, Paredon Records, 1971). It was just one month later, on October 30, that the Nationalists revolted. Some said the uprising was provoked by the government; some, in the government, said it was planned by Albizu, who was a "madman." He was imprisoned, as he had been before, and spent almost two decades in federal prisons, much of it in solitary confinement. On his death *El Imparcial*, in San Juan, called him the heir to "the work of Simón Bolívar."

A REVOLUTION OF OUR PEOPLE

by Gilberto Concepción de Gracia

November 10, 1952

With you, Dr. Gilberto Concepción de Gracia, president of the Puerto Rican Independence Party

Fellow citizens:

Last October 30 a revolution broke out in our land, organized by members and leaders of the Nationalist Party of Puerto Rico. The revolutionary movement spread to numerous towns in the land, with the results that every armed revolution produces. And that movement has profoundly shaken the Puerto Rican consciousness.

I appear before my homeland's public opinion in my role as president of the Puerto Rican Independence Party to present our party's position and that of the Board of Directors in the wake of these events. The following facts must be affirmed in order to understand better the Puerto Rican Independence Party's position.

The revolution of October 30 was organized by men and women who maintain that the road toward achieving our independence is that of armed revolution. Contrary to the movement that espouses that thesis and that for many years has defended it before public opinion, since October 20, 1946, there has existed in our homeland the Puerto Rican Independence Party, over which I have the eminent honor of presiding; a political group of democratic principles, established with the purpose of achieving this land's independence through all the legal and peaceful means at our disposal, in peace and harmony with all the peoples of the world and with all men of good will.

While the Nationalist Party of Puerto Rico calls for voter abstention, permanently and under all circumstances, the Puerto Rican Independence Party went to the primaries in 1948; it obtained 66,141 votes in the ballot boxes and occupied third place among all the political parties in the land, thus displacing the historical parties—Socialist and Reformist—and opened its 1952 electoral campaign the day after the 1948 elections; it has maintained that campaign actively, with the dynamism and enthusiasm it has sustained till now.

While the Nationalist Party concentrates its effort on presenting the case of Puerto Rico in international courts, the Puerto Rican Independence Party, without abandoning that policy, concentrates its daily labor on the task of developing a force of opposition to and control on the government party in Puerto Rico, a force that is capable of serving as a counterweight to the government party, and fully able to defend the interests of the people, the rights of Puerto Ricans, and the physical inheritance of all sons of our land.

These two parties have represented, thus, in the struggle for Puerto Rican independence, the two methods that have been utilized historically throughout the world to achieve people's independence. The task of achieving independence by the first method has been historically the work of select minorities in the call to martyrdom. The task of attaining independence by the second method has been the work of the masses, not by vile hordes who wallow in the mud of personal conveniences of the moment, but rather by masses of superior patriotic caliber—alert, educated masses, responsible before their people and before history.

The method defended by the Nationalist Party of Puerto Rico is that utilized by the United States in its bid for freedom, the very same method utilized by all countries in our Americas, with the exception of Brazil; and the method employed by almost all the nations of the world. The method proposed by the Puerto Rican Independence Party is that utilized by the Philippines in its already triumphant struggle for freedom.

Hence, the Puerto Rican Independence Party's program presents its political goal and the procedure for attaining our independence. And it establishes it with these words, that I copy textually from our program:

"First: Political goal. The Puerto Rican Independence Party is organized with the purpose, primary and foremost, of working peacefully for the constitution of the people of Puerto Rico in an independent, sovereign, and democratic republic. This goal cannot be altered without the party's losing the essential motive for its existence; and those who attempt to stop, postpone or deter its realization will automatically remain outside the party. The governmental work to be carried out by necessity before the establishment of the Republic will be geared to maintain all essential services, to raise the level of life, and to implant those reforms which contribute to the firmer and more rapid founding of the Republic, under a rule of order and justice, whose authority derives from the people.

"Second: Procedure for achieving independence. The Puerto Rican Independence Party will use the primaries as a means to obtain a mandate from the people in order to attain Puerto Rican independence. Once this party obtains a majority in both houses of the Legislative Assembly, the first official act of this body will be the approval of a resolution demanding the immediate recognition of Puerto Rican independence from the government of the United States. As a part of the forementioned first act, a commission will be named to negotiate the fulfillment of the resolution, and to establish, according to the dispositions of this program, the bases of relations that will exist between both countries. No negotiation can have as a basis the disadvantage of the integrity of our territory, nor limitations of the full sovereignty of the Puerto Rican people. All negotiation, to be effective, will have to be finally approved by the people of Puerto Rico. The commission will render periodic reports to the Legislative Assembly, and the latter will report in turn to the Board of Directors of the Party. Within six months from the date of naming the commission, the general assembly of the party will be convened, with the purpose of having the commission give a detailed report on the result of negotiations carried out with the government of the United States. The assembly will approve the means that it deems appropriate for adjusting the action of the party to the exigencies of the struggle for independence."

Up to this point the clear and unmistakable quotes of our political program.

The Puerto Rican Independence Party has accepted, and accepts, the voter struggle, conscious of the vices inherent in the electoral system. It has accepted it, knowing that those vices grow worse in a colony; and even more, when the ballot boxes are utilized as a weapon for freedom, in strife with the very representatives of the system that maintains our people in a state of submission, inferiority, and servitude.

Our party has accepted that, for the men and women who comprise it have absolute confidence in the intelligence, patriotism, and valor of our people, and complete faith in their creative powers. And additionally, because these men and women firmly believe that the path of the ballot box is the most rapid and direct way for obtaining our independence, and the only one that can guarantee the economic stability of the future Puerto Rican Republic. Because they have that firm, unrelenting certitude, the men and women of the Puerto Rican Independence Party have rejected the road of armed revolution and have devoted themselves arduously, religiously, in body and soul, to structure a great party, prepared to obtain victory in the election of 1952, and to achieve independence for our homeland.

For that reason, the events that began last October 30 found all the leaders and members of our party and our radio program series occupied in the mobilization of our new voters for registration this November 4 and 5, so that our forces would be able to participate in the elections that, in accordance with law number 600 of the Eighty-first Congress of the United States (known as the Law of Referendum) can be held in Puerto Rico. We were and we *are* participating in that electoral process, insofar as this can affect the struggle for the independence of our people.

The Law of Referendum is a colonial measure that pursues the sinister purpose of confirming (with the Puerto Rican vote) the unjust political, economic, and social relations that prevail between Puerto Rico and the United States. That measure, which constitutes a fraud and a deception, seeks to pervert the sacred concepts of our struggles for freedom; it seeks to confuse the meaning of those concepts, such as that of the Constitution and the Constituent Assembly, and deceive the people of Puerto Rico and international opinion. That measure constitutes the greatest affront that can be perpetrated on a good and worthy people, who have fought a hundred battles for their liberty and for that of other peoples. It is an outrageous affront to ask this people to tell the world that Puerto Ricans want to continue to be a colony voluntarily.

Historical truth demands that the world be told that the government has sought to impose that shameful measure in Puerto Rico, using all the coercive methods at its disposal, monopolizing all the channels of propaganda and diffusion, using all the agencies and dependencies of the government (including public schools), and placing at the disposition of those who defend the monstrous Law of Eternal Colony through Consent all the infinite resources of the state and all the terrible power of its officials. Besides, the government rushed the registration period and elections foreseen in the spurious statute with the purpose of preventing the adequate organization of those who oppose that infamous legislation, who no doubt count on the support of the majority of the Puerto Rican people, but who lack the necessary economic resources to oppose the corrupt machinery of the government. And all this the government has done with the most vehement protest of the Puerto Rican Independence Party, which constitutes the *only* voice of opposition to that government.

In view of the nationalist revolution, and having before us all the related facts and many others that it would be impossible to discuss with you, our group, convened in Aguadilla, approved on the night of November 1, 1950, a pronouncement judging the events that had occurred in Puerto Rico. Here is the text of this pronouncement:

"First: to ratify the norms of the Puerto Rican Independence Party, stated in its program in the following words: The Puerto Rican Independence Party is organized with the primary purpose of working peacefully for the constitution of the people of Puerto Rico in an independent, sovereign and democratic republic!

"Second: to make the present government of Puerto Rico responsible for trying to impose on the Puerto Rican people, with the name of Constitution, a political measure that constitutes a fraud of the legitimate rights of this people, and that tends to confirm the colonial system in our homeland. We declare to this effect that this outrage to the dignity of the Puerto Rican people has brought one of the most peaceful people of the earth to a state of unrest and protest, which has culminated in the present revolutionary movement.

"Furthermore, we hold responsible the present government of Puerto Rico because, not having made a formal declaration of martial law (with the evident intention of taking away importance from the Puerto Rican revolutionary movement in the eyes of the world), it has committed a long series of violations of civil guarantees, establishing thus, in fact, illegally, a state of martial law. Consequently we call for the cessation of those violations of law and of the vicious persecutions on the part of the government. And we likewise demand complete legal guarantees for all Puerto Ricans involved in the revolutionary movement.

"Third: to hold the government of the United States of America responsible for the historic deed by which for more than half a century of its domination in Puerto Rico it has refused to recognize the right of our people to the enjoyment of their sovereignty. And at the end of that half century it aspires (in combination with the present colonialist island leaders) to discharge its responsibility in Puerto Rico by means of the deception of a false constitution.

"Fourth: to declare the sentiment of the deepest respect of the Puerto Rican Independence Party toward fellow compatriots who have offered, and still offer, their lives for the cause of independence in Puerto Rico."

The resolution quoted above does not constitute an act of solidarity with the revolution, as the Governor and President of the Popular Party, Mr. Luis Muñoz Marín, and his collaborators maliciously declared in commenting on our pronouncement. Far from it. Our party pursues, and will continue to pursue, actively and insistently, the peaceful path of the ballot box to obtain a majority mandate by the people of Puerto Rico in order to achieve independence.

If we supported the nationalist revolution and were in solidarity with it, we would not be here, serenely defending the position of our party in the field of ideas. Surely we would be elsewhere!

Well, now. Our party has to determine responsibility clearly. And it has. It has laid blame on those who stubbornly maintain, from Washington, the colony in Puerto Rico. And it laid blame on those who have sought to impose on our people the fraud of the ill-named Constitution.

Even when we do not believe in the method utilized by the Nationalist Party of Puerto Rico to achieve independence, we declare the feeling of our greatest respect for those who made a holocaust of their lives to the cause that is the direction of our cause. To the cause that nurtures all our dreams: the independence of Puerto Rico. This is not to say that we are to deviate from the political program of our party one bit. This does not mean that we are to abandon for even one minute the channels we have followed in the struggle for liberty. This does not mean that our form of propaganda is to vary one iota, nor are we to change in anything, in our peaceful negotiation toward independence, nor in our respectful observance of the law.

Until October 30, 1950, the Puerto Rican Independence Party was different from the Nationalist Party of Puerto Rico in its tactics. After that date, our party has continued to be (and will continue to be) different in its tactics from the Nationalist Party. And it will be so, until our party obtains in the ballot boxes the mandate granted by the majority of our people, to establish here a democratic republic that will really be "of all and for the good of all," a republic in which we can all live in peace, work in peace, and create in peace; a republic where we all can love God freely, and where the rights of all citizens, rich and poor, black and white, are guaranteed; and where the farmer, the worker, and the man and woman of the middle class can attain true social justice. That kind of republic they have not been able to achieve, and they could never have it in the colony.

Taking advantage of the situation created in the land, the government of Puerto Rico devised a diabolical plan to try to destroy the Puerto Rican Independence Party, knowing full well what it was and the historical reality in which our people live. And we shall adduce some evidence of that diabolical plan.

While the Governor of Puerto Rico told reporters of the

international press that the Puerto Rican Independence
Party legitimately supported independence and aspired
with complete legality to become a majority in Puerto Rico,
in the Fortaleza palace lists of names of independence
leaders were being drawn up, for the latter to be arrested
throughout the land, at the time when these arrests could
better serve the Machiavellian electoral processes of the
government party. They simultaneously worked on other
lists of names of our leaders throughout the island, to arrest
the directors of our party in every single town. And those
other lists were prepared with the approval of the head of
government, mayors of the government party, legislators of
the government party, and by police chiefs in towns where
these are on the side of the government party: the Popular
Party, heretically called Democratic.

The evident purpose was that of crushing the Puerto
Rican Independence Party in the November fourth and fifth
registration period. Because of that, the petition of postpon-
ing the registration, formulated by both the official representatives of our party in the Island Election Board, and by
the president of the party, on November 1, was not even
considered. While we were conferring with the General
Superintendent of Elections, and as we explained to him
that it was impossible to hold voter registration under a
state of undeclared martial law, on that very day arrest
orders were being drawn up against the leadership of our
party, disguising those orders as "subpoenas to testify as
witnesses in an investigation." And those illegal arrest
orders were issued, and those lists were prepared *before* the
board of directors of our party convened in Aguadilla, and
hence before the board made its historic and momentous
pronouncement.

But it is necessary for us to enter into some detail on the
procedure of official demagogy utilized in arresting our

independence leaders. Their homes were broken into without court orders. Bail of any kind was denied them. They were led to barracks and to heavily guarded jails, and certainly in a ridiculous manner, if we consider civil records of our arrested leaders. Their pictures were taken from all angles, with number signs on their chests, like common criminals. And in some cases they had the shamelessness to lead these patriots *in handcuffs* to barracks and jails.

These men were subjected to all types of vexations. Their fingerprints were taken. And while they were held, police and national guards aimed carbines, rifles, and bayonet points at them, as though they were dealing with the most inveterate and dangerous criminals.

Five members of the board of directors of our party were arrested at the time they were headed for the meeting of the board in the city of Aguadilla. And all this abusively, without there existing the remotest justification for their arrests. And at this very moment, one of those members of our board of directors is still being held, without the slightest reason for his incarceration.

The leaders and members of the different committees of our party were arrested throughout Puerto Rico, according to a preconceived plan of the government. Many members of our committees on the island were arrested in towns where not even one Nationalist is known, and where such members are of Socialist, Liberal, and Popular extraction.

It was evident that in those conditions, where a state of undeclared martial law existed in Puerto Rico, and our members and leaders maliciously and unjustly pursued, it was not possible for us to participate in registration. But the Puerto Rican Independence Party was prepared to attend the registrations and to *win* them. We had already placed in the Island Board of Elections the names of members throughout the island, of the local boards of registration, as one can easily corroborate by examining the records of the Island Board of Elections.

We asked for postponement of the registration period because *we wanted* to attend them, honorably. And besides, because we had worked to win them and we were confident, as we are still confident, in having the backing of the new voters.

The government preferred to go without consultation to the aforesaid registrations. And it turned out to be a colossal fiasco for the government, for the government went *alone* to that registration, without opposition, and ignoring the most elementary principle of democratic systems.

And the failure of the registration period for the government is clear and evident. Instead of registration of the number of new voters calculated by the Island Board of Elections, in the neighborhood of some 400,000, only 156,000 in fact were registered. And the panegyrists of the government, instead of accepting this tremendous failure, devoted their energies to deceiving the people once more, comparing in bad faith the last registration results with those of 1948, when the clear fact is that the registered voters who did not vote in the elections in 1944 had been incorporated by law into the voter lists, instead of comparing them with the registration results of 1944 (of six years ago) when the situation was identical to that which had existed for the last registration period; that is, the voters who did not vote in the 1940 elections had been *eliminated* from the voter lists, and *they were forced to register again.*

Everyone knows that the legislature of Puerto Rico had eliminated from voter lists those voters who had not been to the ballot box in 1948, whose number came to 232,000. We know it, and the government knows it.

The failure, then, of the last registration drive has demonstrated the devastating force of the Puerto Rican

Independence Party. The government well knows that force of ours. And it recognizes it, because the government has been holding voter censuses throughout Puerto Rico, and it knew the tremendous number of new voters who had announced their affiliation to the Puerto Rican Independence Party.

With the consciousness of our place in public opinion and of the force of our electorate, we have continued voter work, and we are already choosing the officials who will represent our party in all electoral colleges throughout Puerto Rico, for the referendum elections that will be held on June 4, 1951. And we are strengthening our group for the voter fight in 1952, with the absolute certainty that in those elections we will resoundingly defeat the forces of reaction and colonial status, which the present government party represents in Puerto Rico.

For the elections of 1952, we will register all those who did not sign up in the past registration periods, which have had nothing to do with the general registration of new voters, that, *by law,* must be held for the next general elections.

We are in the fight. We go with firmness toward victory, along the path of legality and democracy.

We are not frightened by the threats of reprisals that appear to be hatching in the brains of twanging politicians, who, scared in view of the imminent defeat that awaits them, seek to terrify tenured public officials who, completely in the right and helped by the Law of Personnel, occupy positions in the government despite being members of the Puerto Rican Independence Party. Those employees and officials cannot be removed from their positions, and should an attempt be made, we will obtain the ineludible protection of the courts for the rights of these independence supporters.

Our party is a party of struggle. Of indefatigable struggle for the liberty of our people and for the happiness of all Puerto Ricans, following the clear norms traced in our program.

Thus will the Puerto Rican Independence Party always be! Thus we will always be ourselves, till the end of our days! Our lives will always be so (without failings, without stumbling, without fear of the powerful) till our souls enter the mystery of eternity. Dedicated to democracy. To peace. To the independence of Puerto Rico. To genuine social justice. To the fraternity of all Puerto Ricans!

EVERYBODY IS QUIET BUT THE NATIONALIST PARTY

by Pedro Albizu Campos

Mr. President of the Lares Municipal Council, ladies and gentlemen. It is not easy to give a speech when we have our mother lying in bed and an assassin waiting to take her life. Such is the present situation of our country, of our Puerto Rico; the assassin is the power of the United States of North America. One cannot give a speech while the newborn of our country are dying of hunger, while the adolescents of our homeland are being poisoned with the worst virus, slavery. While the adults of our homeland must leave Lares (their hometown) in fear and don't even have exit to foreign countries different from the enemy power that binds us. They must go to the United States to be slaves of the economic powers, of the tyrants of our country, they are the slaves who go to Michigan out of need, to be scorned and outraged and kicked. One cannot give a speech easily while this tyrant has the power to tear the sons right out of the hearts of Puerto Rican mothers to send to Korea, into hell to be killed, to be the murderers of innocent Koreans, to die covering a front for the *yanqui* enemies of our country, to return insane to their own people . . . it is not easy. Our blood boils and patience beats at our hearts and tells me that patience must end, must disappear, and that the day of Lares must be the day of Lares, that is, the day of the Puerto Rican Revolution.

This year is the one-hundredth anniversary of the creation of the Cuban flag, and in the speech our illustrious secretary-general made in homage to the flag of Cuba, he compared it and called it the womb of our own flag, for this centennial of the Cuban flag is also the centennial of the Puerto Rican flag in the sense of origin. We have called here those who want the union of our brothers, of our Latin American brothers, and very specially of the Cubans, of the Dominicans, of the Antilleans, for they all love the independence of Puerto Rico as their very own, because as long as Puerto Rico is not free those nations feel mutilated. The Cuban standard was raised by Narciso López, and a Puerto Rican took part in the invasion by Narciso López, General Valero de Bernabé, of Fajardo, who maintained close relations with Iznaga, one of Narciso López's expeditionaries. Valero was then, I understand, the chief of General Staff in the Venezuelan army—our blood has always been on a level with the supreme height of dignity. We repeat our salute to all the heroes and martyrs of the great Cuban nation, we salute on this day especially the youth studying in the University of Havana, the University that has been a principal source of inspiration for the eternal struggle for freedom. It is the only center for higher studies in the world inspired by the sacrifices of the innocent.

Today we come up to a reality of our country, in that the enemy, the United States of America, feels defeated by our rights in the recent decision of the American Commission of Dependent Territories: their recognition of Puerto Rico as a nation intervened by the power of the United States. The U.S. did not dare to attend an inter-American conference for the first time in the history of America. Why? The U.S. had a right to sit there and always has a right to a place in the American Commission of Dependent Territories. Why didn't it attend? Because there, by their own right, Puerto Rican entities would be present. This is the work of the Nationalist Party of Puerto Rico, which in Bogotá achieved direct participation for all entities interested in the situation of military intervention by the United States in Puerto Rico, and the Nationalist Party of Puerto Rico went there with the flag of Puerto Rican independence, not to claim the possibility of recognition within the positive right, the natural right we can demand at any moment, but to claim recognition because within international rights Puerto Rico was a sovereign nation on the date on which the Treaty of Paris was drawn up, and Spain could neither give away Puerto Rico nor could the U.S. annex it, nor the entire world disown it. The sovereignty is irrevocable, and when the United States, through its cannons, forced the Spanish plenipotentiaries to sign the so-called cession of Puerto Rico, it was committing just a typical North American stickup. And this coaction against the Spanish had no part of the Spanish-American War, was never a belligerent against the United States or anyone else, and here the *yanquis* have been at war fifty-two years against the Puerto Rican nation, and have never acquired the right of anything in Puerto Rico, nor is there any legal government in Puerto Rico, and this is uncontestable, one would have to knock to pieces all the international rights of the world, all the political rights of the world, to validate the invasion of the U.S. in Puerto Rico and the present military occupation of our national territory. And the *yanquis* can't sit down at a table with jurists and ask those jurists to tell them that United States military intervention in Puerto Rico has validity, and that is why they did not dare attend the conference in Havana, they intimidated the whole of it, they sabotaged it so it would not meet, they browbeat governments not to attend, they intimidated the whole hemisphere and everything failed. The Commission met and resolved that Puerto Rico is an intervened nation, and expressed wishes that Puerto Rico should have the opportunity to enter the society of the world's free peoples.

They know they have responsibilities before the world, before all the Latin American nations and all the nations of the world, because before the United Nations Puerto Rico has a direct recognition. The Nationalist Party, which disowns the power of the United States in every terrain, got within the Constitutional Charter of the United Nations as an official observer with diplomatic status, to make the voice of Puerto Rico heard and to tell the whole world that the United States, as a nation, is a violator of the constitution of the UN, that these pretended defenders of freedom of every nation of the world except Puerto Rico are mere bandits in the current history of mankind. And that each time they present a report there—because they are under an obligation to render an annual report on the intervention of their administration in Puerto Rico—we also answer to all nations that this report is void and null, is plagued with lies, with perverse and cynical omissions from people dedicated to the most abject slavery and piracy for the demolition of a whole nation with the viruses of tuberculosis, cancer, hunger, of every plague known to mankind, to destroy it, and those who survive this policy of starvation become the cattle the United States needs to pick the crops in Michigan. These are the cattle the U.S. needs to be shipped as cannon fodder to Korea or to any other part of hell existing on this earth. They are looking, my friends, for a legislative base to tell the world in the face of the accusation by the Nationalist Party, by the Puerto Rican Liberation Movement, that we Puerto Ricans have consented, that if there ever was any nullity in their intervention in Puerto Rico, this lack of validity is no longer in effect because Puerto Ricans have ceased to be Puerto Ricans, and, after fifty-two years of *yanqui* occupation, well, we are no longer Puerto Ricans, we are *yanqui* citizens. And as *yanqui* citizens we bow, you understand, to the intervention, to the occupation by the United States and we give up not only our right to be Puerto Ricans but also our right to be *yanquis* because it says in that law, which they want to force upon this country "through the eyes" that Puerto Ricans cannot aspire to become a province of the United States, a badly called state, not that, because in the Senate of the United States, although they claim to represent brown and black peoples, no black can enter nor anyone suspect of having a black grandfather. That's very exclusive, it's called the most exclusive club on earth, they call themselves that. Those are the great democrats. No, today in this Senate it can no longer be an independent nation either, no, Puerto Rico is content to be a possession of the United States. A thing the U.S. can dispose of at its will; they can dispose of the women, the lives, the properties, all of Puerto Rico. The women to be WACs, the sons to be *yanqui* soldiers, they can expropriate our lands, they can decree that all of Puerto Rico become a United States forest reserve park, they can decree that all Puerto Rican monuments are *yanqui* monuments, *yanqui* property administered by *yanquis* and above all that, we are *yanquis* because they say we are *yanquis*.

The so-called law for allowing Puerto Rico to draw up a

constitution begins with an amendment to the existing U.S. law through which they pretend to rule Puerto Rico. The Jones Law is a law of the U.S. Congress, it has been amended by the present law, which is authorized to submit to Puerto Rican voters whether they want to assemble later on to draw up a constitution in which they will say they are *yanquis,* and the present law says clearly that they can meet in any constituency, but upon meeting they cannot say they are Puerto Ricans, they must say they are *yanquis.* The citizenship law is not amended but rather the imposition of U.S. citizenship continues over every Puerto Rican. [Listen carefully, it is true that in Massachusetts, Florida, or New York there exists the so-called citizenship within the state of Massachusetts, Florida, or New York, that's within the existing Jones Law, and there is what is called citizenship of Puerto Rico, but that is a citizenship within the important citizenship, it's a provincial citizenship: the international citizenship is the *yanqui* citizenship—meaning the citizen of New York is a citizen of New York for the purpose of voting in New York, but the citizen of New York is above all a citizen of the United States, and that disposition of the existing Jones Law remains intact.]

This is to say that all the constituents can gather here, yet they cannot say they reject United States citizenship. You will say—well, Don Pedro, and why is that important? A great deal, when they come to seize your son to go kill in Korea, to be a murderer in Korea, what they apply to him is the U.S. citizenship. Listen to what they apply to someone they consider a citizen of the U.S. The first thing they ask is are you a citizen of the United States? Oh yes? Yes, well throw the pack on, to Korea, to Korea, boy, where all American citizens go, and fly. If you are half blind, tubercular, lame, however, no, you still serve to cover some hole, to duck behind the bullets of the Koreans. And I say this because the mobilization in Puerto Rico for Korea has taken 8,000 men, and it is a vile act of the U.S. government to pretend to mobilize by force the Puerto Rican nation so that it can pick up a front for the U.S. in Korea. The U.S. had in Korea the same proportion of men that we have— they have 150 million inhabitants, we have 2, so they have seventy-five times the number of inhabitants that we have, so it would mean they should have 4 to 5 million men in Korea, and they really scarcely have 80 thousand men.

Ask yourself if this is not a shameless act of the United States. Why? Because if they feel obligated to intervene in Korea with all their weapons, let them mobilize themselves. Let them go fight for their interests, instead of taking advantage of Puerto Rico's defenselessness to make it go to defend the sordidness and the iniquity of their policy before the world, that is shamelessness. Well, the law that forces all of us here to go to elections, that law is dominated by the Jones Law. The Jones Law is not derogated, no sir. The Jones Law remains intact regarding the sovereignty of the U.S. in Puerto Rico, that is, in regard to the mobilization of his personal property and the mobilization of his person at the will of the U.S. Congress, in which we have no representation, nor do we want any. When a Puerto Rican goes to register [at selective service offices], when he's called for inscription, you'll say to me, we have to vote in protest—no, no, all those registrations and elections are a big trick. If registrations were good for Puerto Rico, the *yanquis* would never have inscriptions and elections here, nor would we ever have them. Registrations in Puerto Rico and elections are the trap to make Puerto Ricans keep turning the millstone. Yes, so-and-so goes up today and wears out four years, maybe eight years, steals a little and this and that—out he goes, discredited, just another scoundrel in the history of Puerto Rico, but he will be able, in the

Puerta de Tierra legislature, to approve a law for greater taxation, that's fine, lots of taxation. If you are going to sell codfish cakes, you need a license, there's a health inspector with a pistol in his belt, so this fried codfish is fried but uneatable, it poisons the population, etc.—you pay for the license and the codfish is all right, and if you grease the palm of the health inspector then the codfish is delicious. Taxation from every side.

The Jones Law remains intact as regards jurisdiction in Puerto Rico; in Puerto Rico there is only one primary jurisdiction of the only power here, that is, the strength of the government of the United States. The so-called insular government is only a corporation organized by the Congress of the United States, it didn't intervene in making the Jones Law or any *yanqui* law. The resident commissioner over there is resident but he's not commissioned; the poor fellow is just squatting there, he can't vote on anything affecting Puerto Rico. Now poor Fernós wasn't able to vote on the law he himself brought up and that he claims is his; what a rascal, he couldn't vote. I can't explain where those people keep their faces, saying, "This law is mine, we Populares have put it through," when they couldn't even vote on it. For the resident commissioner to speak in the U.S. House of Representatives, he needs the unanimous consent of the House (chamber); any fool over there says "sit down, shut up" and he has to sit down, poor fellow. My friends, these "gentlemen" have lost all sense of honor, for here there is but one jurisdiction and that is the jurisdiction of the United States government. That government of the U.S. has organized, with the purpose of deceit, a corporation it calls "the people of Puerto Rico"; this corporation has judges, prosecutors, policemen, soldiers, even an air force. You pay taxes to maintain an educational system in which the Puerto Rican is no longer Puerto Rican, to tear the Puerto Rican heart out. I have just read the magazine edited by the Commissioner of Education of Puerto Rico, and I have seen the dates to be celebrated in September. Well, in the month of September, the date September 23 doesn't appear. Tell me, gentlemen, if it's not an act of banditry on the part of Villaronga and all his department of education, if this limitless audacity doesn't cry out for the hangman's ropes.

Well, then, this little government's legislature—jails, many jails, there's no money to bring a loaf of bread to Lares, but for a jail in Lares there will be money. So, lots of money for jails in Lares and all Puerto Rico—for schools, yes, because they are to destroy the heart and mind of the Puerto Rican, denaturalize him, prostitute him, corrupt him—for that there will be money. There's money to have the Health Department in Puerto Rico inject the youth of Puerto Rico with any disease that the U.S. government desires, to kill them on a long-term basis, there's yes, money for that—but to kill hunger in Lares, Jayuya, Utuado, in Comerío, in the whole nation there's not a penny because hunger is the policy of the United States. The *yanqui* believes that when a human being is deprived of his loaf of bread, he will surrender and humiliate himself to be kicked by anyone. He will turn in his mother, his wife, his own dignity, so as not to suffer hunger. That's the policy of the United States.

Well, that little legislature now has an elected governor and he signs those laws, those laws which can be annulled by the Congress of the United States; he doesn't dare do anything without consulting his masters, he's conscious of that, poor devil, he has a twinge of conscience yet and he knows he is playing the role of a puppet of the U.S. because nothing is altered. What laws, what constitution can this nation draw up? There will be two constitutions, the Jones Law and the so-called insular government, the corporation the United States has created. This federal jurisdiction is the only one that exists. There it's divided into insular and federal jurisdiction. We have federal zones. Each time the navy wants a house, it comes here and expropriates it. It's interested in that Roman Catholic Church, so let's expropriate it. They need a dance hall for the U.S. officer corps, so it shall be done when they resolve it. They respect nothing. He who does not respect the truth does not respect his own mother.

Well, then, there was a hope held by certain lackeys that when both federal and insular zones were determined, if a crime took place in the insular zone, it would be judged by the so-called insular tribunals—no, it isn't like that. The armed forces of the United States have a privilege here. They can't be tried by any judicial authority, not even the so-called Federal Court of the United States. A U.S. Marine can kill anyone in the streets of San Juan and he cannot be tried by the District Court of San Juan or by the Federal Court, no, he has to be tried by a U.S. Navy court-martial . . . and why this privilege? Because killers need immunity. When one hires somebody else to kill, the first thing is to guarantee to him that he won't lose his skin, in any case. Well, are the armed forces here to defend Puerto Ricans? *To kill Puerto Ricans!!* That's the only government here, the rest are scoundrels, and all that crowd of bootlickers say that this is a democracy—the *yanquis* laugh at them. How wretched, how disgraceful they are. The slaves of their nation dedicated to hunting down their own children, justifying the outrage of their women, the expropriations of their homes, of their monuments, the destruction of their history, and the eventual destruction of their whole future. All this remains intact in the Constitution, this remains intact in the Jones Law. That remains the law, federal contributions here will remain the law, the Federal Court remains functioning in full vigor. There is little change in the so-called Supreme Court of Puerto Rico, a court in Puerta de Tierra that calls itself part of Puerto Rico and is not because it is imposed by the U.S. and is not supreme because there is a source of appeal from its decisions to a tribunal called the Boston District Court. It sounds like an electric switchboard system, doesn't it? . . . All this remains intact. Here anyone who wishes to buy a piece of meat in the Dominican Republic, that passes through the government intervention. If you want a bottle of perfume from France, there's a U.S. customs, if you want to send a postcard to Havana—there's the U.S. mail. A man from Lares wants to send a card by mail to San Juan—the Lares mail, the Puerto Rican mail? No, the U.S. mail. Here the mail administrator is not called mail administrator because he's not Puerto Rican—he's called Mr. Postmaster, and if it's a woman, Mrs. Postmaster. If you touch a wheel of that mail truck, you get dumped into the Atlantic, the gallows of the Atlantic, but that's not all, that's not all. The Federal Court also runs to the Boston Circuit Court, and the Boston court short-circuits back to the Federal Court—this judicial tyranny comes from above and spreads itself out to confuse us, to club us down. There's even more: each secretary, each administrator in the U.S. government has direct jurisdiction over Puerto Rico. The Secretary of Commerce has an office in San Juan to determine if you are importing from the U.S. If you set out to do business with Argentina and you look through the customs laws of the United States for permission to bring in something from Argentina, the Secretary of Commerce will be there to ask how you can buy something from Argentina when it's available in the U.S., this to prevent you from buying in Argentina. The Secretary of Justice, or Attorney General, is by direct jurisdiction the man in charge of all the courts here, except, hear this well, the courts-martial. Notice the military nature of the Puerto Rican government; the U.S. Attorney General can determine who is going to be federal judge here, or insular judge there, or attorney general of the insular government here, but he can't influence anything about a court-martial, by law of the government of the United States.

Customs have their own inspectors, their own policemen. In this way the U.S. maintains here its police state. It makes me laugh when the *yanquis* talk about a police state in other governments. There's no police state like the *yanqui* system. Each department of the U.S. government has its own police force, and each one of these policemen can arrest every policeman in Puerto Rico and every Puerto Rican citizen who is not a policeman, and every judge in Puerto Rico, and every prosecutor, and each governor. Tell me, then, if it's not an act of shamelessness to claim that international relationships are still intact in Puerto Rico. The Jones Law remains intact, you will say, and what the devil is going to change with this so-called Puerto Rico Superior Tribunal to be named by the Puerto Rican Executive, that's all; all the laws that the so-called insular government passes will be subject to reversal by the Congress of the United States. Like right now, that is still what will be in order, a big pact, a big agreement. The agreement, my friends, the agreement that when you give me a cent you take two. The Law of the Funnel, the agreement that Puerto Ricans accept that political slavery of the United States, that's the agreement, the only agreement there will be and that is why you are busy with some new inscriptions, some new elections, a tremendous movement. Well, everyone who inscribes himself first has to say that he's an American citizen. The reason why the Nationalist Party opposes the inscription (of any Puerto

Ricans) is because they cease being Puerto Ricans. The PIP
members tell me it's a trick, that they can fool the *yanquis,*
that they'll inscribe, they'll vote, and when the elections get
to Puerta de Tierra they are going to stand up to the United
States. Well, the fools are the PIP members; the *yanquis* are
very well directed, they know what they are doing, the PIP
members are not that wise, with all the cleverness they
have, which I recognize, to fool these superbandits. They
can't fool the United States.

Today PIP members are caught in the trap of the century,
their sons mobilized for the draft—the PIP members quiet,
the Populares quiet, the Statehooders quiet, everybody is
quiet but the Nationalist Party. Puerto Rico is an atomic
base, no one dares talk about it, but there's more: An
eminent *yanqui* doctor, Dr. Filbert, has said that Puerto
Rico is sitting on top of a powder barrel—Albizu Campos
doesn't say that, Dr. Filbert says that—brought here by the
insular government. Well, I'm going to tell you a secret, a
secret that's been shouted out loud: The U.S. has turned
Puerto Rico into an atomic base and the United States has
in Puerto Rico under the direct administration of the U.S.
Army a vast camp of experimentation for germ warfare, for
bacteriological warfare. One of these laboratories is behind
the capitol, looking out to the sea; this laboratory is
experimenting with all the contagious diseases on earth.
They're experimenting in that laboratory with a disease that
is endemic in the highlands of the Rocky Mountains in the
U.S., which is a terrible fever.

Why bring the viruses, the microbes of this disease to
experiment here in Puerto Rico? Oh, it's because it can
spread and if it spreads here, what's the difference—they're
Puerto Ricans. Didn't they kill a few thousands in Korea?
After the next atomic war there might not be one left—
what's the difference?

This laboratory is in the main entrance artery to San Juan, there they have the cages with the animals that read "infected animals"—horses, cattle, rabbits, rats, etc., and any froth from this animal can fall to earth and this dust fly off and anyone passing in a bus can absorb it and pass it on to the rest of the Puerto Ricans. The legislature, has it said anything about this? No, no, no. They are willing even to burn their whole country so that they can enjoy their privileges. You might say no, this is a great historical investigation. My friends, anything under the direct control of an army, no army is a charitable institution, armies are established to kill, and this is in the charge of the U.S. Army. The medical corps of the U.S. Army, called the *yanqui* hospital service, has not dared to take charge of this experimentation in Puerto Rico. Well, I invite the defenders of the *yanqui* flag in Puerto Rico to study this continuation of infection flying over their country. But there's more, the constitution is written, it's all written, because the master does not trust the slaves, no. The slave, always apart, apart, knows when there's sunshine, he disappears in the sun, when there are shadows he disappears in the shadows, the master never trusts the slave. The master trusts an enemy who is free, because this enemy of his, if free, tells him face to face: "Listen, you go so far, you come to an agreement with me to go only so far, we both respect that frontier." And he signs a treaty with a free man and respects it because that man is free, but a slave gives his signature and it's worthless. This constitution they're going to drive the Puerto Ricans to draw up in 1952 is already written. Why? Because if they're slaves it's not the constitution of a free country. Constituents draw up a constitution, approve it, promulgate it, it's the Supreme Law—no, not that this is going to be approved first by the President of the United States. The President has to say that it's good, has to determine, has to approve, and if the President approves it, then the Congress. Why? All this anxiety over an illusory thing? A thing that is to draw a blind over despotism in the United States? Well, then, all this has to be defied, only as the men of Lares defied despotism, with the revolution.

▼▲▼▲▼▲▼▲▼▲▼▲

XIX. THE POETIC REVIVAL

The wealth of Puerto Rican poetry published between 1930 and 1971 is surprising. Rediscovery of the island's identity led to a rediscovery of the old forms of poetry, and the creation of new ones. In the twenty-two selections offered here one can appreciate the intense poetic revival parallel to the historical changes of the century.

"The Town," by Virgilio Dávila (1869–1943), describes the slow tempo of life in a Puerto Rican setting, while in his "Nostalgia" he sets the theme of return from exile: "Borinquen is pure flame/and here I am dying of the cold." A true nineteenth-century man in spirit, Dávila was a businessman and farmer, teacher and town mayor, whose book *A Little Town of Yesteryear* (1917) combined the traditional and modern forms. His son, José Antonio Dávila (1898–1941), was more sophisticated in his chant to a humble woman, "Letter of Recommendation." The themes of "anguished love of fatherland and love of all beauty" are reaffirmed in "I Remember the Apostle," by Félix Franco Oppenheimer (1912–   ), in "Invocation to the Fatherland," by Francisco Matos Paoli (1915–   ), and in "Fatherland," by Francisco Lluch Mora (1925–   ).

Homage to the island's heritage, in "The Castilian Language," and its natural beauty, in "The Wooden Wall," are the themes celebrated, as well, by Evaristo Ribera Chevremont (1896–   ), a versatile poet, whose "vanguardist" style has influenced many generations of writers.

Latin American "nature" poetry has often been a vehicle for patriotism. It sings the praises of nature in national tones, but in it, man either conquered nature, or was defeated, as a patriot. On the island the conflict rarely existed in poetry. A man was part of nature; he felt "fusion" with it, in the oldest Indian sense. Nowhere was this more passionately expressed than in Julia de Burgos' (1916–1953) famous "Río Grande de Loíza," where the "man river" is her lover—"who kissing my soul has kissed my body." (Interestingly, the Río Grande de Loíza was a sacred river of fertility to the Indians.) In searching the island for physical signs of their "spiritual identity," Luis Hernández Aquino (1907–   ) finds it in the stones, "Elegy Before the Ruins of Caparra"; Gustavo Agrait (1909–   ), in "Find" is bemused to find it everywhere, "in my hand this sea, this blue, this moment"; Francisco Manrique Cabrera (1908–   ) discovers it in the *"Batey,"* the *jíbaro's* front yard; Juan Avilés (1905–   ) remembers it, finds it, and loses it, in his memory of life on "The Coffee Plantation": "The coffee plantation, when it returns, the absent homeland will return to the homeland"; and Olga Ramírez de Arellano Nolla (1911–   ) sees it everywhere, in the "alphabet of tree, breeze, song, God, star," in her "Island of Childhood"; and hopes that, though "a materialistic culture" is beclouding the island with "the most barren moment of creativity," her faith will survive as long as "The Puerto Rican Wild 'Amapola' " will survive.

The surrealist elements of modern life did not deeply affect the poets rooted in the older, rural traditions. In the wise innocence of love, as in "Madrigal" by José P. H. Hernández (1892–1922), and in the harmonies of religious belief, as in "To Saint John of the Cross," by Manuel Joglar Cacho (1898–   ), they found absolution and peace.

But there were a few of the older generation who threw themselves, bodily, into the conflicts of the industrial era. One of these was Juan Antonio Corretjer (1908–   ), a poet, pamphleteer, and politician, first a Nationalist, then a Socialist laureate, who has been called "the Neruda of Puerto Rico" and the "Whitman of the Island." From his many works, the prison poem, "Distances," hints at the intensity of the symbolic clashes that reverberate in his vision of "the trembling homeland," torn apart by contemporary life and irony. Juan Martínez Capó (1923–   ), journalist and poet, searches for the answer to the destiny of Puerto Rico in his *jíbaro* poem to the *bohío* bird, while Jorge Luis Morales (1930–   ) raises his voice in a "Hymn to the Sun" reminiscent of ancient rites, and Violeta López Suria (1929–   ) writes a moving elegy to Jesse Routte, a lovely Negro boy who lived in Puerto Rico and was later killed in New York. Diana Ramírez de Arellano (1919–   ) and Clemente Soto Vélez (1904–   ) represent the first generation of Puerto Rican poets in New York, with selections from their most recent work, while Andrés Castro Ríos (1942–   ) is a poet of the younger Puerto Rican generation in the island.

THE TOWN

by Virgilio Dávila

The little town is picturesque and happy in its way.
It has some old patriarchal homes undented by Time's
    test
And few of younger vintage; all done *al fresco* and gay,
With bay windows a score and with porches all the rest.

The church stands in the center with unpretentious air;
The dome, called "half an orange," is a crimson oval
    block.
She seems proud of her twin towers so genteel and
    debonair,
One of them shelt'ring the belfry and the other one, the
    clock.
Well in keeping with the temple, trim and squarely cut and
    snug,

Around May the little plaza seems a brightly patterned rug
In whose center has been woven a vermilion *flamboyán.*°

The rest? Huddled to the ground in their somber drab and
    gray,
Looking as if all they wished were to hide themselves away,
Are the huts, home of the poor, of the desolate and wan.

° The beautiful tree that borders the highways and grows everywhere
in the island.

NOSTALGIA

by Virgilio Dávila

"Mamma, Borinquen calls me,
this country is not mine,
Borinquen is pure flame
and here I am dying of the cold."

In search of a better future
I left the native home,
and established my store
in the middle of New York.
What I see around me
is a sad panorama,
and my spirit calls out,
wounded by much nostalgia,
for the return to the home nest,
Mamma, Borinquen calls me!

Where will I find here
like in my criollo land

a dish of chicken and rice,
a cup of good coffee?
Where, oh where will I see
radiant in their attire
the girls, rich in vigor,
whose glances bedazzle?
Here eyes do not bedazzle,
this country is not mine!

If I listen to a song here
of those that I learned at home,
or a *danza* by Tavarez,
Campos, or Dueño Colón,
my sensitive heart
is more enflamed with patriotic love,
and a herald that faithful proclaims
this holy feeling
the wail "Borinquen is pure flame!"
comes to my ears.

In my land, what beauty!
In the hardest winter
not a tree is seen bare,
not a vale without green.
The flower rules the garden,
the river meanders talkative,
the bird in the shadowy wood
sings his arbitrary song,
and here . . . The snow is a shroud,
here I am dying of the cold.

LETTER OF RECOMMENDATION
(TO THE PROPRIETOR OF THE UNIVERSE)

by José Antonio Dávila

Sir:
    A timid sweet little old lady
will reach Your heaven shortly;
the lilies of the years blooming in her hair,
and her face smiling like a daisy.
She is the most diligent in the home
where she has sacrificed herself for all;
and she is so good, so good . . .
like the bread she has given to all of us.

In Your house, Lord, with her duster
and her everlasting pulchritude,
she will shake up that stardust
that covers the Lord's throne.
She will wind up Time; she will bring flowers
from Your garden and grapes from Your vineyard
and will paint fresh the colors
of the rainbow, when it fades.
She will polish the metal of the moon;
she will clean the lanterns of Your palace,
and will hang out to dry, one by one,
the sheets of clouds in space.

She will change the wick of the lights
of the Milky Way, and taking her combs,
she will braid the locks of the suns
and the stubborn mane of the comets.
Your tea, of the flower of some celestial linden tree

she will make on winter nights, when it snows;
and at harvest time she will sharpen
the silvery scythe of the new moon.
She will mend tears
in the tunic of the seraphim,
and she will bring sponges and soap
when it's time to wash the cherubim.
She will stitch in the pillow of the fluffiest halo
Your initials with a golden thread,
so You can stretch out when fatigued
by Your immortal worries.

That is how she has been down here: never skimping
of herself in the good of another's fortune;
she is the most unselfish in the house
and the most industrious in the hive.

And that is how she will be up there: in what she can
do for others, she will not be remiss.
Put her on salary, Lord, of just a coin:
the coin of light of Your smile.
Her goodness like her neatness invades the
most hidden corners of soul or memory:
basking, fluffing the welfare of all
is what she has had as glory.

If crossing Your kingdom one day
You catch on her face a sign of fatigue
and she tells You that she has not yet grown tired,
don't believe, Lord, what she tells You!

I REMEMBER THE APOSTLE

by Félix Franco Oppenheimer

I remember the Apostle, the one I've seen and heard,
who standing on the sand of the sea, said to himself:
where are the seven gold candelabra, the seven
stars! . . . , when the galloping of four steeds
enter suddenly in the waters of his eyes, with regal
cuirasses of Vulcan and brimstone; their heads,
like those of snakes: the first was white,
spirited, and dazzling, its arch in black laurel;
the second, reddish, unsettling,
went for sowing of blood; the third was black
and had a measuring scale of wheat
and barley; the fourth was yellow in color,
and with a scythe ready to reap, it planted the seed
of famine and death. . . . On fountains and estuaries
stars fell like bloodless faces;
the waters turned to absinthe, so that the angel
of the Abyss, Abaddon, would have ductile clay
to mold statues in the light of sunset,
in the putrid swamp . . . (While in flight wander
seven beautiful angels with the last plagues . . .)
There, on high, Cain, in his strange witches' Sabbath,
who stokes, with his sheaf of brambles, instigating
impulses in the waters and steps on the dunes,
and in the cold ashes already without eyelids, seeks
the belt of time that ties with its magnets
this stone of Sisyphus sunken in our seas. . . .

INVOCATION TO THE FATHERLAND

by Francisco Matos Paoli

Fatherland, what a happy sun between the trees!
Drunk of burning kingbirds,
from hill to hill it is the wake
of those who gave themselves to the kindled
honor of spring.

Fatherland, while the sum total of your dreams
makes us the skein
to join us to the lilies
on high in your mountain range,
we invoke from the heavens
the energy of all silences
on the horror of the chains.

And we shine the braided bread,
without hatred, like men who remain
ecstatic with light before the redeeming
blood that dreams.

We are the future of the swords.
We are the sandlewood of the blind night.
We are, as ever, a secret joy.

FATHERLAND

by Francisco Lluch Mora

1

I proclaim your sweet name fatherland,
crossed by swift birds,
rocked in the undulations of the palm,
and in the wave that imposes its emerald.
I proclaim that rose you raise
on the high mountain of your clay,
in the chaste thrush, in the legacy
of its perfect trills in the silence,
and in the skein the bowers weave.
In your guava trees I touch the shadow,
that dark backwater that sustains
its untouched flowers. In your little fig tree
I contemplate happiness and hope.
Oh, fatherland of my taciturn blood!
For you I listen to the swaying of the coral trees
carpeting the land in the ravine.
For you I breathe and renew existence,
for you, my sweet fatherland dawning,
eternal springtime raised,
I get up in the clay they gave me,
in the clear substance of my race.
I proclaim your name, sweet fatherland.
The hummingbird wakens in the ausubo tree
imposing its winged tessitura,
its true love song.
Here the sap exhibits its presence
leaving buried roots

and raising to heaven its banner
of bright green. Sweet fatherland,
for you who are the conscience of my life
I give unto you my enthused voice.

2

Ah, fatherland of my blood, of my name!
I seek in you the word that redeems,
the noble heart, the sure honey.
I seek in you the silence of the afternoons,
the rose-apple drunk with joy,
the balsam-apple at the edge of trunks
and the erect mountain coral trees.
I seek in you the humble peppermint,
the fruit orange tree in gardens,
the slender presence of the palms
and the sad paper tree of shadow.
I seek in you the bark of the royal palm and the
    lily,
the hummingbird of dream that in you fosters
its untrammeled river of harmony.
I seek in you the ever-red clay
that dreams silent in shadows.
I seek in you the fluttering of the gray kingbird,
lord and master of the diaphanous air.
I seek in you the substance for dreams.
I seek in you the constancy of my song.
Oh, fatherland of my blood, of my name!
How your voice dreams in my conscience,
how the kingbird cries in the mountains!
That cry goes deep, and moves me.
That cry is the voice and the hope.

THE WOODEN WALL

by *Evaristo Ribera Chevremont*

The wooden wall speaks to me with red voices:
"We were beautiful trees with bright branches.
Our arms fell with the weight of the leaves
and our fruit was the glory of the landscape.

"Bluish birds and vermilion insects
drilled our trunks, walked on our branches;
and in the sweet intimate warmth of their profound desires,
the subtle blood of flames flowed through us.

"One day, woodsmen blandished strong axes
against our shields. Hoarse cries were heard;
and the birds and insects flew. Hard blows
destroyed the black shields of our trunks.

"Now we are the home, comfortable shelter.
Day sings and dreams in our corridors,
and afternoon bestows on us the tenderness of wheat
with golden bread and the honey of the flowers.

"If you have love, we have love: red desires
as in the good old days when we glowed with branches.
Our illusion still wants to feel the green leaves
and the subtle blood of flames still flows through us."

THE CASTILIAN LANGUAGE

by Evaristo Ribera Chevremont

The language that dressed my cradle with words
is the language born in the Castilian soil.
From the romance-poetry to Lope, without any neglect,
it is offered in ballad, sonnet, and quatrain.

Not an atom in my human form is reluctant
to the shining, musical, and perfect peal
of the language that in book, sheet of paper, or memo book
gives, because of its purity, strength to the idea.

The language of classical flavor rises
in writers sure of beauty.
Doctors of song, the greatest purists,
serve it to me in clauses of loftiness and precision.

The language—voice of the centuries—joins my word.
They shall not destroy it, for it is the best part
—the substantial, the eternal—of the whole of my race.
And my race is, in all, faith, sorrow, love, art.

RÍO GRANDE de LOÍZA

by Julia de Burgos

Río Grande de Loíza. . . . Spread in my spirit
and let my soul be lost in your brooks,
to seek the fount that stole you as a child
and the path that returned you in a wild impulse.

Curl upon my lips and let me drink of you,
to feel myself mine for a brief moment,
and hide you from the world, and hide you in yourself,
and hear voices of astonishment in the mouth of the wind.

Get off for an instant the back of the land,
and seek the intimate secret of my desires;
tangle in the veil of my fantasy bird,
and leave me a water rose in my illusions.

Río Grande de Loíza . . . my source, my river,
since the maternal petal raised me to the world;
with you I was brought down from rough peaks
to seek new furrows, my pale desires;
and my whole childhood all was a poem in the river,
and a river in the poem of my first dreams.

Adolescence arrived. Life surprised me in
the widest part of an eternal journey;
and I was yours a thousand times, and in a beautiful
    romance
you woke my soul and kissed my body.

Where did you take the waters that bathed
my forms in a shaft of recently opened sun?
Who knows in what remote Mediterranean country
some faun on the beach will be possessing me!
Who knows in what rain shower of what distant land
I will be pouring to open new furrows;
or if perhaps, tired of biting hearts,
I will be freezing into crystals of ice!
Río Grande de Loíza! Blue. Brown. Red.
Blue mirror, fallen blue piece of the sky:
naked white flesh that becomes black on you

each time night gets into your bed;
red band of blood, when the rain comes
in torrents the hills vomit their clay on you.

Man river, but man with the purity of a river,
for you give your blue soul when you give your blue kiss.
Very dear river, mine. Man river. Only man
who kissing my soul has kissed my body.

Río Grande de Loíza! . . . Río Grande. Great plaint.
The greatest of all our island plaints,
if greater were not the one which flows from
the eyes of my soul for my slave country.

ELEGY BEFORE THE RUINS OF CAPARRA

by Luis Hernández Aquino

Here only the stone
that utters its age-old word!
Man's voice fell silent in nothingness,
only a voice of stone is perceived
in the autumn air;
for the stones speak his language.
It is a language fixed to them by time,
a perfect language
for the past to be understood.

Here Caparra raised its dream;
the tower of its desire grew with the impulse
of Spanish blood.
From it sprang confident heroes,
sappers of dreams and conquests.

Here was a zealous spirit!
Here Spain took root tooth and nail!

Arid and barren earth,
Puerto Rican land, you
who project your name as a symbol,
and maintain your stone like a song,
I hear in your voice the resounding of yesteryear
growing now like a fresh rose
that days make gigantic.

Luis,
Isabel,
Juan Ponce,
you who dream under this earth,
are you watching my passion now?

Here, before some ruins, face to face
with the earth and dust;
below the sweet evening star,
breathing this air that you were
breathing for a lifetime
I feel your blood torment me,
and I take root with neither tooth nor nail
on your earth,
but with song and plaint.

Dreamy Caparra,
see men pass by.
That one is my brother!
He passes by here without seeing your stone
without knowing the strength of yesteryears
without perceiving your breath.
Night fell on his spirit,

the dense night of not knowing his origin,
and he has lost his voice
and grows not in his spirit.
For him, for you
for your name of glory
I raise the flaming verb and the tear.

Caparra: stone and dust;
story of some men and a land;
changing geography, solid fact
that circulates in history,
here I am watching you,
feeling you, affirming you.
My dream sinks its golden root
in the silent clay of your years.

My flesh is face to face with your stone,
and the voice you heard in the past, now
flows from the heart to tell you
these tender words:
On your dust a song shines resplendent;
beside your stone my soul stands guard!

FIND

by Gustavo Agrait

Fields of the south without water or greenery,
smelling of sun, beards of the *júcar* tree,
magic land, perpetual marvel
suspended in miracles of equilibrium
between the blues of seas and heights!

Saltpeter beds of mica reverberate
at the edge of a multiblued sea
in whose white sand and snowy foam
the sea animals gambol.

The bitter cactus nails
its feline caress in the countryside
and the niggardly breezes, planning
in spheres of blue and white,
are redeemed in flesh and rot.

This so rare moment, why now?
Caprices of fortune or infallible providence
older than the centuries?

Childhood, youth, adolescence?
Are they memories, desires, omens?
It is unnecessary to know anything:
this is my land
and in my hand this sea, this blue, this moment.

I can ask for nothing:
look at me in suspense.

BATEY

by Francisco Manrique Cabrera

When the word *batey* perches on my lips
a rain of lights my spirit dawns.
The hills seem transparent to me
like drops of nothingness.
I erase horizons of yesterdays and tomorrows

to be sky and land pure,
of centuries, neighbors, without ever meeting.
Through that word come telephonemes of the past,
shouts of the present,
dreams of tomorrow (on the mountain).

The *batey* resounds.
Who is speaking?
Here Cabrera the stubborn peasant voice
soul of the mountain.
The Areíto songs! Come all!
We shall speak in the voice of the *güiro*,
our common tongue for centuries.
Come, I say, dance on the five letters of the *batey*.
We shall sing in the voice of the *güiro*.
The flesh of our song
will have calluses of slowness and sweet melodies,
I will be red-hot
like dawn in the flower of the royal poinsettia.
Ah, our song and dance in the voice of the *güiro*,
our common tongue,
eternal instrument of the soul of the hills!

The *batey* resounds.
Who is it?
Here Cabrera the brute force
of our land land.
My childhood!
Come on horseback this very instant.
We will call all the neighbor children:
Sky, Moon and Star,
Mountain, Bird and River,
to sing walking
on the five letters of the *batey*.

Our song:
Doña Ana is not here,
for she is in her garden,
caring for the rose
and opening the carnation.

The *batey* resounds.
Who is it?
Here Cabrera the hurricane cry
of muscular soul
that knows rivers and falls.
My old age!
Come but without losing my toys' song,
those that forgot in your shoes
the Kings of the hills,
the Kings of the pools,
and those of the Seis Chorreao.
Then, in clusters, hanging from our "once upon a time,"
we will roll my stories like accounts
through all the ages of our land land
on the five letters of the *batey*.
City, you forgot the *batey*,
you will die without it.
Will you die?
No, take it in my muddy song in flower.
I bring you all the *bateys*,
I bring fresh ones . . .
The *batey* of the voice of the moon,
the *batey* of the song of the ravine,
the *batey* of the strong poem of the sun,
and that of the Seis Chorreao.
Come, comrades, to the public square
of my land land

and help me to declare with trembling love,
with depth of the soul,
with frenzy and madness: *BATEY!*
You will see a rain of lights
that dawns in my spirit,
you will know unshod the voice of the mountain,
and you will feel the land land.
One and all: *BATEY! BATEY!*
and you will dawn. . . .

THE COFFEE PLANTATION

by *Juan Avilés*

I am from the coffee plantation, from up in the mountain,
from the plain and from the hill.
I have willingly climbed the ribbing
of the green shade of the guamá trees.
I am the intimate friend of the cedars,
of the stately capá tree in the ravine,
of the placid locust tree on the hill,
of the giant ceiba, of the inaja palms,
of the milky blue and black caimito,
of the lush guabas in the gulches,
of the weak elms and the oak
that rock hurricanes in their branches.

I know them all. They used to be mine.
They were my childhood companions.

I am from the coffee plantation that yesterday
                    was everything!
            That was the homeland!

In the three flowerings of the coffee tree
I saw the ornaments of white stars
with which the candid peasant then
trimmed his crowns of hope.

More than simple flowers of the coffee tree
they were a promise fulfilled.
They brought the old man's pants,
the shirt, the skirt,
the little powder box of the girl
who was already falling in love;
the ribbons for the fiancée's dress,
the subtle embroidery for the negligée,
the perfumed soap
that was cheap in the trinket store;
the quarter dance on Saturdays,
the Italian straw hat,
and the shoes of the growing lad
who, after the parties, hung them
like a scutcheon of peasant nobility
from the highest beam in the room.

The coffee trees of my days
bloomed with flowers of hope.

I witnessed the indescribable glory
of the three harvests:
of the first border beans
to the green and ripe ones. The voice
of happiness resounded in those mountains!
That was the carnival of the mountain!

I still recall the voice of the supervisor
giving orders to the peasants in the morning.

"You continue here, from this orange tree
to the foot of that inaja palm."
"You continue this line to the elm tree."
"You follow the furrow to the palm tree."

And the peons would undertake their chores.
And you heard the ardent lament
of the boy in love with the girl
who wouldn't say yes. Everything was alive
as though each shorn bean
were going to strike the soul
and tear out a note of joy
that filled the mountain with voices!

The abundant harvest finished
the party began.
The great end-of-season party of other times!
The party of the harvest set aflame!
The party of the coffee plantation, even more of a party
with the loud music!

Long live the native meat pie wrapped in leaves,
and the classic roast pig on the spit!
Long live the burning rum of those times
that warmed throats,
and made brave bold men of cowards,
and graced the girls with rhythmic hips!

And year after year it was
the purest party in the homeland.

Today I sing to the coffee plantation with the sadness
of he who carries in his soul
a painful memory, something lost
in distant times.

The coffee plantation of those days
and the green shade of guamá trees fades;
the cedars and the stately
capá tree in the ravine,
the placid locust tree on the hill,
the giant ceiba trees, the inaja palms;
the weak elms, and the oak
that rocked hurricanes in their branches;
the milky blue and black caimito
and the lush guabas in the gulch—
all gone in smoke.

Today the horizon is more distant
for the mountain wears a different garb.

I am from the coffee plantation that was everything
                    yesterday.
Today I weep for the coffee plantation that is no
            longer anything.
My song to the coffee trees is a sad one.
More than a song it is a prayer.

As I view the barren land
I seek the bush that went away. The homeland
handed it over to the machete and the arms
and the land was left sacrificed.

Perhaps one day not far away
the coffee plantation may arise again in the ravine,
and adorn the plains as before,
and again be lord of the mountain.

The coffee plantation of yesteryear is not far off.
It went on a trip. It will return tomorrow.

And with the coffee plantation, when it returns,
the absent homeland will return to the homeland.

ISLAND OF CHILDHOOD
by Olga Ramírez de Arellano Nolla

ABCDE

Alphabet of *árbol* [tree], *brisa* [breeze], *canto* [song], *Díos*
   [God], *estrella* [star];
an open star in a blue field,
a deep vegetable fiber, luminous,
burning roots on the high roads,
raised from me in intimate horizon,
grown in polished and fragrant air,
ecstatic rose nailed to the earth of the soul.
Transparent in troubled waters, butterflies fluttering
in the mauve cane crests with rose fuzz
or in the wind that tear its gauze heart,
intimate lark sun, slender flower of the homeland.
Climber in fingers of bamboo, luminous,
cooing of doves or ambit of maracas.
The sound of waves breaking in the breeze
overturns on my essence breath of daisies
that envelops the tender memory of childhood.
Rosy conch shells, high sour quenepa fruit,
teeth of balsam-apple or guava meat
in a minimum world of golden songs.
It was born with me, beautiful, from the greenest root
in peasant childhood of the *coquí* and heavy water,
in the round ripeness of sounds, sweetness of *pana* bread,
aromatic and friend in the ripe cashew tree, the pineapple
   and the orange.

THE PUERTO RICAN WILD "AMAPOLA"

by Olga Ramírez de Arellano Nolla

> On the mountain path
> the wild "amapolas" frolicked
> kissing the breeze.

Puerto Rican wild amapola! Flower of my land, flame made silk, silk made petal dragged through the furrows of arable land. Flower of nervous undulating fragrant flame! Blood of hot clay! Voice in red undulation of inborn tendernesses! Purpled lastingly like intense caresses or orange passions. Sweet in the breeze, you gambol along curls of soft moiré on the surface of the hills or exploding in vertical arrows on the horizon of peaks.

Humble and solitary flower, who fills with warm light the wild cycloramas of the meadows and is born, timid and intimate, of the sun like dawn itself. They say your origin goes back to black Africa of wild rhythms and that you came, like that blood, across the same path of waves and wind. There are those who assert that you were native of South America and that you beat your red banners along the path of the Conquistadores.

But you are—on this land of transparency, as your corollas rise under the breeze—a prayer in flower or an ecstatic weeping raised in the air and bit by vital fires. You are wild flower in my Puerto Rican land, that cradled your seed with motherly hands and procreated you in her breast, carrying you, intimate tropical song, on the loving panorama of her fecund harmonic body.

Some insensitive men destroy you and burn your bulbs cruelly, knowing not that they are immolating beauty on their funeral pyres. I cannot forget the day when, on an excursion to some near-by spot, I saw you lying on a hillock, your petals open in profusion, trembling with dew. I asked the owner:

"Are they amapolas?"

"Yes, there are hundreds of them. They cover more than three acres. Come on this side."

On a hill a silky blanket of you twinkled in the light, gentle breeze, while you, multiplied, went up hills to the terrace of a singing pool.

The man added: "I'm going to destroy them in spite of the fact people are mad about them. But they're useless. . . . Why do I want a plant that gives me no material gain?"

A tear inside me made me defend your splendor and think, plunged into a profound hyperaesthesia of beauty: Is a utilitarian logic going to dominate our people to the point of annihilating emotion and spiritual and artistic sources? Are we becoming matter before we reach that stage? Are we already what we will be in death?

A materialistic culture can drag us—I thought—to the most barren moment of creativity, to an extraordinary exhaustion in a world without song, but filled with gold pyramids, megalithic and absurd. And with the hope of a shipwreck that wishes to save a treasure, I took from your seed all that my arms could hold and I returned with them to the warmth of my mountain. I dug furrows and planted your flower root, humming a tune of love and faith; faith, that through me, your beauty would continue to live on my island.

MADRIGAL

by José P. H. Hernández

(*Theme: to heavenly eyes*)

If God one day
blinded all source of light,
the universe would be lit
by those eyes of yours.
But if filled with bitter anger
for such blasphemy, God tore out
your pretty eyes,
so that the world at dawn
were not lit by your pupils:
even though He wanted, God could not
extend the Night on Nothingness. . . .
for the world would still be lit
by the memory of your glance.

TO SAINT JOHN OF THE CROSS

by Manuel Joglar Cacho

That which I seek most . . .
—ST. JOHN OF THE CROSS

Learned creator of the divine canticle
that nurtures the flocks of the Lord
for more than four hundred years
you have ascended on the wings of your trills!

The stone on the road is already dust
which caused injury to your bare feet,
but your lyrical and strange verses
yet drip dawning dew!

I should like to go where you are,
my soul free from worthless things,
dying in what you die and die not. . . .

Lend your hand to my poor palm
and permit me to be what you are:
eternity dressed in harmony!

DISTANCES

by Juan Antonio Corretjer

When my heart said: Outside,
in front of the jail bars Consuelo
waits in vain to see you,
I thought . . .
. . . what a man whose look
is plunged into the night of nothingness
and wants to see the sky thinks.

When a long absence
that a childhood memory
filled with its presence
in inhospitable foreign shores
(that strange fragrance
that nocturnal birds exhale softly,

or that gentle noise
of the little bird that abandons its nest,
either cast from the branch to the ground,
or from the wind in the willows along the way,
or the wandering movement of the brook
between the new blackened sand,

or that phantom of presentiment
which reaches us in the wind
and makes us look through the window
as though the heart felt alarm
and feeling, could
see dawn written in the night),

my heart used to
feel the Epiphany
of nearby distant things,
drink its poetry
and not feel the cold
solitude of things so far.

Luck the agile boy
with a simple heart plays
who knows how to live humbly and bravely!
I will never be prisoner
in enemy hands, so oppressed
that my breast breathes not freely,

and illume the darkness,
and leap over the wall
and to my fatherland swiftly fly,
where the colt mounts the hill
and in the dew-tipped flower
the buzzer flits!

But here is the wall,
the bars, the mortar,
soulless, that keep watch
between your vain wait at the door
and my awakened anger,
which wavers toward a futile decision.

Never had it occurred before to the mind
that distant things
having been formerly so near,
the sweet loved treasure
so near my side
they forced it to such far distances!

For sure in this moment
what is absent is not remedied
by sweet imagination that foretells fortune
and in the distance aspires soft essence.
This suffering is not cured
"except by your presence and your figure."

These present distances:
that machine gun,
the sweaty khaki
the leaning gun
and even the sun silhouetted
and rationed like a precious balm,

are outrages that invite the heart,
call and request
even irrational temperature.
But my triumphant faith
is sustained by what transfigures
your loving person at the door.

And this I think tonight in La Princesa:
the fight never ends.
All of life is a struggle
to obtain desired freedom.
The rest is nothing,
but surface and style.

Fatherland is knowing the rivers,
valleys, mountains, huts,
birds, plants and flowers,
the mountain trails and the plain,
the waters and high peaks,
the shadows, the colors,

with which the east is painted
and later the west is unpainted,
the tastes of the water and the land,
the multiple aromas,
the grasses and the hills,
and in the terrifying night

the thunder that resounds in the blackness,
penetrating thickets
seeing as in a lightning bolt the path
and in a fast drink
the wind of the hurricane,
recognizing enthused animals from the farm.

The fatherland is the beauty
with which the letter, book, and verse
erect its magic statue
dressed in glory,
seeing it cross history
toward the fullness of the universe.

Take its cardiogram
and see how its health
inflames flushness.
Kiss its flag,
dream its daydream,
love its loves.

But in the hard test,
when the fatherland irrigates
our own life in the current:
the trembling homeland
that wears our life like a cuirass,
that demanding fatherland

that imposes its silence or its word,
and works with its hands,
on the bloody mass of pains
with lightning blows
the form of a star,
a song of resplendencies,
a certain moment, a day,
behind the cold wall
of the prison, a prisoner
will ponder that game of distance
between his mute room
and the nearby bewitchment
that tells his heart: "Outside,
outside the prison bars your Consuelo
waits in vain to see you."
And he feels the same as he whose
look is plunged into the night of nothingness
and wants to see the sky.

PEASANT

by *Juan Martínez Capó*

Man of my country,
illustrious old man of this land in spasm.
Challenge anchored yearning on the *batey* of the island
forgotten above and by races;
you are like mimosa under the plow
of the solitary churlish world.

Over anonymous hills you will go running wild or child
with eye filled with foals and poppies,
the soul nodding with a fateless desire
and a chronic question on your face.

Bohío bird, in your wingless anguish
you dream pulp of trills
and you begin to swarm from hill to hill
a grimace of *güiros* and guitars.
One day you will dawn hurricane-like—
voice and accounts paid—
with your sack of hungers on your back
you will become an arm of God over men
and you will wield your destiny in your advance.

Man of my country,
any other morning
the cock of farewell will crow your sugar crop.
You will go, early riser—just dew—
along the main road backward.

You will go cast down upon my heart
like a millenary mountain range.

HYMN TO THE SUN

by Jorge Luis Morales

I honor my heart singing to you: Sun.
You burn this ray of God in which I drown
to make my conscience live, daily,
and to cross myself with lilies, untouched by man.

I see nightingales raising prayers to you,
at the point where the sunset is amazed at itself,
larks blessing your perfection of infancy,
when in the east breaks forth a fire of angels
who grant us the liberty of wakefulness.
Why, if I am so brief: am I to believe myself
neither nightingale nor lark, lark nor nightingale,
so that I persist in not being your guest
and demanding you be guest in my dwelling?

I am brevity: you are eternity.
It is just that earth looks always toward heaven
and aspires to be assimilated in the heaven's vastness;
but, on the other hand, it is unjust for looks to come
from heaven to earth. It is more the father's son
                              than the son's father.

Let me go to you: Father Sun.
Let me grow in your eternities,
for, if you come to me, only death
would fill my hours.
Remain on high, for a day will come
when my misty brevity will be transfigured
and I fuse with you who have kept the secret.

You know the secret: my Father.
You and I were the same substance, the same joy
before ships struck out for the high seas,
before the affable season of the harvest
milked the fruit of the trees like cows.
Then there were not yet those clouds that, walking,
                    whistle to me,
like white serpents, wanting to burn me,
so that I do not preach your Evangel of lights.
Then, dynasties of Oblivion succeeded themselves.
Man pronounced not words, but stars.

Lives hasten, like the waves of the sea;
and I, like a wave, will reach my shore.
Be still, shore, let the wind move you not,
though it come armed with storms.
Father Sun, my Father:
You the shore, I the wind.
Ay, the storms the world has filled me with
so that the hour of silence fall upon you
and men extinguish their own flames!
I can no longer endure so many storms,
that hand me over, daily, telling me:
Declare war, right now, on your father.
And go on, go on, for love redeems not:
with love all graves are nurtured.
Be still, shore, let the wind move you not,
though it come armed with storms.

I who am of your origin; I who come from you,
as fragrance from the flower;
I understand:
I the fragrance, you the flower;
but the fragrance I, whom, I recall not why,

the gods have cast to this crackling war,
to find an ill-fated destiny of dust.

ODE 1962

> *by Violeta López Suria*
> (*To Jesse Routte*)

> (. . . *J. G. Routte, 20, killed in N.Y. He was tied
> to a bed, gagged and stabbed, and an attempt had
> been made to strangle him—apparently with a
> wire coat hanger twisted around his neck. Officers
> said* . . .)
>
> —SAN JUAN STAR, *P.R., July 3, 1962*

You were filling yourself with silent flightless mirrors.
Black child limited in light, lacking plains to recognize
There was at your side an introblivion of stone, of blows, of
   silence,
a silence, impossible hinge, rising
like a trembling skyscraper church.
A sightless silence in the background,
raised inert in its smashed branches.
Perhaps a silence, dead aluminum, before being,
without dreaming of having been what it had been.
   There you were standing with a smile
split in two. In two possibilities
of teeth dressed in snow.
Young bone teeth, saved,
sustained by that unaccustomed clay
that equalizes us in separating us already different.
   There you were, with your arms
sweetly black
and your legs, nubile stalks, dark

stars. There must have been a deep wound
behind you, or below your forehead, on your forehead
   kissed
only by what you wanted faith to be,
on your forehead already longly wept
before being born.
Velveted boy, of linen
and glass and purple.
Pure child with Christ beside recognizing himself,
frightened by your own pain.

   Asphalt child
with pristine glass within,
lost in his origin,
placed in a land foreign to his pain,
a land so far from his steps
for him to be washed by the yet
unclosed wound of his mother.

   Followed by nails,
nails that hurt you
from before,
much before,
when it was the fragrant
nail in the caves
of comprehension,
become a musty spike
of a rancorless iron,
to pass, no doubt,
through bramble needles
sunk in noncomprehension,
segregated, without exit.

   You foresaw all.
There was in your walk
a crude resolve.
You never sang to yourself,

that sin was
not yours.
You never furled
the voice of the poem
to sing to yourself.
Perhaps the rest
hurt you so, those
who brushed by you and
you always forgave them
with a soft smile,
tenderness made moss
in your hands.
You always forgave them,
they who only
tripped on your
dark skin,
skin stuck to your soul.

   Dark child,
shrouded, in a lewd
frightful bite.
Indefinably mutilated, from
where man is the blackest
well,
from where man
is the wretched dust
become pointed ruin
in seed.

   From where man
is larval monster in dung,
thorns of dried quartz.

   From where man
unloosens himself in
lapless traps,
in traps with licentious

empty tentacles
like a frozen star.
    Under the ground, in an already
white shadow,
the rush-like enchantment
of your black body opened.
Child wrapped
in the silky sheet
of final absence,
empty absence feeling sorry
for itself, without hearts
to water.
You offered the lush flower
of your heart
in your adolescent transparency.
Ah, carnations denied in wood,
cold carnations, funereal.
Child with the aroma of salvation,
now that you are not timidly absorbed
with your innocent grace,
you have something to tell us
with your silky word of dawnings,
your chest in pieces of black bread,
crucified,
thinker made skew
of what could have been
without the chosen torch
of your tragedy.
    Smile at us.
The earth became mirrors
to shroud your shadow.
Dead child, undone,
fragile, fragile being toward
our salvation.

Between the newly arrived miracle,
hear us. . . .

TO A POET

by Diana Ramírez de Arellano
(To Enrique Ramírez Brau, on His Death)

Vanquished verse: subsequent origin
to the dialogue flooded of oneself.
Vanquished verse: volatile monument to our
delirium.
Interior myth of dream and evidence
in the transdepth of anyone who could
attempt, as I, translucent sense.
Its nature not ignored.
Vanquished verse, and not attenuatedly exists;
yet, cannot be apprehended and cannot be
expressed
but as it has remained within itself denied.
Point without relation, asleep,
unlinked and mute,
limitless a limit gyrating around itself,
the vanquished verse.
Silent the word. Irreality swims.
Senseless and yet something,
something as essential and memorable
as this twenty-seventh of April absurdly tied
to the improvised flightiness of my life,
and to the unapprehendable certainty of his
death.

THE PROMISED LAND

by Clemente Soto Vélez

(*Fragment*)

The promised land
fights
　to
enlarge herself
with elegance immune
to the honey of praise

drawing in
the disturbed word
the word
　that
　senses
　the skin of the word
　with
　healthy spirit

　word
　that
withstands
judging
　of the animal acting of her mind

　of word
　that
　prefers
　to run
　for the present

by
the
shooting of the mirrors

  of word
that
  is not
  a towrope of stranded death
  of word
    that
originates
her forehead of frugal gratifications
    of
word
that
  does not
    break
    the
        crystals of Innocence.

FOUR VOICES OF PUERTO RICO

by Andrés Castro Ríos

1: Voice of the *güiro*

I am the song, the sorrow, the cry
of my Antillean land;
I bring the infinite love
of the light in the morning.
At my early cadency
the mountain lives secluded,
the air, the sun, the cottage

and the kingbird, who in his bill
brings the voice of Puerto Rico
and the heart of my affection.

2: Voice of the maraca

The stone is my heart
and I bear the song for a soul,
the hand covers like a quilt
the life of my frame.
I raise the annunciation
of my primary sound
in the planetary air
and in my innocent land,
then I embrace the watershed
of that imaginary cry.

3: Voice of the *cuatro*

My *cuatro* climbs the hill
and the brambles of the road
embracing the peasant
with its dove song.
The essence of the countryside
appears to my heart:
flower, elm, kiss and pineapple
whirl around singing
and leaving their voices
on my Girl's breast.

4: Voice of the peasant

I am the bird of the mountain
and the man of the plain,
the voice of the thicket,
the blood of the horizon.
At my cry let no one appear
for I shall break my shackles;
stranger, get yourself together and go
in the light of new day,
for in my fiesta and my persistence
the voice of the machete sings.

▼▲▼▲▼▲▼▲▼▲▼▲▼▲▼▲▼▲▼▲▼

XX. THE PASSION OF HISTORY

On an island where a few decades ago 90 per cent of the inhabitants lived in rural villages or in the *campos* (the fields), today 60 per cent of the people live in urban areas and suburbs. The change was so sudden, and abrupt, that the social planners did not have time to "bury history beneath a superhighway." So the novelists of that social change have been haunted by the presence of the past. In his searching novel of the Nationalists' revolt and defeat, *Los Derrotados* (*The Vanquished*), César Andréu Iglesias (1910–) found himself transcending the event and wondering, do we "invent" our history, and ourselves?

The uprising of 1950 is related by the frenzied words of the "existentialist novelist" José I. de Diego Padró (1896–). In "The Fish Sing," from his novel *A Cowbell with Two Clappers*, the act becomes a single moment in time. While in Julio Marrero Nuñez's (1910–) story of the tourists and the guide at El Morro fortress in San Juan ("The Interpreter"), the tourist becomes so agitated by the guide's love affair with the fortress she archly accuses him of a "passion of history." The guide replies, quietly, "El Morro has a soul." Enrique A. Laguerre (1906–), the leading novelist of this century in Puerto Rico, traces in his first novel, *La Llamarada* (*The Flare-up*), the social consciousness of the 1930 generation. We have chosen two selections: a cockfight and a strike. The "Socialist leader" is depicted in the novel in ancient terms as

"An old Moor, a bad Christian." Laguerre, whose style is akin to Hemingway and Hammett, and whose themes, in half a dozen novels, have often been urban dramas, nonetheless is "softened" by the ever-present Borinquen traditions; as when, at the end of "The Strike," the old man says in a *jíbaro* voice that is almost Indian, "God grants to man only what he can't use."

THE COLLAPSE

by César Andréu Iglesias

I have had the strangest meeting. Cheo Cruz, maker of saints' statues, came back to life. At least I had thought him dead. And suddenly he stepped out on the road. Who knows if he saved me from something worse!

I felt a volcano surging in my chest. All the ridiculousness of a sixth-grade graduation made me laugh, and I was ashamed of my laughter. I blamed my curiosity for having attended. I decided to leave. When I was getting ready to leave, Sancha appeared, dragging her granddaughter by the arm.

I again laughed, this time at the face the girl made: rebellious and submissive at the same time. I think she was about to cry. Because of that, or because it was beginning to rain, or to get rid of Sancha, I made my mount tear off wildly. Heaven knows what drove me to do it! Perhaps the desire to spot Gogui's white suit with mud. . . . And I crashed.

I crashed against Don Cheo's house. I must confess his story impressed me. Perhaps, like him, I heard a voice that dictated a destiny to me?

But there are no voices. Nor were there any even in Cheo

Cruz's case. If he abandoned his work, it was true that he could no longer handle the saw. A neighbor told me . . .

"He's crazy," was the first thing he told me. And when I asked for details, he told me that one day Cheo Cruz returned from the woods saying that he had heard the trees talking. People laughed in his face. A joker urged him to tell what he had heard, and he replied, "They speak a language I don't understand."

Since then they took him for a lunatic. And the cause of his madness was not the trees exactly. The neighbor affirmed with biting cynicism: "It was a woman." Shortly after becoming a widower, he brought home a prepubescent girl. Work with the saw fell off. The hearth was lit only to parboil some green plantain bananas. No one was surprised when the little wife threw herself into the arms of a younger man.

That was the coup de grâce for Cheo Cruz. He remained several months shut up in his shack. When the door finally opened, he was seen in the middle of the little room carving saints' figures. He ceased to be a lunatic for his friends. His eyes, till then wandering, became placid. A beatific calm colored his countenance. And he lived in this way till very recently, when it was begun to be rumored that he had lost his faith.

Cheo Cruz himself gave rise to rumors by lamenting: "The saints don't turn out right for me now." Can a greater tragedy be imagined: a maker of saints' statues without faith?

His look again wandering, Cheo Cruz remained mute, looking without seeing, absent from the world without being in any world. . . . Can it be that my trip back returned his life to him?

An endless chain of gestures besieges me. But what is

certain is that all of them can be reduced to just one: can it really be necessary to believe?

There are beliefs and beliefs. Can all have a common thread?

Believing in an image that one has himself carved, isn't that funny? But perhaps I myself, like the most able, have not modeled my saints. And in general what has history been but a factory of wooden saints?

We spend life making images with the sole purpose of inspiring valor in ourselves. It is a way to accompany ourselves. And we do it for the same reason that the boy whistles passing near a cemetery. We live desirous of company, and when we do not have it, we invent it. Even he who flees from his peers does it only to take refuge in a world peopled with his own image.

But the accompanied solitude of Cheo Cruz can be of no use to me.

THE FISH SING

by José I. de Diego Padró

It was the year 195–. On March 2 the local morning papers published the sensational news in big red-letter headlines. The event described in the report had taken place the day before, in Washington, the capital city of the nation, and was limited to the following:

Five members of the Congress of the United States had been wounded in the House of Representatives by four rebel patriots from here, among them one woman, who opened fire with their pistols from the visitors' gallery, with shouts of independence for their homeland. . . .

Suffice it to say that this bloodbath, unprecedented in

that nation's history, served to disturb and worsen things, already bad enough in themselves, in this country.

Since the year before and in what had passed of the present one, the liberating movement had been booming once more in the course of events, and this territorial dependency of the Caribbean had become a madhouse. It wasn't even known exactly what time it was.

But indeed it was known on pretense, and openly, that there was a hidden force that lent a hand to the insurgents, and that this force dealt, as a part of its dissociating policy, in sowing discord between the patriots and the government agencies, and even among the former, to take advantage thus of the situation and achieve its particular goals in a progressive manner. Now, the thorn of the matter was that there was no way to unmask the components of that force, identify in that jumbled river the deceiving harmful fish from the innocent.

Everyone in the revolutionary movement fought for the same cause of liberty, justice, rights, human dignity, and other analogous values that in the workers' paradise were not regarded favorably or had been completely discarded. In justification of their armed violence they were merely repelling unjustified aggression, defending themselves from gratuitous persecutions and from the brutalities of the government's bailiffs.

Be it what it may, the fact of the matter is that the country was crossing through a crucial period of uncertainty and alarm that made one recall the bloody nightmares of other memorable years when the hidden torrent of revolution had again broken through to the surface and poured forth, impetuously, through cities, towns, and country.

The capital was the center where protests began and where police fury was more conspicuous against the insurgents.

Once more one heard the repetition of those sporadic shoot-outs, explosions of Molotov cocktails, clashes between government forces and patriots, attacks on the police, student uprisings, strikes, acts of sabotage, multiple and arbitrary arrests en masse.

Malicious acts of arson broke out again, and more frequently than ever—with material losses calculated in millions of dollars—not only in the large commercial establishments belonging to foreign owners (especially North Americans) as has ordinarily occurred before, but in the same manner, in important commercial and industrial installations belonging to native concerns.

Mysterious assassinations continued to occur, perpetrated with frightening skill, and whose authors, in the vast majority, remained indefinitely unpunished after all was said and done. . . .

More than an uprising of patriots, what had developed in the country was a wave of terrorism that sought to level everything, and before which the government had no other choice but to force its hand and adopt the most drastic measures in order to safeguard public order against the provocateurs. It renewed persecutions, breakings in and searches, frisking individuals right in the street by the local authorities. FBI reinforcements were sent in. The police in the capital and the provincial guard were put on a state of alert. Members of both forces, and of the Corps of Criminal Investigation patrolled the streets and avenues in the city, wearing steel helmets and carrying clubs, revolvers, rifles, carbines, and machine guns. It was officially stated, numerous arrests had been carried out; and arms were seized from many individuals and from some houses. With all this, the forces of public order, as far as it was known with any certainty, could not find a definite trail toward arresting the authors of these offenses. The police, as always, refused to reveal details, using the old argument that these could prejudice the investigation of innocent persons arrested in the forming of an uprising or in any other act of violence.

In view of the seriousness of the situation, the regional legislature passed urgently a law called the "muzzle," to enter into effect immediately.

THE INTERPRETER

by Julio Marrero Nuñez

1

Why does El Morro fortress have such an attraction for visitors, besides its physical structure? What do they seek in El Castillo, the Castle, as it is called? What is its secret? Its secret is Morales—the interpreter—a robust man like the tree of life, with the contagious smile of a fourteen-year-old boy and the appearance of a peasant from Comerío who still has not gotten rid of the banana stains.

When Morales explains the history of El Morro, the fortifications are charged with meaning and rise like a marvelous show of stone and geometry. His clear eyes are lit with happiness and his body is simply that of a truthful man, a friend of reviving historical things with love.

The Castillo is for him a place where one is invited to reconstruct the past from the present. The history of the Plaza Fuerte (Fortress) is like a river, in continuous movement, flowing toward our days. For Morales, each one of the worn stones preserves the spiritual treasure of our history, and the sentry boxes graceful as stone pavilions are the witnesses of ever-present heroic gestures. They are not dead remnants of the past but living stones, emanating from new illusions through the flight of the ages.

The rustle of arms and the galloping of horses are no longer heard through the ramparts. Now instead of soldiers with lances and blunderbusses, those who walk through the arms patio are men from distant lands who wear multicolored shirts. Many show their faces like toasted shrimp, and others happily change their skin like lizards. The hand grenades have been transformed into complicated photographic equipment. There is no doubt tourists like to "camouflage themselves" as natives with necklaces, clothes, and hats in appealing colors. It is another innocent way of having a good time when away from home. At times some seem like robots, empty lives in search of adventure.

It is a pleasure to hear them ask for El Morro. The "rr" seems to have been adopted without consulting previous visitors.

2

Irma also decided, finally, to visit the Castillo that afternoon. She went up Norzagaray Street and with a nervous step walked the whole Boulevard del Valle. She contemplated angrily the little *bohíos* with green roofs in La Perla district. She murmured a few words and continued walking like a somnambulist. From a window two children kept watching her, because she walked almost without touching the ground. "There goes the madwoman from Caguas," one of them cried to her as he laughed innocently. A dog growled hearing her pass by. She was a strange woman. The wind mussed her hair, giving her the look of an abandoned being.

A bit tired, she reached the visitors' room of the Office of the National Park Service. She said hello timidly, and without looking up inquired:

"May I join the excursion that is going to visit the Castillo this afternoon?"

The municipal clock had just struck three.

Irma's face was strange. She suffered a lot. Her hands trembled and her wandering look indicated she had not slept for nights, that she only cried.

The visitors' room impressed her as a place where people from everywhere congregated. And she was right, for through there passed daily rich men and poor, happy women and unfortunate ones, and the most mischievous and sad children in the world. All of them wrapped in the most interesting adventures, passions, and dreams.

The interpreter who was going to accompany the visitors that afternoon was Morales.

"I've never visited El Morro," Irma declared in a whisper, sadly.

"Madame, I'm sorry to tell you that you are not a good Puerto Rican if you don't know the Castillo," the interpreter commented with a certain good humor.

"I'm a tourist in my own country," she answered, making a great effort to smile. The words came out like a flock of timid doves. She fixed her hair a little. And the interpreter saw two large, lovely eyes appear. She was no doubt an attractive woman.

After signing the register she began to read the pamphlet and waited for them to give the signal to begin the excursion.

3

At three-thirty sharp, Morales approached a group of fifty-two people gathered to visit El Morro. There were more foreigners than Puerto Ricans.

"Ladies and gentlemen: I am going to begin the last excursion of the afternoon. My name is Morales and I shall be glad to answer any questions. The afternoon is beautiful and promising. I assure you an excursion full of agreeable surprises. The Castillo is going to reveal to us this afternoon its most intimate secrets. Follow me, because we are going to travel 'backward in time.'"

They walked through the green area of El Morro till they reached the monument that commemorates the defeat of the besiegers of 1625. He reconstructed the story of the Dutch general and pointed out the magnificent series of ramparts that runs like a stone rabbit from El Morro to the Castillo of Saint Christopher.

"To bring about this marvel of walls, the Spaniards must have possessed great military qualities," a man said very seriously. He spoke with the arrogance of a veteran of two world wars. "To achieve works of this magnitude it was necessary for the Spaniards to be men of persistence, patience, and great fortitude."

"It was an idea that grew and grew with the years till it became larger than the men themselves," Morales replied, adding splendor to the fortifications. His words, full of life, revived a whole heroic past.

The walls shone in the sunlight, exhaling a smell of great sacrifices.

A woman who blinked incessantly did not tire of saying: "Wonderful, marvelous, incredible."

The visitors were all eyes before the spectacle that the

city of enclosed walls offered. A few contemplated, amazed, in silence. A girl with a body like a Mexican jug could not contain herself:

"It's terrific!"

There are moments when words get in the way, and this was one of them.

The palms, uncombed sentinels, watched the road that led to the main gate.

A blond girl in a black and white striped dress, like a Picasso harlequin, made insistent gestures. Finally she approached Morales, and whispering, asked him where the rest rooms were.

The group followed the interpreter's explanations attentively. Irma, the sad woman, tried, too, not to lose even a single word.

They were taking a real excursion through the heart of the Castillo. One woman, enthused, exclaimed: "This is what I was looking for, someone like you, an interpreter who could teach me the ABCs of this Castillo." And handing him a small card she added: "If you ever visit the state of Oregon, you can reach me at this address."

Irma looked at the interpreter and a smile withered on the sadness of her mouth. The acrobatic antics of the photographers to take the best shots of El Morro were surprisingly funny.

"Unbelievable!" a man of somewhat advanced age almost cried out. He had a childlike air, long hair, and melancholic eyes. He gave the impression that he lived lost in the clouds.

4

When they reached the Castillo, a sprinkling of rain fell. They entered vault number twelve, and from the small iron balcony they saw a large cloud that was falling like an enormous transparent butterfly. In an instant the horizon grew dark with mountains and pines. Before the spectators, Cabras Island, with its little old sixteenth-century fort, disappeared as though by magic.

It was one of the last days in May. While the rain drummed on the blue skin of the sea, the dolphins frolicked merrily in "hide and seek" like children. The waves, in turn, with their white crests, leaped like steeds on the rocks.

With the same rapidity with which it arrived, the rain left. It began to clear up. The pines and the mountains appeared again with humid, soft silhouettes. The submerged island, like a criollo Venus, was born from amidst the shining waters. The floating Castillo appeared in the rain with the colossal surprising force of a galleon prepared to continue the route of the Indies.

The sea shone like a tray polished by the murmuring of the wind. A small boat entered the bay with its sails full, leaving behind it fliers of foam. It was coming from the Lesser Antilles, escorted by a school of silvery dolphins. All of it was a great scenic transformation. The wind was filled with swallows.

How was the idea of El Morro born? This Castillo was built because the bay of Puerto Rico kept dreaming of it for centuries with a maternal desire. Few were the enemy sailors who dared look at the Castillo face to face.

For many, that military fortress was a Hispanic monster. For Francis Drake it was a high and dry dragon who guarded day and night the main entrance of the Antillean sea.

Morales repeated with pleasure that phrase expressing bravery and fearlessness: "Spanish sailors know how to go out naked to the sea when the King commands."

The city with its canvas of shades was a magnificent

example of colonization. The Castles, the Cathedral, the Municipal Building, Fortaleza Palace, the Red Palace, the Administration Building were one more irrefutable proof of the transplant of the Old World to the virgin lands of America. History for our interpreter was not a narration of isolated and dead episodes. He sought with intellectual sympathy the spiritual materialization of a past era.

5

The rain stopped and the group walked toward the man from where the district of La Perla was seen. The road to the cemetery, foreboding, bewitched, mysterious, also stood out.

Below, the little shacks, *bohíos*, like nests acrobatically placed between the walls and the sea. The arduous, multiple life of the suburb. The infinite and fiery life of love and hate in perpetual change; the panoramic view of that barrio of strong men and weak women evoked the painful world of the unemployed, orphans, sickly children, the naked with paunches like drums, victims of parasites, extreme poverty, flights to New York, unions and separations, marriages behind the church, faces scarred by knives, tattooed arms, trafficking in drugs and narcotics, eyes thirsty for marijuana, the little world of jealousies and envies, of the smell of urine, of fried food, of hot lard. A world of contacts and solitudes, of insults and vulgarities, of blasphemies and curses, of nickelodeons vomiting horrible howls and radios blaring torturing ads for beer.

Down below, those men of the suburb also contemplated that ideal landscape of age-old stones. The Castillo on its promontory, challenger of hurricanes, contrasted with the frailness of the *bohíos* and was for them a consolation, the living expression of an illusion.

The visitors, with simplicity, with perspicacity, observed that world of men and women who lived at the base of the Castillo. At that moment the landscape was strong and serious, like an engraving by Tufiño.

A man with an ostrich neck, repelling that human beehive, exclaimed:

"Disgusting, very disgusting."

A weak romantic voice rose to inquire: "And the Garita del Diablo, the Devil's Sentry Box?"

The interpreter's hand pointed out the diabolical structure suspended between the sea and sky.

"Is it true that persons who wait for twelve o'clock in that sentry box disappear?" Irma asked rapidly, desirous that her words be true.

They strolled till they reached the highest part of the fort. The impression was that they were in the prow of a great stone ship.

From those heights Morales spoke of the conquering of the past. Nearby the lighthouse rose, happy, like a symbol of life, truth, and liberty.

The imprudent, mischievous wind played tenaciously with the women's skirts till it made them blush.

"Aren't you tired of coming to El Morro every day?" asked a man, a wholesale dealer in nails and tacks from New Jersey, who looked with cold respect at the walls.

"No, sir," Morales answered promptly; "El Morro is a gift of nature. Here the strong and the beautiful are joined. It is so beautiful to see the sun rise through the cannon holes with its sword of fire and to hear the swallows and the waves in their age-old ebbing and flowing!"

A man with the appearance of a seminarian, who heard all the explanations without becoming enthused, commented: "And to think that all you admire has been the scene of so many bloody episodes."

Morales understood the intention of the question and said about the bellicose history of El Morro: "The destruction the attacks caused wasn't the worst part, but rather the moral annihilation and the tremendous havoc that they brought along with them."

In the Santa Bárbara rampart the bronze cannon maintained absolute silence.

Morales' face was transformed when he spoke of El Morro, of war, of history. His greatest pleasure was in making the past true-to-life for the visitors. He tried to exalt that which was permanent, alive. For that reason the Castillo was not a petrified mummy for him, but rather something plethorically full of vitality. Hence his words were able to move thought, fantasy, and the hearts of his listeners.

A woman with a bronze-toned face, her arms full of jewels and her body as thin as a parasol handle, commented with refinement:

"You live the Castillo with more dramatic intensity than other guides."

"Madame, I am its interpreter."

"You possess the passion of history."

The greenish sockets of the woman were the frames for two piercing eyes.

"And so many times we say through ignorance that we have no history," commented a Puerto Rican student, thinking of the mythical condition of El Morro.

Morales blazed with joy hearing the comments of his visitors. The Castillo fulfilled its mission to stimulate, inspire, and make people think.

"What a shame the great deeds of history are not repeated," the student added nostalgically.

"That's so," Morales affirmed, "but man is always the same."

All these so diverse digressions were possible because El Morro appears to the excursionists as a living body. It has smell, color, sound, and taste. The salt in the air, the fleeting murmur of the waves, the sonorous flight of the swallows, the ocher, gray, and red of the walls, surrounded by a sea and sky of undulating blue make of El Morro an enormous strongbox of memories that gives off energy, solidarity, and youth.

"El Morro, besides its features, has a soul," Morales recalled emphatically.

"You are a happy man," an old woman with a kindly face exclaimed jubilantly. In her tiny eyes there was a hidden happiness.

"Madame, I am a privileged man. You know the happy man is not he who has happiness, but rather he who seeks it," he replied joyfully.

His heart burned intensely as he spoke of all that he recognized as the great traditional and humanly undeniable legacy.

It was a joy to caress those walls which represented the triumph of a virile people. All that anonymous effort seemed now like an insuperable human expression. And the miracle of enjoyment of those ramparts and sentry boxes was possible because of the interpreter's clear words, without vanity or conceit.

6

A man of short stature—he was hardly five feet tall—with an enormous head covered with black hair, standing on end like a porcupine, with thick eyebrows, joking eyes, mischievous and prominent, and a sensual mouth, approached the group of people, and touching the interpreter's shoulder, inquired in a cross tone:

"Why in devil's name do so many people come here?"

The little man with the enormous head, in spite of the fact that he was smiling, spoke with a strangled soul. He stood out from the group because of his bitter look and because of his questions, which seemed rather like whacks from a tiger's paw.

"To live," Morales answered quickly and clearly.

This simple truth did not fit in his head, in spite of its being quite large. Our little man spent the whole excursion scratching his head as though he had lice.

Silent, simply contemplating, the secret of that landscape so full of history surged forth.

"In the fort every day the world dawns and life grows," Morales continued to comment joyfully.

"Well, I've come to photograph the sharks." And in the mouth of the little man the roar of laughter broke out. The echo of that tiresome laugh resounded between the walls and darted through the sentry boxes like the cry of a condemned man.

Poor Irma contemplated the dying of the waves, absorbed. She mumbled, very low, "I've come in search of Death." No one except her tortured soul heard her words. "I'm coming, Death; I'm coming already."

While the interpreter pointed out to the deepest part of the Atlantic Ocean, Irma slipped along like a snake and with the greatest calm approached the balcony. That night she intended to sleep with Death. Her profound eyes were bitter, like two abysses. "Oh, Death, I come out to meet you, I'm coming . . ." And entering between the bars she prepared to leap into space.

She felt herself held back by a powerful arm. Where had

it come from? Why did it butt into her life, rather, into her death? She hadn't asked to be born. Well, at least let her choose her death. Why prolong the suffering? She was frightened to live again. A cry of pain crossed the air like a resounding lightning bolt. The Castillo filled with the agony of her voice, and her hands trembled.

Irma had never felt so constrained in her life. She noted that she was becoming ever so small and that she just about fit into the interpreter's hand. That horrible emptiness made her despair. She cursed, threatened, begged, but it was all in vain. Her face was the portrait of a crumbling world, of a ruined life. Her disillusion weighed on her like lead.

Fright was immediately revealed in the visitors. Some did not emerge from their astonishment. The small man with the large head coldly exclaimed:

"Preposterous!"

Many things were said for and against the unfortunate woman. The sentry boxes, suspended in the air, and filled with impressive tenderness, trembled before the tragedy of that woman who knew not the pleasure of living.

The interpreter carried her, still half faint, to the chapel of the Castillo. The old woman with happy eyes approached to fan her.

Morales begged the visitors to reassemble in order to give them the final explanations. All thanked the guide for his attention. A Jewish businessman tried in vain to offer him a generous tip.

Taking the sidewalk to the right, they returned happy and a little tired to the hulk of San Juan.

7

In her delirium the poor woman asked questions in sentence fragments:

"Don't the sentry boxes ever sleep?"

Irma's voice was sad, like that of a poor beggarwoman. The straight flight of a bird filled the sky with mystery. Irma's eyes sparkled. She felt her heart reborn to the intense joy of living.

"What a beautiful sunset!" she exclaimed, breathing in deeply the blue air from the sea. She had known the greatness of the Castillo for the first time. It had given her back life when she wanted to throw it away. Night fell serene, and in the mirror of the bay the moon flirted, while the colossus, with its century-worn bricks, contemplated the passing of time.

THE COCKFIGHT

by Enrique A. Laguerre

Juan Pedro, Don Florencio, and I went to the cockfights. It was the first time I had attended such a spectacle. Some yards from the place of the fight, on the road, we began to see groups of people playing "heads or tails." On seeing us in the distance, many stopped, thinking perhaps of the police. There were a few cars; they took advantage of the fact that the road was dry, for in times of continuous rain they are inaccessible because of the mud pools that are formed. We entered through a little wire door into a spacious patio, with the living quarters in one corner. Farther on, the gambling area, behind the house and between mango trees. One could hear the cries of the crowd.

There were many people even in the patio. Groups could be seen here and there. Everything was being gambled: tossing coins, cards, flipping things.

Some of the individuals gambled the salary earned in the hell of the cane fields. They forgot the tragedy of the dividing lines and the impious weeds. They forgot the cruel servitude of the machete and the hoe, the indifferent whiplashes from the foremen, the fury of the circle of fire, the horrible sharp pain of sweat, the martyrdom of being bent over day after day. . . . Everything, they forgot everything, even the hunger of their youngsters and their anemic wives, their debts to the tavern. What are they supposed to answer when their poor wives scold them: "You've taken the bread out of the mouths of your children"? In other words: "You, father of these creatures, do you forget our eternal lack, our hunger, our anemia?" But, heaven knows, those men forgot life. . . .

In one group a man, at ease on the ground, was cutting a dirty deck of cards, while the bets were heard: "I'm for diamonds," "I'm for hearts," etc. And the oaths: "a peasant girl," "a great big peasant girl," etc. In another group a diminutive whipster pressed two cents on the ground to toss them in the air and wait for heads or tails. There, in a little gathering that was playing flipping coins, was La Bruja, the Witch, hunched up, "playing her pennies," as she said.

At the edge of the maya cactus under trees or in some other place, the players' horses were lined up. Almost all were skinny nags, sad remains of the vigorous horses of the Conquerors, those "strong and agile" steeds. How the tropics wastes them! The spirited horses are patient, sleepy little nags, as though they imitated the burro. The same thing happens with many people. They are pale, weakly men. Effects of the climate, arthritis or negligence. Many seem to be slaves, because of their lassitude. The poor lack means to combat the effects of the tropics, on account of the inadequate conditions they suffer, the moral, physical and spiritual slavery in which they live. It is indeed a great shame.

It was the same people I see on pay day every Saturday. The male and female innkeepers were not absent: the hippy Negress with the checked kerchief, the weak little white girl, the loudmouthed, slangy fellow, the boy with the brown sweets. . . . Sales made in the home to help the "little beast of burden" in maintaining the home.

The owner of the game place came up to receive us. He was a swarthy oldish man, with a certain cash prestige in the district. Besides, he was a so-called political boss, very useful in days of strife. He said:

"Pleased to meet you."

"Here we are, Chelao."

"Good; come this way. Look here, you! Tie up the horses near that little hut over there."

La Bruja drew near to take care of the animals, and shortly after we followed toward the cock ring, which was crammed with people. At that moment one match had just ended and another began. While the cocks were being excited, bets were offered. Not another person could fit in the benches, which went up to the straw roof. There were even spectators on the beams. We settled down with difficulty, and with the ill wishes of some fellow spectators. Below, in the center of the place, surrounded by the stands, the enclosure, a dusty round circle. Behind us, the little cages where they kept the little devils. A disagreeable strong stench of chicken shit hung in the air.

The first match we witnessed lasted quite long, because one of the cocks fell unconscious, and in order to revive it it was necessary to press down on it with the thumb, bite its crest and tail a couple of times. But the second contest lasted but a few minutes.

The cock on which Don Florencio bet grabbed the other one's vein in the first attack. The poor victim's gizzard filled up with blood, and from time to time it lowered its beak till it touched the ground. An intermittent, unstoppable hemorrhage of blood dripped from its beak. The spectators roared with laughter. And suddenly the loser dropped dead.

The owner began to shout: "How much do you give for the fallen?"

They gave him a few cents which he accepted, uttering curses against the dead animal. The "prey," in the buyer's hands, displayed its languid, red, swollen neck. The victor was showered with praise and bathed with mouthfuls of rum and water.

I went out for a few minutes to breathe the clean air because I felt a queasiness I could not control. All that is disgusting!

In these matches savagery is exalted in an atrocious manner. And then that foul stench of damp feathers, blood, dust, tobacco. All this is repulsive! As sickening as the attitude of the animalized player. I cannot stand the swearing, the laughter, the rotting-place of false emotions of these people. I just cannot understand how people of certain lofty ideas are confused with the strong passions of the cock ring. Perhaps they are dressed in other spiritual garb on these occasions. I do not know if it is the atmosphere of the ring, for I see two cocks battling in the straw-littered ring and it even interests me. In the cock ring I experience a sense of repugnance.

I was overwhelmed by a torturing boredom. I met Balbino, who doesn't work on Sundays; we remained talking for a few minutes, and then I went back to the cock ring with the intention of excusing myself from my companions. I wanted to return home. But Juan Pedro begged me to wait for him, for he would be going soon. And yet several more matches were held and he wasn't leaving. Now it was Jesús who was introducing his cock. He had a match. He drew near to tell me:

"Don't you want to bet anything, sir? He's a razor shot."

"No, thanks, I don't bet."

"Okay. You'll be sorry."

"Don't you believe it."

Don Florencio cursed. He whispered in Jesús' ear, advising him to use "some little trick." Jesús smiled, quite pleased. Then Don Florencio explained to me: "There's no time for Mass in times of war." And I thought of him: "He who has played bad tricks, will never or belatedly forget them." How well this proverb fits Don Toribio de Palmares.

As Jesús bent over, I saw he had a revolver in his pocket and a knife in his belt underneath his shirt. He wasn't the only one. There were many. The cashier sprinkled his cock with water and handed it to the caretaker, whose lips were red with the blood of the necks he put in his mouth.

When they were released, the rival had the advantage. The cock didn't grab the other, and Jesús scratched his head, cursing wildly. He was in a very bad mood, a rare thing for him. He declared:

"Damn, if you don't grab that cock, I'll smash you to smithereens on the ground!"

Several minutes passed in that manner. Suddenly Jesús picked up the rival cock and held it to his nose. He then threw it to the ground, shouting furiously:

"Damn! That cock is greased. It smells like bee's honey. You're a thief!"

The other man jumped into the ring. He said nothing and stood glaring at Jesús. He was a big swarthy fellow with slow movements and a cold stare. The man's silent, hostile attitude forecast something bad. Jesús insisted:

"It's a fraud! Your cock is greased."

Then the other man spoke lazily: "Here I am, man. Take me on."

And as Jesús had made a gesture of bringing his hand to his pocket, the other man added: "Don't bother. It's very easy to be brave with a gun in your hand. Be a man, hand-to-hand combat."

Jesús turned his hand away, risking taunting and boasting:

"I'm a gambler and I can bet my life when it's my turn, but you're just a thief. So just go slowly, man."

The other remained silent, again looking him over from head to foot with his cold stare; Jesús continued:

"So you already know. I'm ready for anything. You beat me with luck? Well, . . . and if I beat you?"

He paid no heed to the others' pleading. He had given a piece of his mind, and for him it was a pleasure to speak out. Then Chelao intervened with his notorious informality:

"Okay. Okay. It's over! Whoever wants to fight, step outside!"

It was like putting sticks to the candle, for Jesús gave him a punch that was taken by one of the shock absorbers in his face. Chelao stepped forward to put an end to the fight, and trouble broke out. Some weapons shone; many people threw themselves into the ring. Others ran. A small, heavy-set man tried to go through some wire and got caught for several minutes, without being able to get out on one side or the other.

In the meantime they tried to calm everyone down. Three of Jesús' friends dragged him away forcibly, as soon as the opponent had said, with his customary tranquility:

"I'm not going to fight here, and even less, among so many people. If you want, later tonight."

"Okay. Tonight."

"At your service, sir," and he serenely bent down to pick up his animal.

Jesús' father, who was in a nearby grocery, reached the patio and made his son come with him. The latter followed, swearing to take care of "that little matter" in due time. In the ring things returned to normal and shortly afterwards the shouting was heard inciting the cocks that were killing each other in the ring. The danger passed, commentaries were listened to, some comic, some serious. They had the small man vexed with their comments. And he excused himself, saying:

"Sometimes running is wise."

"Yeh, yeh," they answered ironically.

We left before they finished the match. Don Florencio assured us:

"This'll end badly."

THE STRIKE

by Enrique A. Laguerre

And in effect it happened. At night the two men met and held a duel with knives. When people intervened, they were covered with blood. The swarthy fellow's wounds were quite serious. The following day the event was well commented upon, even when other happenings came to reduce its preeminence.

And it happened the following day, Monday; the flag of protest waved on high. A week before, I had received news of signs of conspiracy but I didn't give them credence, and I didn't even try to find out if it was true. Now the sudden eruption surprised me. Segundo was the leader of the movement, and although he said he regretted having to assume this responsibility—taking into account the estimation with which he singled me out—he was forced to go beyond the laws of fairness and justice. At the beginning I was aggressive and challenging, but I was to calm down thinking of Don Polo. However, I remained dull-browed and reticent, speaking sarcastically. Segundo in turn demanded dramatic attitudes and gestures. He told me: "I cannot avoid the call of conscience! They, Juan Antonio, are condemned to seed and prod the weeds that yield them so little."

I foresaw the approaching disaster. Within me there was taking place a fierce struggle. On one hand, my sentiments of justice, my sympathies for the oppressed, Don Polo, Segundo, the face of Ventura! I was deeply moved thinking about this. My heart was an open bleeding wound. But on the other hand, my economic independence, the memory of my worries as a student, my duty, my position as farm colony chief, Don Oscar, my subjection to the interests of headquarters. . . . But finally I calmed down and there was a truce. I thought: "It's better to be calm." And I told Segundo:

"I'll send for someone from headquarters, someone who has more authority than I."

"In Palmares they're having a wild time, too. They tell me the strike broke out in headquarters itself on Saturday."

He spoke to me apparently to give me a simple bit of news; nonetheless, clarions of victory and pride in the words resounded in the air. I even thought I noted a certain veiled threat. I shrugged my shoulders and suggested:

"They'll lay the case before Don Oscar."

"Very good, Don Juan Antonio."

He left. He slowly descended the slope and went to join

the peons near the pool. The fact that Segundo had called the cane a weed caught my attention. Weed! What could he have been thinking of when he said that? I was pondering the expression when the overseers came to obey my orders. I sent Lope to where Don Oscar was and Balbino to take a walk around the plantation.

I looked at the countryside that extended before my eyes. Cane fields, pasturage, groves of trees, the sea. The coral trees were already beginning to bloom, red spots in the distance. I remembered that the day of my first outing I contemplated that same landscape from this very site. It then was the royal poincianas that were blooming, and red blotches were seen here and there. My first outing! What an ingenuous joy overwhelmed me! Now it was different. How the attitude of the peons worried me! I felt burdened by obligations and I could not avoid a certain profound mortification, as though a poison had infected me.

I mounted my horse and went out to meet the peons. I wanted to speak to them, persuade them to return to work. I said hello when I reached them. Many of them, in spite of being on strike, said with their eyes: "Forgive me." The gesture was too great for them. For others no. Others received me with a defiant gesture. A terrible hate had poisoned these fellows. However, I spoke to all, inviting them to return to work, for the crisis did not permit salaries to be raised. I appealed to all the persuasive means available, but it was in vain.

I then spoke alone with Segundo, trying to convince him, but my attempts were to no avail. He spoke to me of the hardships of these lives, "which have come into the world to serve as dust for all footsteps." "All they ask for now is a few scraps of food, because, believe me, they deserve to be treated like human beings and not like beasts of burden." Some of them, by dint of living in perennial subjection, have

lost the notion of the ideals that distinguish men from
beasts. They live miserably. Since they live that way,
without hearing the good word, they have come to feel
without right to life and they don't rebel in view of their
conditions. One must shake up their dormant conscience.
Some deserve the strong reproach and even blows to carry
them from anger to the reclaiming of their denied rights.

He began to speak clearly, but as he spoke he got carried
away till he finished with an aggressive apostrophe. And he
left me with words in my mouth, silent. I then followed the
path to Don Florencio's house. On the way I met some
groups of peons, who glanced at me. When I was already
near Palmares some men gestured coarsely.

Don Florencio was furious. His aspiration of the moment
was to have, like Jupiter, a thunderbolt in his hand to
fulminate so many brigands, as he confessed to me full of
profound rancor. The idea troubled him. Hate spewed from
him like a consuming flame. It was a terrible hate, capable
of setting the whole world on fire. I could not pacify him.
When I said we should be reasonable, he replied:

"Speak of reason to them!" And he added, bitingly,
"Well, you can speak like that. Your peons correspond. See
how they don't abandon the work. Your method is excellent.
I forgot to congratulate you, lad."

His mordacity mortified me; if I don't control myself I'll
rebuke him pitilessly. I was content to say: "And what are
you complaining about? Jupiter can lend you his thunderbolt at least for a few minutes."

He looked at me with a troubled glance, troubled like the
waters of a restless river. He then went out onto the
balcony, looked toward the groups of strikers, and exclaimed, full of hostility:

"Let's see who can avoid their being peons!"

I couldn't endure such vicious arrogance, and I told him: "You're a fine Christian! No wonder you go around under the priests' habits!"

"So you sympathize with them?"

"I am reasonable. And I've done more than you to control the strike."

"Why don't you become a striker, too? Since the peons pay your salary, you ought to correspond."

"What do you get with your hate?"

"And you, with your Christian feelings?"

"At least I believe they're men like you and me."

"Animals, you mean! Those people hate because they can't stand others being in better conditions than they."

"After all, what does this argument lead to? I have come only for us to reach an agreement."

"Just let the headquarters official arrive."

"Then, I'm going."

"Wait. I'll go out with you. Paquita! If anyone calls for me, tell them I'm going out with Juan Antonio. Did you hear?"

"Yes, sir."

We went out toward Santa Rosa. Passing by a crowd of people we heard murmuring, and from behind I felt hate climbing my horse's haunches. It was like a lugubrious phantom, a compendium of all the looks and gestures of the peons.

Near the black portal of Santa Rosa many people had assembled. Segundo was there. Spirits were becoming angered. If the headquarters representative didn't come soon, it would be necessary to call the police.

"There's Don Florencio."

"The flower of the flowers?" I heard someone say, Segundo, I think, because of his voice. "A healthy man and without malice, ehem!"

Fortunately Don Florencio didn't hear it because he was staring at a car that was approaching. The automobile passed by like a vapor, and then he addressed me:

"I think the machine is going to have to be drawn by cars."

At this, some youths were driving a herd of oxen toward the corrals at Santa Rosa. The majority of them were old animals, with long horns and enormous hooves. They went along, pressed closely, some raising their head on the next one's rump. The sound of horns striking each other was heard as they approached. They lowed silently. As they stopped they lifted a cloud of dust, hurried by the cracking of whips and shouts: ooh, ooh. . . .

Already nearly noon, the headquarters representative arrived. He was a man on in years, one of the principal employees with whom I had not formed a friendship. However, he treated me like an old friend and cursed out Socialists "who only serve to cause strikes and take advantage of things."

"You see how the tobacco sellers, carpenters and demagogues of just yesterday govern us. There is no longer any shame in the country. The situation is unbearable. Where will we decent people wind up if they succeed in having a definitive triumph?"

His hate was a pestilent swamp from whence his words flew. Oh, he couldn't endure the arrogance of the rabble, he addressed all strikers, calling them "good Puerto Ricans who deserve all kinds of considerations."

"Headquarters," he said, "wished for their well-being and wants to afford them means of life in the measure of their reach, but you know what the situation is."

No agreement could be reached, and the man kept uttering curses at the "insolent people." Don Florencio had proposed they look for strikebreakers, but the delegate decided against that. The mediation commission was already on alert and was expected any minute.

After midday there was a demonstration of strikers, and the red flag waved on high. Segundo went from one side to the other. From the nearby town they had been informed of the situation, and they also awaited a Socialist leader. There were some shouts and insults. They stopped a few moments to listen to Segundo's words, while the red flag floated on the green of the countryside like a trembling wound.

The red flag was a threatening shout that the wind caused to float, a tongue of fire that announced rebellions, inviting to set fire to the straw rotting-places of prejudice and abuses. It shouted: "Damned be castes! Down with oppression!"

When the Socialist leader—a small fat man, advanced in years—arrived, there was silence, and all looks shot at him like arrows. The first moment of expectation over, some "vivas!" were heard. The leader climbed on the car's running board and began: "Comrades!" The masses clamored around him. Don Florencio approached me, stopping to hear the "buzzing," as he called it.

The leader's speech was not long. He spoke to them of "the right you have to participate in human happiness," of the outrages committed with impunity, of the inconceivability that being the producer is "for enriching the pockets of the bourgeoisie, while you are the victims of hunger and nakedness," of the necessity of having to "end this state of things. . . ."

He then indicated the need to be united always, to go arm in arm toward the realization of the ideal; and among other high-flown sentences that very few understood he

ended his harangue. Segundo was radiant with joy. He could
also speak of those things; he had read so much in Don
Polo's books! He expressed his happiness with stentorian
shouts.

Don Florencio made a gesture of discontent and looked
angrily at Mars. I also felt mortified and proposed to call his
attention. . . . Oh, yes, what imprudence! In spite of the
fact the crowd could hardly keep up with those shouts.
Shouts that seemed to tear out their weak humanities.

Before leaving, the leader assured everything would be
fixed, that he was going together with the mediation
commission of San Juan to confer with the directors at
headquarters. Between exclamations of some of those
present, the car started up, carrying the "comrade" on its
comfortable cushions.

Don Florencio and I withdrew, Don Florencio to his
house and I to Don Polo's house. I wanted him to help me
control Segundo's impulses. I found the old man alone, with
a book in his hand. He showed signs of joy upon seeing
me.

"How are you, boy? Praised be to God, you haven't let
yourself be seen for so long!"

"How are you, Don Polo?"

"I'm fine, lad. Did you hear the speech? Good, it
wouldn't interest you. . . ."

"It did interest me, a lot," I answered with a smile that I
fancied would lessen my bitterness, "especially because he
spoke from the running board. I would have been interested
to hear him about the partitioning of the land."

"It's natural that a trip from San Juan to here has to be
made by car," Don Polo answered, tolerant, "don't you
think so? Now I want you to know that that man was a
victim of all the outrages in the beginning of socialism. He
was beat up by the police, jailed some twenty times,

pursued like a rabid dog. . . . Together with the others he
has conquered rights that the proletariat didn't enjoy. He
fought stubbornly, with exemplary obstinacy. I assure you
there are many scars on his body. Don't you believe that
now that the government respects the party he has every
right to a little happiness? Oh, yes, it's natural. At heart he's
the same as ever: a child who wants to reach the moon. He
embraced me, tightly, and after so many years of absence,
the word 'comrade' that he pronounced was like a fresh
bath for the heart; it was something that moved me
profoundly. Look, boy. I cried. My eyes filled with tears.
And then: 'Do you remember this?' 'Do you remember
that?' . . ."

I wanted to contemporize. I remained silent. I didn't
want to offend the sensitivity of the old man. It was better
that way. And through my mind flashed the history of the
social struggles, like a filmstrip. True, the workers' party had
had titanic struggles; its endeavor had been inflexible. It did
something for the workers: at least, it shook them in their
lack of will; but the greatest benefit was obtained by a
group of leaders who reached the governmental offices. The
anonymous mass obtained little benefit. Good laws were
promulgated, but many of them without effect. It thus
happens that great quantities are spent on employees'
salaries, while the suffering workers are hardly attended to.
That Party, which, trampled and martyrized, rose up
fighting, which was a Christ in His *via crucis,* finally raised
the tattered banner of egotism. And all was reduced to a
handful of mutilated ideals. The bitter truth grieves me. The
anonymous mass has continued to be a multitude deprived
of rights!

At the beginning, after his misfortune, Don Polo carried
on a correspondence with his comrades in arms, with those
who accompanied him in victories and defeats in campaigns

and in jail. Little by little his messages ceased to be answered. First, a few lines; then nothing. And Don Polo smiled, full of tolerance.

He was also a friend of the principal leader; he hadn't seen him for years nor had he personal news of him. From time to time Manuel got him the paper and then he knew something. Presently he is a leading figure in island life. And Don Polo, filled with dreams, watching the parade of days, hours, minutes pass by . . .

Luckily Manuel is extremely kind, and he has something to read. He remains seated in his wheelchair—this chair, a miniature *Clavileño* (wooden horse)—with his dreams of redemption repaired. He constantly thinks of the fortune of the infrahumanity that suffers. Poor people!

I admire Don Polo. While his old comrades enjoy privileged positions and are already called "honorable," here is Don Polo, with his healthy ideals, far from the rotting-room, erect in the middle of the field like a lump of granite that challenges all the storms that strike him.

"My roots do not die," he has told me. "In my life of ideals there are no dead roots. Alive, yes, nurturing in the heart."

How far from Don Polo this man is! How far from the "evil of others that hangs on hair." A great cavalier of the ideal, Don Hipólito Cabañas! To live like that, far from life, dreaming on the back of his *Clavileño*, tortured by the conviction that he is sacrificing his son! And yet, anyone would say that he does not suffer, because he is always smiling, because bad moods do not assail him. And now that he spoke of roots, I thought: "I feel my flesh crack! The hungry roots of a handful of ideals open fissures in my heart and sink in my clay with desires of reaching the clear water of the feelings that flow in the spirit. I feel the penetration of the roots! God grant they don't put poison in my waters!

It would be a horrendous martyrdom after suffering the roots' penetration! May the bud announcing the sap in each molecule not be wasted."

I was going to confess to the old man. "I am the first to recognize the reason that attends those unfortunate men! The iniquitous thing is that they live in such painful subjection! They have rights to a more dignified existence. It isn't possible for them to endure any more! They are martyrized enough! I'm with you, old man. I will say nothing to Segundo. He is right to rebel. He's right, he's right, he's right." It was something that was hammering away at my brain. All my anxieties pounded in my eyes, and the old man smiled. A clear, understanding smile. I felt it inside, deep. And when I was going to open my mouth to make confession, it happened that the small worries, the worries that fill daily life, the same ones that on a memorable occasion wanted to put RIP on my feelings of love, the same ones that made fun of the heart, cried to me: "You wouldn't commit such madness, boy! You will not be able to live if you make of your heart your guide. On guard!" It was a long cry, entangled in my life like a perverse bush rope.

The change was sudden. My mind again trod the field of my student struggles, the sacrifices, renunciations, in favor of the affirmation of my future. And then, my airs of a conqueror the first day on the job. It would be, truly, a madness to obey the heart! So it was that I whispered:

"Don Polo, I come to ask you a favor. You know how much I respect you."

And I told him of the refractory activities of Mars, to ask him then to intercede, advising the boy to suspend his rebellions. Don Polo looked at me tranquilly, with a pious glance, with profound commiseration. I couldn't resist his mute protest, and I explained:

"I respect you all very much. I don't want to harm Segundo. And I am under the obligation to fulfill my duty."

"All right, my son. I will do what I can."

And then he pronounced these words, which, because of the softness of his voice, because of the somberness of his attitude, made me shudder:

"But remember they, too, are children of God. The poor things live like that, pulling away from death a little piece of shroud with which to protect themselves from the cold of the night."

It was a graphic image, like a gunshot in the night. What a mysterious, subjugating influence his words had! They set me to pondering. I remained silent, without knowing what to say. And he, with a trace of disconsolate bitterness, affirmed:

"And I don't exaggerate, my son. Have pity on us."

His words impressed me so profoundly that the sentences stuck in my throat. I was afraid to let myself be convinced by his love. But no. My duty above all! I almost jumped into the chair where he was sitting and exclaimed with firm resolution:

"I'm going, Don Polo. I think Rosado is waiting for me. Good-bye."

However, I remained standing, beside him. The "good-bye" had a deeper reach. I went away stuck to the walls of a fictitious indifference, like a criminal. He understood me. And he saw me leave, spirit in hand, and moved his head from one side to the other, hardly vocalizing a sound of ineffable anguish. With the "good-bye" I pronounced, I felt carried away from center. I left with the desire not to visit him again: I feared his words. I took flight, spirit in hand, to take refuge in my "duty."

There, in his wheelchair, was Don Polo. I saw him leaner of flesh, his eyes more illuminated, his life purer. I experienced a terrible remorse and yet I confirmed my escape:

"Good-bye!"

"Good-bye, son."

"Good-bye!" It was better for him to think so, but I didn't want to visit him again. I left pursued by a hallucination, my gesture sullen, my eye bewildered. My small worries justified my treachery, my flight. "You're a hero, boy!" You deserve honors of a fighter who challenges death. Hurrah! Hurrah! But I felt off center. I fancied that the afternoon heat was going to dissolve me. I perceived the murmur of the cane field, and I grumbled, with naïve and even puerile satisfaction: "Bad grass! Damned grass!"

I went in search of my colleague. I now had to creep up his sleeve, so to speak; I could well forgive his pedestrian attitudes. He was my colleague, after all! I would take refuge in his desolate life. After my escape, spirit in hand, I could be in any place! I felt a piercing despair.

Don Florencio asked me: "You been in the Cabaña house?"

"Precisely."

"And how are you?"

"I'm fine, and yourself?" I asked somewhat jokingly.

"So, so. And what did you think of our friend's speech?"

"I don't know what to tell you."

"The same old song to close eyes to the truth. Don Oscar will take care of giving him a little banquet and let there be peace. . . . He'll also whisper a few things in his ear, you understand? You see, he'll spend the night in Don Oscar's house, for it's said they're old friends, born in the same town."

"The leader seems to me to be a convinced person."

I was lying. I was lying miserably. And why? I wanted to

hear Don Florencio speak, to feel myself ensnared in his jokes, to forget Don Polo's words. . . . This is a confession and I must say it! I must say it: the whole world has defects! And I am not to be the exception. Even Don Polo commits the inconceivable sin of being too human! That is the greatest of sins!

"Our friend the Socialist has the reputation of being a fine gourmet. Besides, he is a jewel, and Don Oscar has him where he wants him. . . . The times I've gotten soused with him have been legion!"

I understood his perverse intention, but I refrained from mortifying him. He continued talking for the mere pleasure of plunging in the poison. Referring to the leader, he commented:

"An old Moor, a bad Christian."

Which sounded just marvelous to him. Suddenly, the name of the old man sprang from his lips, and I trembled from head to foot as though I felt surprised. He said to me:

"Careful, for this . . . (here a word I dare not transcribe) this Don Polo! Fortunately God grants to man only what he can't use."

XXI. THE ORDINARY LIFE

If the Romantics wrote with poetic and traditional symbols, and the Realists wrote of vast social changes, the Naturalists wrote of both, as they exist and conflict in ordinary life. Antonio Oliver Frau (1902–1945), a lawyer whose fame rested on a single book, *Narrations and Legends from the Coffee Plantation* (1938), wrote what at first glance seemed to be a simple, rural story, "The Red Seed," until, with one word at the end, he symbolized the cataclysmic change that had occurred to his characters. In Wilfredo Braschi's (1918–) vignette, "The Hunchback's Zeppelin," the denouement is subtler, and swifter. The dream and reality, the old and new, the Spanish and English, confront one another as harshly, but with more easy-going and *jíbaro* humor in "Peyo Mercé Teaches English," from the book *Terrazo* (1947) by the traditionalist Abelardo Díaz Alfaro (1917–), who writes for nontraditional television and radio. But it is the Puerto Ricans on the "other island" of Manhattan who face the schizophrenic conflict most cruelly. It begins in San Juan, when the *jíbaro* of José Luis González's sketch, "The Letter," writes his mother how he has "made it," but has to beg for a postage stamp to mail the letter; then he journeys to New York, where in "The Passage" the reality of the homeland has become a murderous nightmare. González, a self-exiled writer, living in Mexico, heralded the style and school of ghetto writers that was to arise from his books *Five Blood Stories* (1945) and *The Man in the Street* (1948).

THE RED SEED

by Antonio Oliver Frau

Early, at dawn, while the fire of the stars still kindled in the peaceful blue sky of the farm, the children, Juancho and Maruca, weak and vexed by heat and sadness, awoke. They had awakened at the racket of the animals stamping in the barn and hitting their heads on the firm pavement of opaque, dry stone. Besides, farther out, on the silhouette of the mountains, the roosters had already sent forth the noisy rebellious cries where the abundant, fruitful branches kindled their aromatic fragrances of resin. And that call of the birds, that timbre of country joy was the awaited sign, which cast out of their warm comfortable beds the light humanity of the two of them: country brother and sister, children of robust farmers, like real country oak.

But the perspective of that morning was changing. The fresh bubbling laughter fled from the poppy-red lips of the children, putting in its stead clouds of sadness on pupils tormented by fear. And half-opening their lids, they spoke, guessing each other from behind the curtain that separated them, like the dividing line of their frontiers. They talked with each other so slowly, between hesitant tears, confidentially, plunged in the dark shadow of the main room of their father's farmhouse, old and crumbling. He was a skinny, bony young lad, with eyes broached and penetrating like an aggressive knife blade, representatives of the desolation, desire, uncertainty, and ambition of those people of the coffee plantation, who formed a legion of misery, far from the prosperous sectors graced by the hand of God. She was lively and shrewd, with immense black eyes, where superstition, suspicion, sweetness, and meekness of farm women, rustic and simple, slumbered like the dusty white water that flowed past the mill wheel, at the edge of the cottages, speckled and scattered. . . .

"They're throwing us out!" he cried.

"They're throwing us out!" she accentuated.

Outside, the moon climbed, doing pirouettes like a clown on the green trapeze of the trees. A dog barked at the moving carts that exhausted the night between the immense windings of the road. And confidentially, almost in each other's ear, brother and sister recalled the cut thread of their memories. It had happened the day before. From the city arrived some gentlemen, wrapped in large coats and with paunches, slow and lazy in gait, with spools of paper under their fleshy arms. They got off their mounts and entered the house, like a master who sets his foot squarely on a gained possession. The children's father went to meet them, followed by Manuela, the old woman. Don Antonio begged for postponements and asked for reasonable periods for the payment of the interest. The gentlemen, like stiff inanimate stakes, spoke not at all, said nothing, but conceded nothing either. They were the powerful and demanded their payment: the immediate eviction of property to avoid spells to take away legality. The little ones trembled, terrified, behind the dividing wall. Manuela implored favors from the image of the Virgin, stuck on the back of a yellowing cardboard.

Tears, supplications, and beseeching crashed against the visitors' indifference. The strangers read strong, severe things. Then they withdrew. Behind the fences, the frightened silhouette of the boy moved restlessly, and his lips vibrated with rebellion and anger: Crooks!

Lunchtime arrived. The benches, long and uncomfortable, provided seats for the old workers and the two children spoiled by health. No one unbuttoned his lip, no one dared break the religiosity of the moment. The watchword was given, silent, mutely. Only from time to time did glances meet, frightened, and then they were lowered, rapid and silent, filled with secretiveness and fear. When the meat was finished, the black coffee drunk, the father thought it time to speak: The farm was no longer theirs. The times had been bad; the harvests had grown meager, and the prices were far too low. All the mortgages were due, and the interests were excessive. The foreclosure papers had been presented that morning, and new owners would take over the plantation. But that wasn't all. Whims of fortune! Things of luck! Nothing. Here or afar the daily bread could be earned honorably. The family would set out on new roads. The children would go to other schools to continue the mastery of reading and writing. Writing would make them strong and would free them from the power of the greedy rich, full of pride and satisfaction.

The meal finished, they got up from the table, sad and gloomy: the girl's eyes filled with light; the boy's clouded with shadows, and on his lips there appeared a frown of anarchic rebellion. The following day everything had to be readied for the imminent departure. And through the property brother and sister went gathering armfuls of memories in the clouded recesses of silent alleys, pouring raptures of daydreams plucked and broken in their childish memories. The girl, foreseeing days of journey, continuous

journey across the countryside painted red by lights and
disperse colors, pursuing new paths of fortune and prosperity; the boy, between serious and silent, with the presentiment of days of misery, hunger, and want, exploding in
helplessness and shelter. They returned to the house late,
having unwalked the favorite paths, trekked through the
fields redolent of thyme, where golden doves of their lost
childhood fluttered; they returned when night already had
taken hold on the distant bare horizon, burning with dust
and mist. Dinner took place between sentences of boredom
and weariness sprinkled with mutual comfortings and
hoped-for yearnings. After the rosary they withdrew to their
little rooms to wait for the new day's announcement, giving
the order to leave. And so the hours slid down the clock of
their souls till dawn, when the cocks crowed their song of
bronze and silver, trembling with rhymes and harmonies.

Through the small window brother and sister saw the
animals laden with packages and bundles of clothing. A
potpourri of domestic objects: footstools, little railings,
wooden ladles, white fabric, plates and figwood spoons,
agave cots, and another heap of utensils that offered
accouterment for the animals loaded down with weight and
volume. "And now, brother, where to?" she asked. He
confided his hopes, his concerns, his new paths to her. They
would ask the old man permission to work in the city. He
wanted to free himself from the oppressive tyrannical
countryside subject to that order of things; from the
countryside orphaned of schools, library, without books or
ideals. He wanted to go to the city to continue learning to
write, in order to know a lot, even more than the
schoolteacher. Then he would settle accounts with those
gentlemen in redingotes and glasses, who had torn from him
the miserable piece of land bequeathed from father to son,

from generation to generation, till it was lost forever. It was necessary to fight, become upper class, government people, unconcerned and arrogant, who ordered at will the underdogs, his people, an unconscious mass, kicked about by despicable adventures. Yes indeed, when he rose he would remember the flock, and he would help them resolve their problems, to be people of importance, to awaken from the rock dream in which they were frozen. His sister listened to him, enchanted, astonished by that string of absurdities, as one who hears a distant music that is scarcely perceived. The boy's countenance lit up and he continued: "Sis, you'll see, you'll see. . . ."

The caravan set out on its journey. The mounts trotted onward, and the landscape bent before the nomad family seeking rejuvenated perspectives. The lad remained behind, taking care of the grandparents' farm in order to make legal delivery of the property to the new owners. Later he would undertake the journey to reach the family at a distant resting place. In the boy's eyes there continued to burn that light which, like a burning wick, crept into his immense pupils. The reddish embers grew successively larger; it seemed a wave of anger formed them, and grew and grew like an enormous red pyre. Then his eyes began to water, and he gave free rein to his tumultuous wild desires. The old farmhouse sparked, wrapped in a belt of fire and crumbled like a paper castle. From the neighboring hill the boy savored the honors of his work, his soul aching with memories and his heart wild with anger and vengeance: "Down with thieves!" And overcome and victor at the same time, he wiped away a big tear that, like a handful of lead, slapped his weakened face. From the nearby hills the peasants came down, like domestic masses, torpid and ignorant; they watched the flames with a childlike fright and then asked the same question: "What's happened? Why?"

The roads ran uphill and down. Above, the spires of the church were faintly perceived; below, the limits of the far-off coffee farms were delineated. For the boy, there was no indecision. He turned toward the right and fixed his gaze on the distant spires, clothed in mist. He advanced a few steps, took the fragile book found in the dead grandfather's ruined chest, and read secretly, joining letter to letter its devastating words in order to understand the ideas. On the cover of the old book was sketched, in profile, the prophetic figure of the schoolteacher, and on the wrinkled picture a whole program of force, a complete symbolic name stood out: Karl Marx. The boy's eyes became more and more inflamed, and the sun, in full twilight, poured into him, into his soul, till it consumed his heart, smoking of struggle and combat!

THE HUNCHBACK'S ZEPPELIN

by *Wilfredo Braschi*

He had the sad, squalid appearance of a boy from the slums.

Large black eyes, the mouth of an old man and a tired gait, as though he had entered the world loaded down with years, with prior lives in the dry skin, or with all the calendars of time between his chest and his back. His chest was sunken, concave, and his back stood out like a boil or furuncle. That is how I see him: books and notebooks riding on this hunch of a little Job, minuscule Quasimodo, perplexed and dull-sighted, on the streets of stone, asphalt, and mud.

Few spoke with him at school, and I—son of the teacher

and half a savage with a clean fist—did really esteem him. His father, he said, was the owner of a zeppelin, nothing less than a dirigible swelled like the dream of his long, shiny, shaved head. He assured me very seriously that one day we would get in the silvery vehicle. How could I not go with Balthasar to his house and from there undertake the circumnavigation of the nutshell that is the earth?

What a beautiful universe is that of the child! Balthasar, hardly four feet tall on the dust of the road, insisted on taking me before the hero of his life, who, according to him, used to take him up with the rapidity of air or light.

We went to see him. I relive today the trek to his house, beyond the fence that divided his district from mine. Here one heard the *toc toc* of the cobbler's hammer, there exploded the ruby of fire in the ironwright's forge and his bellows made hot sparks leap.

Once in the district, Balthasar's house appeared, smashed and kneeling, and in the frame of the door—I then did not know who—the magnificent and fabulous owner of the zeppelin: his father. His ugly face, a bed of warts, his chest hairy like a monkey, his large hands hanging. He spit tobacco between the shovel-like ruins of his teeth.

Balthasar's voice rose from his old and newborn mouth— now I remember that his lips changed: at times they seemed of an old man, at times of a baby—and he uttered his request:

"Papa, here is my friend. He wants you to take him with me in the zeppelin. You'll take him too, right, dad?"

I have never seen anyone as furious or a human being so beside himself. Balthasar's father, his face flushed, his temples swelled, and his lips spattered with white froth, thundered:

"Besides being hunchbacked, you're crazy! Accursed be the hour of your birth!"

I do not know what I thought or said. I do remember hunchbacked Balthasar, the size of a tear, so crushed as the Graff Zeppelin and his dream world in ashes.

I felt that my boxer's fists in blossom served for nothing.

PEYO MERCÉ TEACHES ENGLISH

by Abelardo Díaz Alfaro
(*To my "comae" Margó Arce, from Peyo Mercé*)

After the talked-about episode of the introduction of Santa Claus in Cuchilla, the prevailing animosity between Peyo Mercé and Rogelio Escalera, the supervisor, became more bitter. The latter, in a virulent letter and in drastic terms, ordered the old schoolteacher to redouble his efforts and teach English at all costs: "under pain of having to appeal to recourses not at all pleasant to him; but healthful for him, for the good march of progressive education." He knew quite well this obliged ending of the supervisor's letters, and with a scowl of disdain he threw the unfortunate letter aside. The curious aspect of the case was that with it also arrived some strange books with shining covers and landscapes in bright colors, where some well-dressed and better-fed children showed their faces.

Peyo seized one of the books. In black letters was written: "Primer." He meditated a while and scratching his ear he mumbled: "Primer, that must derive from *primero*, and hence with that book I must begin my new *via crucis*. Another pain! And Peyo Mercé teaching English in English! Like it or not I'll have to adapt myself; my daily beans are in it. It will be Cuchilla style. And if I don't chew it well, how am I going to make my students digest it? Mister Escalera wants English, and he'll have what he likes." And he

thumbed rapidly through the small pages of the recently
edited book.

The hubbub of the peasant children entering the old
classroom drew him out of his reflections. The simpletons
with shirt neckbands stained with bananas, lazy brown
locks, their little feet lumped with the red clay of the
footpaths, and on their faded faces the faint gleam of the
eyes of hunger.

The anger that the supervisor's letter had produced was
dissipated as the classroom filled with those children of his.
He loved them because they were of his same nature and
because he had a foreboding of a destiny as dark as a foggy
night. "Good morning, Don Peyo," they would utter and
with a slight lowering of the head they would walk toward
their seats. Don Peyo did not like to be called "mister":
"I've been a sweet-potato vendor from Cuchilla, and I'm
proud of it. That 'mister' sounds to me like the haughtiness,
jest, and boorishness they're now trying to sell us. I'm
marked with banana stain and the shoots of the bushes."

He leaned out the badly cut-out window in the rustic wall
as though he wanted to catch his breath. On the leaden
green of the hills veined with swaying tobacco fields, some
white clouds filled their luminous sails with sunlight. In the
red flames of *bucayo* trees mozambique birds burned their
black wings. And he felt a repugnance, a weakness of spirit
invade him, impelling him instead to channel his class into
the study of the land, the fecund land that fructified in a
trickle of light, in a coalescence of rubies. The return to the
daily work was painful to him on such a sunny day. And
painful to have to teach something as arid as primer English.

With slow steps he walked to the front of the classroom.
A laugh, forerunner of effrontery, was insinuated on his
slightly parted lips. A bitter thought erased this laugh from
his wrinkled face. He again thumbed through the intruder

book. He found nothing in it to awaken his pupils' interest;
nothing that adapted itself to the circumstances. Joyfully he
discovered a picture in which a crested rooster displayed its
luxurious tail. The pompous cock raked its long curved
claws where a coin of Isabel II of Spain could very well
nestle. "That's it; my boys will have rooster in English."
And somewhat more animated, he decided to face his class
serenely.

"Well, children, we are goin' to talk in Englis' today."
And as these words, sprinkled with suffocating hiccups,
emerged from his mouth, he cast his harsh glance on the
astonished faces of the pupils. And so that the "storm" of
words not escape them, he asked in a treble voice,
"Understan'?"

Absolute silence was the answer to his question. And
Peyo felt like scolding the class, but how far was he going to
get doing it in English? And he again leaned out the little
window to gain strength. A wood lark sailed through the
blue abundance—a petal in the wind. And he felt his
suffering more intensely. Desires of freeing himself.

He took advantage of the moment to try out pronouncing
the word he was going to teach. And making a grotesque
gesture followed by a sound similar to that produced by a
sneeze, he mumbled: "Cock . . . cock . . . cock." And fed
up, he grumbled: "The devil's tongue!"

And he decided to try a method that deviated from that
recommended in the annoying pedagogical sermons of
erudites on the subject.

Silence ruled in the classroom. Peyo was loved and
respected by his pupils. Such an inexplicable thing for
Rogelio Escalera! Peyo did not know the latest studies on
the personality of the teacher and less on child psychology.
He did not like to attend the "prepared model classes,"
which supervisors did not pay much attention to.

A flood of bright light entered the little window, turning red the pale faces and shining nervously on the free-flowing hair.

"All right, boys, today let's recite a little in English, pure English." And as the words emerged laboriously, he intended to give a little speech referring to the advantages of what he was going to put into practice. But sincerity was his main defect as a teacher.

He felt a curse word forming in his throat, and with his convulsed fingers loosened the knot of his discolored tie to free himself from the oppression. In the most remote part of his subconscious he cursed out a few things, among others the supervisor who wanted him to swim where he who is not proficient drowns. And he mused, resigned: "With whip and spur any horse travels better." And the peasant proverb took on all its painful reality in his mind.

And Peyo searched in his imagination for all the devices recommended in books versed in the teaching of English. Peyo's mind was shadowy, like a night of foreboding. "A shortcut, a path, a trick to get me on the right road," he exclaimed. And rocking his pained head between his rough hands, in view of the pupils' amazement, he dropped these words: "What a paradise this would be if it weren't for the supervisor and his gibberish." And convinced that his efforts to conduct the class in English would be fruitless, he negotiated in his own way, as on other occasions, a "compromise," as he would call it. And he chose to make a mixture, a knot, a grafting. "And let it come out duck or coot."

He raised the book above his pupils' heads. And with his index finger stained with tobacco, he showed the picture where the proud cock strutted. "Look, this is a cock. Repeat." And the children began to repeat in chorus the word in a very unharmonious way: "cock . . . cock . . .

cock." And Peyo, his nerves excited, his head congested,
shouted wildly: "Stop, more slowly; these kids have made
the cock ring right here on me!" The untuned voices fell
silent. Peyo was drowning from the heat. Once more he
went over to the little window. Sweat soaked his colored
shirt. He needed air, a lot of air. And he paused for a
moment, his hands grasping like claws the uneven frame of
the window.

Unconsciously, he fixed his gaze on the water pouring
from the nearby cascade—a fresh tear in the rough rock.
And he envied Petra's son, who submerged his dirty face in
the waters pearled in sunlight.

Fed up, he decided to get out as soon as possible from the
jam he had gotten himself into. He went to the head of the
class with nervous steps: "Now you know *gallo* is 'cock' in
English, in American." And he again pointed out with his
tobacco-stained finger the strutting cock. "This is 'cock' in
English; *gallo* is 'cock.' Let's proceed slowly, for that's how
one breaks in a stallion, if it doesn't run wild.

"What's this in English, Teclo?" And the latter, who was
amazed by looking at that rooster, answered timidly, "It's a
turkey-hen rooster." The old room shook with the jingling
of children's laughter. Peyo, hiding the fun those words
produced in him, frowned so as not to lose moral strength,
and replied scornfully: "I know it, this one gets in Don
Cipria's cock ring. And what a turkey-hen cock! This one is
a tame rooster, a respectable cock, not a clipped one like
those fighting kinds."

And he again asked: "What is this in English?" And the
children entoned the monotonous ditty: "Cock, cock, cock."
And Peyo felt quite satisfied. He had escaped Scot free from
that bloody fray. He distributed some books and made them
open to the page where the showy cock's story was told.
"Let's read a little in English." The pupils looked at the

page with surprise, and they could hardly contain their roar of laughter.

His face paled. A shudder raced through his body. He even thought of presenting his irrevocable resignation to the supervisor. "Now they really burned the pig's tail." And with tripping steps, stuttering, his tongue heavy and a taste of pineapple on his lips, he read: " 'This is the cock, the cock says "cock-a-doodle-doo." ' " And Peyo said up his sleeve, "Either this cock has pip disease, or Americans don't hear well." That was the last straw. But he thought of his daily bread.

"Read with me: 'The cock says "cock-a-doodle-doo." ' " And their voices tuned the morning breeze. "That's good. . . ."

"Tellito, how does the cock crow in English?"

"I don't know, Don Peyo."

"But look, boy, you've just read it. . . ."

"No," moaned Tellito, looking at the picture.

"Look, dummy, the cock crows 'cock-a-doodle-doo.' "

And Tellito, excusing himself, said: "Don Peyo, that must be the song of the American rooster, but the cock at home sings 'cocoroco.' "

Don Peyo forgot all his modesty and gave out a loud guffaw that was accompanied by the children's fresh laughter.

Frightened by the hubbub, Don Cipria's Camagüey cock flapped its iridescent wings and wove in the blue silk of the sky a clean, metallic "cocoroco."

THE LETTER

by José Luis González

San Juan, Puerto Rico
March 8, 1947

Dear Mother:

As I used to tell you before leaving, things here are going well for me. Since I arrived I found work at once. They pay me 8 dollars a week and with it I live as well as Don Pepe, the administrator of the sugar factory over there.

Those clothes I agreed to send you I haven't been able to buy yet because I want to get them in one of the best shops. Tell Petra that when I come home I'll bring her baby a little gift.

I'll see if I have a picture of myself taken one of these days to send to you, Mom.

The other day I saw Felo, the son of *comai* Maria. He's working but he earns less than I.

Well. Remember to write to me and tell me everything that's happening over there.

Your son who loves you and asks for your blessing,

Juan

After signing it, he carefully folded the paper, wrinkled and full of corrections, and put it in his shirt pocket. He walked to the nearest post office, and upon reaching it put the frayed beret over his forehead and sat hunched up in the entrance to one of the doors. He contracted his left hand, making believe that he was maimed and extended the open right hand. When he had collected the necessary four cents, he bought the envelope and the stamp and mailed the letter.

THE PASSAGE

by José Luis González

They met by chance at the subway exit of 103rd Street, and Juan—who had a job—invited Jesús—who didn't—to have a beer.

Juan preferred the grocery of a fellow countryman, "The Flower of Borinquen," where they served beer in cans at two little tables in the back. The grocery was farther from the subway station than the bar owned by the Irishman who knew Spanish and lived with a Cuban woman, but Juan explained:

"I'll be damned if I stop before a bar! My kidneys are shot, brother, and my feet are so bad off I can't stand."

"From work?" asked Jesús.

"You know what it's like standing all day tightening the tubes in the radios they send you on that damned assembly line?"

"And what, you can't sit down?"

"Ask the owner of the company why not. I'll tell you one thing: this country is death, death in a large basket. Hey, here's the grocery."

They entered. Juan greeted the grocer: "What's up? Gimme two cans for the back."

"What brand?" asked the grocer.

"Any one you damn please, old man. All beer here is horse piss."

"If you want, I'll send out for an Ital from Puerto Rico."

Juan stopped at the entrance to the back.

"No, you made a mistake. What I drank in Puerta 'e Tierra was Ital."

"Ah, that's right, for you're from Puerta 'e Tierra! Listen, by the way, did you see the *El Imparcial* that arrived this morning?"

"What's it say?"

"Santurce clinched the championship from San Juan in the final series. They ought to be ashamed! After they won the first game so easily!"

"Bah, don't worry! Next year we'll make up for it!"

"Next year nothin' doin'. When they have a pitcher like Rubén Gómez, then we'll talk."

"Ahah. Let's see if one of these days another Satchel Paige is born. Okay. Bring us two beers and don't talk gibberish."

They sat at one of the two little tables. The other was occupied. Jesús asked:

"Listen, Juan, how much do they put you at your job?"

"Thirty-five a week."

"Damn, if I got a salary like that!"

"Don't be a fool. I thought the same thing in the beginning. And now I feel like quitting!"

"Why?"

"Didn't I tell you that I leave the factory every day completely worn out?"

"But anyway you're better off than me!"

"You haven't found anything yet?"

"Find what? Yesterday they told me there was a job as dishwasher in a cafeteria and I went over there. But when I got there they'd already offered it to somebody else."

"A Puerto Rican, too, no doubt, because here the only ones who wash dishes are us Puerto Ricans. Even the blacks don't want those jobs."

"Just to show you, the one who told me was a little Negro from the West Side who left that job to work in a laundry."

"Let me tell you. That laundry must be one of Ray

Robinson's, where only Negroes work. And he does well to protect his people, damn it! But us Puerto Ricans, even for that we're dumb, man. When we had a world champion boxer, who thought of setting up a business to give work to our fellow countrymen? He bought himself a sugar cane plantation in Barceloneta. And who filled the stadium each time he fought, if it wasn't the Puerto Ricans from Harlem?"

The grocer came in with the two cans of beer.

"Ah, that's what you brought?" asked Juan, looking at the cans.

"What, didn't you say the brand didn't matter? That everything here was horse piss?"

"You're right, kid; you won that one."

"No, you said it. I like the beer here. Why would I fool you?"

"Yeah, right. I know you like everything here. Be careful one day a friend doesn't ask your wife to go to the movies."

"Whadya mean! Listen, do you want glasses for the beer?"

"No, it's better straight from the can."

The grocer went back to his counter and Juan, raising his can of beer, said to Jesús: "Well, my friend, to your health. Hope you get a job soon."

Jesús didn't lift his can; he only said, with his glance fixed on a fly that was making off with the grains of sugar scattered on the table: "I think I'm getting out of here."

"Ah?"

"I'm getting out. I'm goin' to Puerto Rico."

"To Puerto Rico? To do what? To cut cane?"

"Anything. It's death here. I have a brother-in-law, a mechanic, who works in General Motors in San Juan. Maybe he'll get me a job."

"Maybe."

"The worst part is the damn passage. I don't have the money."

"And don't you know anyone who'll lend it to you?"

"From where? Since I don't have a job here or there, nobody takes the risk. They think that I am not going to be able to pay them back."

"Damn, if I had it . . ."

"No, man, don't worry, I know you'd do it willingly, but . . ."

". . . but as you yourself say, from where? Okay, kid, drink that beer, it's goin' to get warm. Somethin' will turn up, don't worry. It's always like that in the beginnin'."

"Yes, I knew that. They had told me over there before I came here. But I've already been here three months."

And Jesús raised the can to his lips and said no more.

A week later Juan left the subway station exit at 103rd Street and decided to have a beer before returning home. He thought of the nearby bar owned by the Irishman who knew Spanish and lived with the Cuban woman, but his back and feet hurt and he preferred one of the little tables in the back of "The Flower of Borinquen."

Upon entering the grocery, he was surprised by the grocer, who before greeting him, asked him, very close:

"Listen, Juan, what was the name of that guy that was here with you the other day?"

"Which one?"

"The one who drank beer with you in the back."

Juan tried to remember for a few moments.

"Ah," he finally said; "it must have been Jesús. Why?"

"D'you see the *Daily News* today?"

"Not yet. What . . ."

"Well, look."

And the grocer, showing him the newspaper, pointed out the picture that occupied half of the first page. Juan looked. A man appeared stretched out on the floor of a delicatessen, at the feet of two policemen, who were smiling at the photographer.

"Look at his face," the grocer said.

Juan looked at the dead man's face in the picture.

"Isn't he the same one?" asked the grocer. "I think my memory doesn't fool me, and below it says the name. Just look: Jesús Rodríguez. It seems your friend became a robber with a knife—with a butcher knife, just imagine!—and the police wiped him out."

"Yes, it's him," Juan said, paling, and then added, mumbling so the grocer hardly heard: "The passage."

"The passage?" the grocer asked, not understanding.

"Yes, the friggin' passage," Juan repeated, threw the paper on the counter, and went out into the street. And the grocer remained without understanding.

▼▲▼▲▼▲▼▲▼▲▼▲▼▲

XXII. THE CROSSROAD AND THE PROTEST

His commentary in the newspapers and the radio was titled "The Human Condition." A man of the times, Manuel Méndez Ballester (1909–) in his time has been a journalist, novelist, dramatist, and politician. Elected to the legislature, several times, as a leader of the Popular Democratic Party, he observed well the life he critically depicted in his literary works. The "schizophrenic state of the contemporary Puerto Rican" is presented in his play *Crossroad* (1958), archetypically set in New York, in the climactic scene where the two brothers, Mario and Felipe, fight, intellectually at first and then physically, about what it means to be Puerto Rican. As the brothers draw familiar blood the two worlds clash, and the idyll of the "earthly paradise" is gone, forever. In *The Protest*, Luis Quero Chiesa (1911–), who has lived in New York since 1929, writes of the bewilderment of the intellectual who has left Puerto Rico and must face the suffering of the masses.

CROSSROAD

by Manuel Méndez Ballester

(*Selection*)

MARIO *and* FELIPE *come in through the main door. They have been out all night and are a little happy.* FELIPE *enters with his guitar, greeting in a loud voice. He is much happier than* MARIO.

DON ALFONSO: (*Looking at his sons*) Morning! At a fine time, boys!

FELIPE: Good morning, Father! (*Hugs his father*)

DOÑA PATRICIA: (*Entering through the kitchen door*) What time of the day to arrive is this?

FELIPE: Good Morning, Mother! (*Hugs his mother*)

DOÑA PATRICIA: Good, eh? Coming in at ten A.M. to say good morning. Where did you spend the night?

FELIPE: At a rowdy party. (*Sits on the sofa*)

DOÑA PATRICIA: And you, Mario, the cat got your tongue? Don't spend the night on the street again on me!

MARIO: Do I have to go to bed early as though I were a child? I'm a free man.

DOÑA PATRICIA: And I'm your mother.

MARIO: I'm sorry, Mother.

DOÑA PATRICIA: Aren't you going to kiss me? One thing
has nothing to do with the other.

MARIO *smiles and kisses his mother.*

DOÑA PATRICIA: (*Putting on her shawl*) Marta, serve
Mario and Felipe coffee, please.

MARTA: I'm coming, Mother. (*Enters the kitchen*)

DOÑA PATRICIA: Let's go, Alfonso. (*To the boys*) None of
you is going to Mass?

MARIO *and* MARTA *answer no with a gesture.*

FELIPE: (*Gets up*) No, Mother. It seems to me that if I
go to Mass, I'm committing a sin. (*Pause*) I
haven't been to church in fifteen years. (*Hangs
his guitar on the wall*)

DOÑA PATRICIA: *Ave María Purísima!*

DON ALFONSO *gives his arm to* DOÑA PATRICIA, *and they
leave with great dignity.*

ANTONIO: (*Enters*) I'm going down to look for the newspaper. (*To* MARTA) Do you want me to bring
you something up from the street?

MARTA: No, thank you.

ANTONIO *goes out the front door.*

MARIO: Who can that guy be?

FELIPE: Maybe he's a Russian spy.

MARIO: No joke. I think he's suspicious.

FELIPE: What do you think, pretty little sister?

MARTA: He seems a good person.

FELIPE: He's not your type?

MARTA: No, he's not my type.

MARTA *leaves the room to go to the kitchen.*

FELIPE: (*Sitting at the table*) Listen, brother, what a drunk we had! I must have had twenty shots of Scotch.

MARIO: (*Absorbed*) What a pretty girl, that one from Mayagüez. (*Sits next to the table*)

FELIPE: That one's a real woman, and the rest are all rag dolls. She had your head with its eyes there bulging like a crab. And you, like a good cock, dedicated a poem to her. Where did you get those beautiful verses?

MARIO: From Peache. A Puerto Rican poet.

FELIPE: Recite them again.

MARIO: No, man. Not now!

FELIPE: Please, brother, please.

MARIO: (*Recites*)
If God one day
blinded all source of light,
the universe would be lit
by those eyes of yours.
But if filled with bitter anger
for such blasphemy, God tore out
your pretty eyes
so that the world at dawn
were not lit by your pupils;
even though He wanted, God could not
extend the Night on Nothingness. . . .
for the world would still be lit
by the memory of your glance.

FELIPE: (*Applauding*) Bravo! You're an intelligent poet. Too bad you have those ideas . . . You know . . . Crazy stuff in your head.

MARIO: Cease politics.

FELIPE: You think you're big, eh? You think you're a wise guy.

MARIO: Are you going to get drunk with me?

FELIPE: (*Gets up violently*) I'm not drunk! (*Pause*) What I am is confused. What they call completely disoriented at forty. (*Smiling*) My dear brother, you who know so much, tell me what I ought to do.

MARIO: Learn to speak Spanish.

FELIPE: (*Joking*) Wouldn't it be better for me to become a Nationalist?

MARIO: You're good for nothing. (*Gets up*)

FELIPE: (*Following him*) You, on the other hand, think you're a patriot, and you're only a *buscabulla*, a troublemaker.

MARIO: Why don't you take a shower and go to bed?

FELIPE: (*Without paying attention*) Do you want me to speak frankly?

MARIO: You don't know how to speak. (*Lies lazily on the sofa*)

FELIPE: How deceived I've lived with you! Since you were a little boy. . . . You always thought saintly and good everything you wanted. Even when you put on the black shirt imitating the Nationalist cadets and began to march with that stick gun. (*Laughs*) How much your little friends laughed at you and how I scolded them because I thought you were an exemplary little boy, a patriot.

MARIO: I suppose you stopped admiring me when you joined the *yanqui* army.

FELIPE: Yes. When I became a soldier and traveled throughout the world, when I was meeting boys like you everywhere I went; in Germany,

Italy, and the very ends of the world. All were like you for me. For them there was only one good country in the world—their own—and everything bad or evil was blamed on the rest of the world.

MARIO: What do you know about anything!

FELIPE: I don't know anything, but I've seen a lot. At the fall of Berlin, I was drinking beer in a bar, and there was a Russian sergeant with a glass in the air shouting and saying the Americans were capitalist pigs. If you could see the punch a Texas cowboy gave him! It broke his jawbone.

MARIO: (*Sitting up on the sofa*) Listen, Felipe, do you want to do me a favor?

FELIPE: What do you want?

MARIO: Don't speak any more of the war. You've spent the whole night rehashing the same thing.

FELIPE: (*Without paying attention*) Do you know who you also remind me of? An American soldier who was stationed in Morocco. Each time he went to a bar and there wasn't any chewing gum or Coca-Cola, he began to curse out the entire country. He called everyone "native" who didn't speak English, till one night, in Casablanca, they cut off one of his ears and threw it to the dogs. (*Laughs*) Take note, old man. Whenever a guy like you appeared there was trouble. (*Falls into a chair near the table*)

MARIO: Don't you remember where you degraded yourself with gambling?

FELIPE: (*Gets up angrily*) Don't throw that damn gambling up in my face! What do you know? (*Sits in the easy chair*)

MARIO: Marta, the coffee! (*Gets up and sits at the table*)

MARTA: (*Offstage*) I'm heating the milk.

FELIPE: (*To himself*) I always remember Aunt Consuelo, picking her teeth with a toothpick and saying at all hours to me: "Felipe, always follow the straight path." Hum! The straight path. (*Throws a cheroot*)

MARIO: Listen, Marta, bring him black coffee, let's see if it gets rid of his drunk!

FELIPE *begins to laugh. He gets up and sits at the table, facing* MARIO.

FELIPE: Listen, Mario. I'm going out tonight with the Irish girl from Fourteenth Street. Do you want to go with her sister?

MARIO: I can't. I'm going to speak at a rally tonight. Come with me so you can be taught.

ANTONIO *enters with the newspaper, crosses toward the left, and stops, listening to the conversation.*

FELIPE: I know those speeches by heart. They all say the same thing: "We want liberty for Puerto Rico." Drop that, Mario. Our country is just fine with the United States. If you had traveled like me, you would have realized the great deal of liberty there is in Puerto Rico.

MARIO: How drunk you are! We are people without sovereignty, a colony.

FELIPE: Ay, ay, ay! Don't give me that worn-out argument. I know well enough what a colony is. I was in the English colonies in Asia. You have to see how those people live in squalor and ignorance. Why should I tell you?

MARIO: You speak like a real *yanqui*.

FELIPE: Because I believe in them from head to foot and I'll say so anywhere. You are a jerk. You spend time talking like the Spaniards, . . . of honor, dignity, and heaven knows whatever other nonsense, and yet you live like an American, dressing, eating, and drinking like them. And what's even more serious: you're in love with an American.

MARIO: Don't meddle in my private affairs. (*Gets up*)

ANTONIO *withdraws to his room with a gesture of reproach.*

FELIPE: (*Gets up*) Okay, kid. Lorna is a great girl.

MARIO: (*Pushing him away*) Leave me alone already!

FELIPE: You know what's the matter with you, kid?

MARIO: Don't speak to me in English.

FELIPE: You know what's happening to you? You hate the Americans, and at heart you admire them. You tell everybody our grandfather was a Spaniard to put on airs. Why don't you admit Father was the son of a peon? (MARIO *looks at him, angry.* FELIPE, *repentant, gives him an affectionate slap on the shoulder.*) You didn't like that, right? Well, endure it, 'cause we're brothers. (*Laughs*) My dear Mario, you live in a confusion. You can't live that way. I can't, and don't go around making false promises. I'm with the Americans 100 per cent. (*Sits on the sofa*)

MARIO: You don't have to tell me. You're a good example of the Puerto Rican generation of today. You only worry about money. You admire everyone who makes dough, even if he's a racketeer. You make fun of learned people, and you only read comic books. You think that to be a man means being an athlete and knowing how to throw a punch in time. You're a superficial man. And the only thing that makes you unique is *yanqui* vulgarity.

MARTA *enters with two cups of coffee.*

FELIPE: Have you finished?

MARIO: Yes.

FELIPE: Well, go to hell.

MARIO: (*Shouting*) Stop this nonsense, because . . . !

MARTA: (*Facing her brothers*) Let's stop this damn argument.

FELIPE: Hey. Take it easy, kid!

MARTA: What do you think this is, a club to spend all day bickering over politics? There are more important things to do in this house.

MARIO: And what's the matter?

MARTA: We have to pay for the apartment, the grocer, and a dozen other things, and you haven't given me a cent this month. Are you just here as tourists?

MARIO: I give my assistance to Mother.

MARTA: Some help! Five dollars a week. And the rest, what do you do with the rest?

MARIO: None of your business.

MARTA: Wasting it on that foolish magazine and going around making speeches. You can preach whatever you damn well please, but remember charity begins at home, and we're in hock up to our ears. You ought to be ashamed of yourself. And I say the same thing to you, Felipe.

FELIPE: You leave me completely calm.

MARTA: You're calm enough with what you did last
            night.

FELIPE: Shut up!

MARIO: What did he do?

MARTA: He gambled and lost the money I lent him.

MARIO: So you're back to gambling!

MARTA: And when ten dollars is so needed in this
            house.

FELIPE: Shut up! I'll come up with the money that's
            needed. Your help won't be necessary, Marta.

MARTA: I'm glad to know it, because I'm out of a job
            since yesterday.

The doorbell rings. JACK *enters.*

JACK: Hello, everybody.

MARTA: Hi! You come to collect the rent?

JACK: That's right.

MARTA: Jack, you couldn't wait a week?

JACK: A week?

MARTA: It's the first time we're behind.

JACK: True enough. But the landlord doesn't care.

MARIO: All those Americans are the same.

JACK: Oh, no. The landlord isn't American. He's a
            Puerto Rican who lives in Miami.

FELIPE: (*With a roar of laughter*) So! He's a sellout.
            Listen, Mario, why don't you tell the landlord
            you're a fellow Puerto Rican and ask him to
            wait three months for the rent?

MARIO: Marta, how much money is needed?

MARTA: Seventy-five dollars.

MARIO: Felipe, you can't get that money around here?

FELIPE: Where in hell's name? (*Pause*) Jack, come on.
            (JACK *approaches.*) I'll give you the rent next
            Saturday without fail.

JACK: Okay, Phil. Your word is good enough for me.

FELIPE *sits at the table and drinks coffee. A hot mambo breaks out in the neighborhood.* JACK *smiles and listens.*

JACK: That's it, boy. (*He begins to dance.*)

MARIO: (*To* JACK, *as he dances*) You're a brazen one!

JACK: (*Smiles and continues dancing*) Please, Mario.

NEIGHBORHOOD VOICE: Please, stop the music; we're praying.

The music stops. JACK *stops dancing.*

JACK: (*Opens the door*) All right. So long. (*To* MARTA, *jokingly*) Good-bye, Mario. (*Exit*)

MARIO: To have to endure a guy like that. It's humiliating.

FELIPE: It would be humiliating for them to throw us out of here. (*Pause*)

MARIO: Marta, why'd they fire you?

MARTA: Because I don't know enough English. (*Sits down on the sofa*)

MARIO: That's a lie. For the same reason they wouldn't rent you an apartment in the West End.

MARTA: The apartment was already taken.

MARIO: Wait. (*He takes the newspaper, opens it and shows it to* MARTA.) Here's the ad. It's still vacant. The fact is they don't rent to Puerto Ricans. It's the prejudice, the scorn the Anglo-Saxon feels for the Latin.

MARTA *gets up and goes into the kitchen.*

FELIPE: (*Comically resigned*) Again the sermon.

MARIO: And you evading the responsibility you have toward your people.

FELIPE: You're a bastard, a real bastard!

MARIO: Jerk!

FELIPE: (*Crossing his arms and fortifying himself with patience*) Brother, what do you want me to do?

MARIO: Defend your people. What does an animal do when it's trapped, when it's pursued and pushed into a dead end? Fight tooth and nail. . . .

FELIPE: (*Intrigued*) What do you mean? (*Gets up*)

MARIO: (*Challenging*) We have to make justice ourselves! The same thing that Puerto Rican boy did when they didn't want to play with him. He went up to his father's room, grabbed his revolver, and from the window shot into the air. Below, the kids who were playing were frightened. And since then they admired the boy and played with him. And that's what we have to do, you and I and . . .

FELIPE: (*Approaching him*) Just a moment! With terrorism, no! Stop that right now. You're going to get us all in a jam.

MARIO: My truths wound you. Coward!

FELIPE: (*Grabbing him by the collar*) Me a coward? Me who they hung with a bayonet from a tree so I could save myself. Me who they made a cross on my chest with a razor, who spent all night, no joke, almost eaten by ants, till I myself pulled the bayonet out. (*Sets him free with a shove*) I have my convictions, but they're not yours. Do I have to think the same as you, as if your ideas were the only truth? Hear me well. What are truths for you are lies for me. What do you or anybody know what truth is?

MARIO: Get away from me, you're just like my father: a
          mercenary!

MARIO *throws* FELIPE *on the couch, smashing three punches
in his face.* MARTA *runs in, lets out a cry and shoves* MARIO
aside. ANTONIO *enters.* MARIO *walks to the door, opens it
and disappears.* FELIPE *gets up, full of rage, and walks
toward the door with his fists clenched.*

MARTA: (*Stepping in front of* FELIPE *and trying to stop
          him*) No, Felipe! Felipe, please! (*Seeing she
          can't stop her brother, she falls on the sofa,
          weeping.*) Good God! This had never hap-
          pened before in this family!
FELIPE: (*Stops, with his fists clenched, next to the door;
          full of rage he closes the door, approaches the
          table.*) If he weren't my brother . . . (*He drops
          a terrible blow on the table.*)

THE PROTEST

by Luis Quero Chiesa

When Dr. Manuel Medina reached the building, the police
already occupied their positions before the main entrance
and along the sidewalk. On seeing them—strong, solid,
impassive under the thick October mist—he felt an agreeable sensation of safety. After all, one had to walk carefully
with that Harlem riffraff all around.

He passed by them with a slight smile of approval, as
though to indicate to them that he was on their side. He
crossed the street and entered a small café whose neon sign
blinked through the window. He ordered a cup of coffee

and went to sit near the window, from where he could observe the scene discreetly.

Outside a shower began to fall. From the river blew a cold gust that lifted the rain from the sidewalk, bent it, and threw it snapping against the walls. It was one of those narrow melancholic streets of old New York that end at the Hudson River, in the lower part of the city. A section of food shops, where the pitchy smells of the docks mix with the vapor of sugar and the sharp stench of fish and rotten fruit. The buildings are old, unpainted, rusty, and through the jaws of their wide doors trucks empty or receive their enormous loads. Like something incongruent in that prosaic, broken neighborhood, the modern building of one of the most important newspapers of the city stands out markedly.

Why had he come? All that was repugnant to him. A man of books and peace, he hated popular protests. For him the most complex problems were solved between the four walls of his study, in the warm atmosphere of a literary soirée. Picketing was, to his way of thinking, a violent, vulgar protest: the favorite instrument of subversive organizations. For that reason, when he received the flyer announcing the picket line that was going to be set up around the newspaper building, he threw it scornfully in the wastebasket. With his fine sense of smell he had recognized several troublemakers among the sponsors. No; he was not going to get messed up in that affair. Nonetheless, as the date drew near, a profound preoccupation had grown in him, a strange desire to witness the protest, to see it fail, as all the others in the area had.

That morning he had arrived early at the university. He had taught his first class automatically, with his thought fixed on that damned picket line that would be assembled at eleven. At ten he could endure it no longer, and gathered

up his books and papers, said he felt sick, and took the train
to the lower part of the city.

In the doorways of some buildings about half a dozen
Puerto Ricans took shelter from the rain. He knew them
from afar. "With this rain and the Puerto Rican lack of
punctuality," he told himself, "nothing's going to happen
here."

From his pocket he drew out the copy of the newspaper
in which the last of the articles on Puerto Rican emigration
was appearing. He finished reading it. There was no doubt!
Those articles were pretty strong. Especially the photos.
That was what bothered him most: those photos of peasants
on horseback, ruined huts. With so many cars that there
were in Puerto Rico! And those beautiful homes in Santurce! . . . Besides, the articles were not as insulting as they
were made to appear. My Lord! If that riffraff that was
coming from Puerto Rico was . . . it was tremendous! He
was even ashamed he was Puerto Rican. More than once he
passed for Argentinian, and since he was not dark and
swarthy . . . All could be remedied with a letter to the
director of the newspaper. A little letter written in good
English, polite, firm, if you will. But these people had loused
things up with their damned picketing.

Across the street, under their raincoats, the police strolled
along the sidewalk. From the newspaper building one of the
workers crossed the street, running, and handed the waiter
a thermos to be filled with hot coffee:

"Bad weather, eh, Joe?"

"Yeah, what's happenin'? Why so many police?"

"We expect pickets. The spiks."

The wounding word was like a whiplash. Dr. Medina
became irate. But he did nothing. Those ignorant people
were not to blame. The real blame fell on those Puerto

Ricans who because of their deplorable conduct made themselves hated. They had never called him "spik." He had never been the victim of prejudice or social injustice in the United States. The insults, the injustices, those he had suffered in Puerto Rico.

He had been born poor. He grew up among the symbols of failure. He recalled his humble town, agonizing among the coffee fields that one day gave him life and prosperity; his home, a crumbling mansion that lodged his grandparents in luxury and ease; his poor father, defending his job tooth and nail. And sunk in so much misery he, young, ambitious, heir to the love for the aristocratic life of his forefathers.

How many humiliations his childhood held! Sundays . . . After so many years those Sundays of his youth still hurt him. At one in the afternoon he was already in the square, waiting for his friends. They would arrive, all dressed up, ready for the casino party. He would stick to them, fawning, full of jokes, in the vain hope someone would invite him to the revelry. But it never happened. At three o'clock the first strains of music were heard, and someone would say: "Let's go up there," and they would disappear through the wide casino hall as though he did not exist.

An overwhelming despair seized his soul. The sad little square seemed sadder, more desolate to him. The church, lazily sitting in a corner, yawned from tedium through its wide doors. The little spurt of water in the fountain, as it fell, was like a malicious mocking laugh. The dusty mastic trees projected the heavy warm shadow of their branches on his soul. And the townspeople, airing their rags and gossiping in the sunlight of the midafternoon, were of an unbearable vulgarity. He felt fenced in. On one occasion he ran into the church seeking consolation; but in the quietude of the old chapel the musical harmonies and the laughter of the guests were heard with even more despair. He sought distraction in his books, in vain. And more than one Sunday he went into the coffee fields, and seated beside the river, gave free rein to his bitterness with enormous sobs that were lost in the thickets.

The siren of a police car sounded up the street. The vehicle stopped in front of the building and the sergeant in charge of the patrol approached and greeted the official. They exchanged a few words and the car turned the corner silently. Nothing was going to happen there. Once more the Puerto Ricans had demonstrated their irresponsibility. Surely at the last moment they had fought with each other and the redeemers had stayed home. What a lack of discipline! Why wouldn't they learn from the Americans? He had wasted the morning miserably. He wrapped himself in his jacket, put on his gloves, and went out into the street. He walked toward the subway.

Suddenly the muffled sound of shouting reached his ears. Then he saw a massed crowd that overflowed the width of the street and advanced toward the newspaper building. With a leap he sought refuge in the opening of a doorway.

They passed by him in a few moments. At the head of the group was a handful of youths carrying a bunch of posters. Behind, a compact human mass: men, women, and children. There were all kinds, all types. One saw in their faces a firmness of purpose, a grave dignity that overwhelmed him.

The police took rapid action. One group took up position at the entrance of the building, nervously clutching their nightsticks. The others herded the crowd toward the sidewalk.

The protest line was organized promptly. Leaders arose to distribute the masses in small patrols; posters were also given out. The march began slowly and firmly under the rain. Someone shouted in vibrant voice a cry of protest: "Puerto Rican women are not whores!" The groups took up the cry and amplified it with a powerful note of indignation that repeated untiringly, and drowned out the noises of the great city.

Before that clamoring crowd, between the police and the press photographers running from one side to another, Dr. Medina felt an uncontrollable fright. His hands and legs trembled. However, he advanced toward the protest line. At the edge of the sidewalk, among the curiosity seekers who were milling around there, he stopped to observe the picket line closely.

He was surprised to see among those who were marching several prominent figures from the colony, ladies of distinguished appearance, members of religious groups. But the vast majority were simple people, eminently Puerto Rican in their features and gestures. Their calm attitude, their serious, serene faces inspired a great respect. Looking at them, from his memory arose shadowy figures of childhood: his grandfather looked like that little old man who walked around with short steps in the rain; that bent old woman was his Aunt Amalia or Doña Encarna, the old friend of the family and his mother toward the end of her days; those extinguished, docile eyes were his father's, asking him for forgiveness for his failures; and that slender youth with an irate glance, had the same tortured look that shadowed his own adolescence. No, those people weren't the coarse, violent horde he had imagined. They were simple human beings—good and bad—who at that moment forgot their private feuds and were uniting in order to protest. Protest! He never protested. He wept bitterly, he flattered; but he never had the courage to protest.

Scrutinizing faces, observing gestures, he was able to

recognize a few of them. They were people from his own town whom he hadn't seen for years. There they were, some disfigured by winter clothing, but essentially themselves. There was something in them, permanent and insoluble, that challenged time and change. He saw them pass by in a knit group and he felt like calling to them, but he was unable to remember a single name. He waited for them to return, and he stopped before them. They passed by without recognizing him. The desolate little square of his home town opened before him and he again felt the old, desperate solitude of his childhood Sundays.

He then saw walking toward him a little girl with a sad face who, indifferent to the cold wind, soaked by the rain, clutched a little Puerto Rican flag framed under glass against her chest. With the same unction, he remembered having seen holy images carried in religious processions. He did not know that little girl from his land, but in those moments she seemed to be a symbol to him.

When the girl passed beside him, Manuel Medina raised his hand to his hat and took it off. Then he picked up a poster that someone had abandoned and raised it over his head. He kept walking toward the homeland.

XXIII. SONGS
OF ROY BROWN

"Like flowers of the field no one knows where the fighters for independence grow. They grow wild," said Rubén Berríos, the leader of the Puerto Rican Independence Party. He was talking of the youth, who were a significant part of his movement. The troubadour of these youth is the poet and folk singer, Roy Brown (1946–   ), whose songs are hymns to the activists. His protest songs, from the album *Yo Protesto* (*I Protest*) (Vanguardia, San Juan, 1970), are uniquely and poignantly touching in the way they combine the romantic patriotism of the older *independentistas* with the bitterly realistic and social lyrics of blues and rock music, as in "The Mind Is a Sleeping Soul," "Old Bastions of Borinqueños," "Paco Márquez," and "Monon." (Translated by Maria Cristina López Kelly and Stan Steiner.)

THE MIND IS A SLEEPING SOUL

> But, no, no, I can't comprehend
> pain, the mirror of love—

The mind is a sleeping soul
dreaming and wishing one day
truth will be known—

The soul is a holy flame
illuminating the way
of men who wish to be free—

Life is time that passes
a man who forever
searches for his identity—

A man is a rebel who weeps
when he confronts a dream
by nailing himself to the Cross—

> But, no, no, I can't comprehend
> pain, the mirror of love—

Tears weave a golden cape
upon the shoulders of a man
who thinks he is better
than his fellow man—

Laughter is a cool breeze
enrapturing the man who seeks
peace after the heat—

And sleep is an intimacy
that our senses call by name:
Listen to me, my friend:

    But, no, no, I can't comprehend
    pain, the mirror of love—

A woman exalts a man
who seeks to know
the meaning of love—

The man is a man who loves
his country, his lover,
and his own God—

And it's senseless for sleeping
people to live boasting, there
are no better worlds—

    But, no, no, I can't comprehend
    pain, the mirror of love—

Our world is a lonely being
that follows a schedule
that ends in ruin—

But, if it's true that everyone
has a definition, I define
my world as a great vision—

To extend my hand to a friend—
to give my woman a noble kiss—
and to offer my country my life—

But, yes, yes, yes, I can confront
pain, now, I can feel love—

But, yes, yes, yes, I can confront
pain, now, I can feel love—

OLD BASTIONS OF BORINQUEÑOS

Old bastions of Borinqueños
I have come to sing:

That man borrowed money
on everything he owns,
even his own shirt;
just to sell his soul
to a gringo with a gun—

Simplicio thinks
he is a great man
since the Yankees came—

The fields and hills of
my love were stolen
by thieves and now they
want to sell them for
a pile of dollar bills,
to stroll with their
women, who are not ugly,
nor pretty, just gossips—

The palm trees are tall
and the sun is rising,
But, oh, my good friend,
it is getting very hot—
so tell me, Doña Pancha,
where the King has gone?
It has been so very long
since he has been seen—

> Simplicio thinks
> he is a great man
> since the Yankees came—

PACO MÁRQUEZ

As the wind sings
        his song of grief,
so the dead man cries;
        but wait, enough
of poetry, tomorrow they
        bury him.

Chorus:

Paco Márquez and Betances
were men of ideals,

fighters of the evil
that enslaved our people.

With a gun in his hand
    my brother's buddy
thought he could right
    everything wrong;
but wait, enough of
    poetry,
tomorrow they bury him.

Chorus:

The banner is unfurled
and the people sing
    and dance,
    joyously;
but wait, enough of
    poetry,
tomorrow they bury him.

MONON

Mr. Jiménez came out
when Monon was born
in the bathroom of the bar
at the end of the alley
and he said:

Monon you are a man without equal;
a man of God, fruit of evil—

The thief who crosses the seas
came to the island

when Monon was growing up
in the sugarcane plantation
and he begged to sing:

> Monon you are free as the wind,
> if you are tired you rest,
> if you want you can leave,
> Good-bye—

The man who said he was the treasurer
grabbed poor Monon and told him
it was his duty to go
and put him on a plane
and yelled:

> Monon you are a man of fate,
> you are the one
> who came to save the world,
> who will preserve our tears—

Many men are like this
who make up dreams,
who sing to a world that lies moaning—

And the children are frightened
because the man of fate,
the one who never came,
is dropping bombs and digging graves—

> with electronic power—
> with nuclear minds—

They dig graves in Lares—
They drop bombs in Vietnam—

They throw bombs in Nigeria—
They dig graves in Siberia—

And the children are frightened—
And dying men are dying
in silence—

And the Indian of the Andes,
And the Indian of Father Hidalgo,
still wait
for the man of fate
the one who never came
who walks with science—

And a young man in penance
cries in anger:

FIRE! FIRE!
        the World is on FIRE!
FIRE! FIRE!
        the Yankees want FIRE!
FIRE! FIRE!
        the Yankees want FIRE!
FIRE! FIRE!
        the Yankees want FIRE!
FIRE! FIRE!
        the Yankees want FIRE!
FIRE! FIRE!
        the Yankees want FIRE!

XXIV. THE
ODYSSEY
OF A JÍBARO

It is said that the first islander to migrate to the mainland was Ponce de León. In 1521 the first Spanish governor of Puerto Rico landed in Florida in search of the Fountain of Youth, one hundred years before the Pilgrims arrived in North America. And so, the popular joke: "A Puerto Rican discovered America!" Ponce de León died as the result of an Indian arrow, and ever since, the migrating islanders have been suffering the slings of social misfortune, insult, and discrimination in the inhospitable climate of the north. One *jíbaro*, who came to New York in the 1930s, tells of his experiences with the tenacity and humor of the hills, in "The Odyssey of a *Jíbaro*" (*The Islands: The Worlds of the Puerto Ricans*, by Stan Steiner, New York, Harper & Row, 1974); while an earlier pioneer, who came before World War I, Jesús Colón, a lifelong community leader and political writer, bequeaths his experiences to his relatives who remained behind, in the poignant and passionate "Grandma, Please Don't Come!" (*A Puerto Rican in New York*, by Jesús Colón, New York, Mainstream Publishers, 1961).

THE ODYSSEY OF A JÍBARO ·

I was illegal . . .

When I came to America, I came in style. I traveled in a lifeboat on the deck of a United States Army transport, as a stowaway. That was in 1933.

Everyone on the ship was wearing khaki or white uniforms. But me. I was wearing a black suit. That was because it was the only suit I had.

How I made it I don't know. Somehow I made it wearing a black suit.

My father died when I was a little boy. And my mother was so poor, she had too many children to feed. She could not feed us. And she had to send us to different places. I was sent to a home for orphans. Even if I was not an orphan, I was an orphan. Later, when I was older, I joined the Army, maybe because it was like a home for orphans. That's how I knew about the Army transport.

In New York City I went up to Harlem, to 116th Street, because I heard some Puerto Ricans were living there. But, I didn't know any of them.

So, I used to sleep in Central Park. I had no room. I had

five cents in my pocket. And the grass was nice in the park. I liked to sleep under the stars.

Every day I looked for a job. I didn't know there weren't any jobs, in 1933.

One day I was sitting on a stoop on 116th Street. I still remember it. Some pieces of paper were lying in the street. I picked them up and smoothed them out with my hand and decided to write some letters. But, I didn't have a pencil. So, I borrowed a pencil from someone. You will never guess who I wrote those letters to. I wrote to Mayor Fiorello LaGuardia, who was Mayor of New York City, and President Franklin Roosevelt, who was President of the United States, and to Santiago Iglesias, who was Resident Commissioner for Puerto Rico.

And I asked them to get me a job!

The stoop I was sitting on wasn't my address, because I didn't have one. But I wrote it on the letters, anyway. And then I had to borrow some pennies for stamps, because I didn't want to spend the five cents I had in my pocket.

After that I waited every day on the stoop, for an answer. On the second day I got an answer from Mayor Fiorello LaGuardia. It wasn't a letter. It was a social worker.

She told me that I could get Relief. That was what they called Welfare in those days. It would give me money for a month's rent, so I could have a room full of cockroaches to sleep in. I think that she thought it was unhealthy to sleep in the park, in the open air.

No! I told her. I didn't want Relief and a room full of cockroaches. What I wanted was a job. She shook her head and went away, saying, *Another one of those crazy Puerto Ricans!*

In a few days I got an answer from the President of the United States. He sent me one of *his* social workers, who offered me the same things: Relief and a room full of cockroaches. But I just shrugged. No! I told her. What I wanted was a job.

Of course, the Resident Commissioner for Puerto Rico, Santiago Iglesias, took a little longer to answer. It always takes a Puerto Rican a little longer. He has to think about it. That's something a *yanqui* doesn't have to bother with. Anyway, the Commissioner sent me *his* social worker, who suggested I walk across the street. On 116th Street, in those days, there was the Puerto Rican Government Office. It was right across the street from the stoop where I was sitting. So, I walked it.

They had no money to offer me, because Puerto Rico was too poor itself. But they offered to get me some Relief and that same room full of cockroaches.

In America, I thought, there is no work. There is only money.

So I kept on walking. I walked so much looking for a job, that my heel fell off my shoe. And, as I told you, I had only five cents in my pocket. But, five cents won't pay a shoemaker. I went to a Puerto Rican shoemaker I knew, and I told him this:

Let me sew my heel on my shoe and I will sew some shoes for you. I know how because I learned how to sew shoes on the island. That way I will pay you by helping you in the store. That was how I got a job in New York.

A man who gets something for nothing loses something. His soul. His pride. His manhood.

They tried to buy my manhood from me with Relief money. I learned that is what they try to do to Puerto Ricans. They are still doing that. They yell about Welfare, but they like to give it. It is like the war. They yell about it, but they fight it. If they didn't like it, they would stop it. Welfare is like that. It is a cheap way to buy a Puerto

Rican's manhood. It is a lie to say a man will come to New York to sell his manhood.

He comes because he is dreaming of a break. And he gets broken.

GRANDMA, PLEASE DON'T COME

by Jesús Colón

Please, grandma, don't come!

I know they have sent you the airplane ticket, and a dress just your size with black and white squares all over the beautiful taffeta silk. But please, grandma, don't come!

They have sent you the photographs of your little darling grandchildren born in New York. True, you have not seen them yet. You would like to leave your tropical sun and mountains and the little rivulet bathing the base of the fence in your backyard and the tall avocado tree right by your kitchen door, just to see and embrace those darling grandchildren. But again, I say, grandma, please don't come!

I know you are not well-to-do. But you have been living on what your sons and daughters send you every month from the states. I know there is need and poverty around you. And discrimination and economic and cultural oppression there. Something called imperialism sees to it that these things are not wiped out. But I think this is not the kind of letter in which I should go all out and try to explain to you why some people are so terribly interested in keeping people poor and ignorant. Still I think I ought to tell you that the most important men and forces interested in keeping people poor and ignorant and fighting wars one against the other, have their offices in one short street in this

New York to which your relatives are trying to bring you. The many companies with offices in that street and their counterparts in other great cities own the United States and of course, Puerto Rico. Eisenhower and Muñoz Marín do what they ask them to do. It might sound ridiculously amazing to you. But believe me, grandma, this is nevertheless a fact. But enough of this "deep" stuff for today. All I am asking you, grandma, today, is please don't come!

Yes, it is nice here in a way. It is nice if you are young and willing and able to go down five flights of stairs two or three times a day. If you can "take it" in a crowded subway where you are squeezed in tight twice a day as if you were a cork in a bottle. It is all right in a way—and remember—I only say in a way—for young strong people. We come to New York young and leave old and tired. All the fun and joy of life extracted from us by the hurry-up machine way of living we are forced to live here. In Puerto Rico, nobody pushes you, you walk slowly as if the day had 48 hours. Persons completely unknown to you say: "Buenos Días" ("Good morning"), with a reverence and a calmness in their voices that reveals centuries of a quiescent, reposed, unhurried way of life.

No matter how many photographs they sent you of Times Square at night, or the Coney Island Boardwalk, grandma, please tell them "NO." A forceful, definite "NO." All those things you have not seen are lots of fun. Don't misunderstand me. New York has many things that are grand. But at your age you will not really be able to enjoy them. You know what snow is? What sleet and snow is? The real physical burden of 20 additional pounds of calico and muslin on your old bones? Puerto Rico's climate doesn't require any more. Grandma, please don't come!

You should see hundreds of Puerto Rican grandmas like you on a wintry snowy day, standing by the window and watching the snow fall, as Ramito our folk singer said when he came here: "Like coconut flakes falling from the sky." At the beginning snow is a novelty. But after you have seen it once or twice, you wish you were back in Puerto Rico, looking out at your avocado tree and at the tall dignified royal palm piercing the deep blue Caribbean sky with its sheer beauty.

In Puerto Rico you will be chatting your head off in your own language with the other grandmothers. Nobody will shout at you: "Why don't you talk United States?" Or even threaten you with a beating because you are speaking Spanish. It has been done, you know. People have been killed because they are heard speaking Spanish. So, grandma, please, don't come!

You will be looking so sad, so despondent, so alone when everybody goes to work and you are left all by yourself in an apartment peering through a window at the passersby down below as they go back and forth splashing the grey, dirty, cold snow in the street and on the sidewalk!

All people, North Americans and Puerto Ricans alike, are looking to the day when they can spend the last years of their lives on a tropical isle—a paradise on earth surrounded by clear blue sea imprisoned in a belt of golden beaches. A land perfumed with nature's choicest fragrances. For many of us this is a dream that will never be realized. The boasted "American way of life" has taken out of us the best of our energies to reach that dream.

Grandma, you are there on that beautiful isle. You were born there. You have been there all your life. You now have what most people here can only dream about. Don't let sentimental letters and life-colored photographs lure you from your island, from your nation, from yourself. Grandma, please, please! DO NOT COME!

XXV. PUERTO RICAN PARADISE

So many Puerto Ricans have come to New York that nobody knows exactly how many have come, and gone. The census takers of the government estimate one million, or so; but the community leaders of the barrios say the number is nearly one million and a half. No statistic tells the whole story; for so many islanders come, and *return*, each year, that probably not one, but two, or three, million people have lived in both worlds. In "Puerto Rican Paradise," a chapter in his *Down These Mean Streets* (New York, Signet Books, 1967), the chronicler of barrio life, Piri Thomas, tells of how not only the people, but their dreams, are suspended in between the worlds of memory and reality. Thomas's tale is in the immigrant tradition of Jewish, Irish, and southern black novelists, but its Puertorriqueño ethos and gusto are unique. This is especially so in his later work, *Savior! Savior!* (New York, Simon & Schuster, 1972), where the seeds of urban barrio culture flower in aesthetic richness.

PUERTO RICAN PARADISE

by Piri Thomas

Poppa didn't talk to me the next day. Soon he didn't talk much to anyone. He lost his night job—I forget why, and probably it was worth forgetting—and went back on home relief. It was 1941, and the Great Hunger called Depression was still down on Harlem.

But there was still the good old WPA. If a man was poor enough, he could dig a ditch for the government. Now Poppa was poor enough again.

The weather turned cold one more time, and so did our apartment. In the summer the cooped-up apartments in Harlem seem to catch all the heat and improve on it. It's the same in the winter. The cold, plastered walls embrace that cold from outside and make it a part of the apartment, till you don't know whether it's better to freeze out in the snow or by the stove, where four jets, wide open, spout futile, blue-yellow flames. It's hard on the rats, too.

Snow was falling. "My *Cristo*," Momma said, "*que frio*. Doesn't that landlord have any *corazón*? Why don't he give more heat?" I wondered how Pops was making out working a pick and shovel in that falling snow.

Momma picked up a hammer and began to beat the

beat-up radiator that's copped a plea from so many beatings. Poor steam radiator, how could it give out heat when it was freezing itself? The hollow sounds Momma beat out of it brought echoes from other freezing people in the building. Everybody picked up the beat and it seemed a crazy, good idea. If everybody took turns beating on the radiators, everybody could keep warm from the exercise.

We drank hot cocoa and talked about summertime. Momma talked about Puerto Rico and how great it was, and how she'd like to go back one day, and how it was warm all the time there and no matter how poor you were over there, you could always live on green bananas, *bacalao,* and rice and beans. *"Dios mío,"* she said, "I don't think I'll ever see my island again."

"Sure you will, Mommie," said Miriam, my kid sister. She was eleven. "Tell us, tell us all about Porto Rico."

"It's not Porto Rico, it's Puerto Rico," said Momma.

"Tell us, Moms," said nine-year-old James, "about Puerto Rico."

"Yeah, Mommie," said six-year-old José.

Even the baby, Paulie, smiled.

Moms copped that wet-eyed look and began to dream-talk about her *isla verde,* Moses' land of milk and honey.

"When I was a little girl," she said, "I remember the getting up in the morning and getting the water from the river and getting the wood for the fire and the quiet greenlands and the golden color of the morning sky, the grass wet from the *lluvia* . . . *Ay, Dios,* the *coquís* and the *pajaritos* making all the *música* . . ."

"Mommie, were you poor?" asked Miriam.

"*Sí, muy pobre,* but very happy. I remember the hard work and the very little bit we had, but it was a good little bit. It counted very much. Sometimes when you have too much, the good gets lost within and you have to look very hard. But when you have a little, then the good does not have to be looked for so hard."

"Moms," I asked, "did everybody love each other—I mean, like if everybody was worth something, not like if some weren't important because they were poor—you know what I mean?"

"*Bueno hijo,* you have people everywhere who, because they have more, don't remember those who have very little. But in Puerto Rico those around you share *la pobreza* with you and they love you, because only poor people can understand poor people. I like *los Estados Unidos,* but it's sometimes a cold place to live—not because of the winter and the landlord not giving heat but because of the snow in the hearts of the people."

"Moms, didn't our people have any money or land?" I leaned forward, hoping to hear that my ancestors were noble princes born in Spain.

"Your grandmother and grandfather had a lot of land, but they lost that."

"How come, Moms?"

"Well, in those days there was nothing of what you call *contratos,* and when you bought or sold something, it was on your word and a handshake, and that's the way your *abuelos* bought their land and then lost it."

"Is that why we ain't got nuttin' now?" James asked pointedly.

"Oh, it—"

The door opened and put an end to the kitchen yak. It was Poppa coming home from work. He came into the kitchen and brought all the cold with him. Poor Poppa, he looked so lost in the clothes he had on. A jacket and coat, sweaters on top of sweaters, two pairs of long johns, two pairs of pants, two pairs of socks and a woolen cap. And under all that he was cold. His eyes were cold; his ears were red with pain. He took off his gloves and his fingers were stiff with cold.

"*Cómo está?*" said Momma. "I will make you coffee."

Poppa said nothing. His eyes were running hot frozen tears. He worked his fingers and rubbed his ears, and the pain made him make faces. "Get me some snow, Piri," he said finally.

I ran to the window, opened it, and scraped all the snow on the sill into one big snowball and brought it to him. We all watched in frozen wonder as Poppa took that snow and rubbed it on his ears and hands.

"Gee, Pops, don't it hurt?" I asked.

"*Sí*, but it's good for it. It hurts a little first, but it's good for the frozen parts."

I wondered why.

"How was it today?" Momma asked.

"Cold. My God, ice cold."

Gee, I thought, *I'm sorry for you, Pops. You gotta suffer like this.*

"It was not always like this," my father said to the cold walls. "It's all the fault of the damn Depression."

"Don't say 'damn,'" Momma said.

"Lola, I say 'damn' because that's what it is—*damn*."

And Momma kept quiet. She knew it was "damn."

My father kept talking to the walls. Some of the words came out loud, others stayed inside. I caught the inside ones—the damn WPA, the damn Depression, the damn home relief, the damn poorness, the damn cold, the damn crummy apartments, the damn look on his damn kids, living so damn damned and his not being able to do a damn thing about it.

And Momma looked at Poppa and at us and thought

about her Puerto Rico and maybe being there where you didn't have to wear a lot of extra clothes and feel so full of damns, and how when she was a little girl all the green was wet from the *lluvias*.

And Poppa looking at Momma and us, thinking how did he get trapped and why did he love us so much that he dug in damn snow to give us a piece of change? And why couldn't he make it from home, maybe, and keep running?

And Miriam, James, José, Paulie, and me just looking and thinking about snowballs and Puerto Rico and summertime in the street and whether we were gonna live like this forever and not know enough to be sorry for ourselves.

The kitchen all of a sudden felt warmer to me, like being all together made it like we wanted it to be. Poppa made it into the toilet and we could hear everything he did, and when he finished, the horsey gurgling of the flushed toilet told us he'd soon be out. I looked at the clock and it was time for "Jack Armstrong, the All-American Boy."

José, James, and I got some blankets and, like Indians, huddled around the radio digging the All-American Jack and his adventures, while Poppa ate dinner quietly. Poppa was funny about eating—like when he ate, nobody better bother him. When Poppa finished, he came into the living room and stood there looking at us. We smiled at him, and he stood there looking at us.

All of a sudden he yelled, "How many wanna play 'Major Bowes' Amateur Hour'?"

"Hoo-ray! Yeah, we wanna play," said José.

"Okay, first I'll make some taffy outta molasses, and the one who wins first prize gets first choice at the biggest piece, okay?"

"Yeah, hoo-ray, *chevere*."

Gee, Pops, you're great, I thought, *you're the swellest, the*

*bestest Pops in the whole world, even though you don't
understand us too good.*

When the candy was all ready, everybody went into the
living room. Poppa came in with a broom and put an empty
can over the stick. It became a microphone, just like on the
radio.

"Pops, can I be Major Bowes?" I asked.

"Sure, Piri," and the floor was mine.

"Ladies and gentlemen," I announced, "tonight we
present 'Major Bowes' Amateur Hour,' and for our first
number—"

"Wait a minute son, let me get my ukelele," said Poppa.
"We need music."

Everybody clapped their hands and Pops came back with
his ukelele.

"The first con-tes-tant we got is Miss Miriam Thomas."

"Oh no, not me first, somebody else goes first," said
Miriam, and she hid behind Momma.

"Let me! Let me!" said José.

Everybody clapped.

"What are you gonna sing, sir?" I asked.

"Tell the people his name," said Poppa.

"Oh yeah. Presenting Mr. José Thomas. And what are you
gonna sing, sir?"

I handed José the broom with the can on top and sat
back. He sang well and everybody clapped.

Everyone took a turn, and we all agreed that two-year-old
Paulie's "gurgle, gurgle" was the best song, and Paulie got
first choice at the candy. Everybody got candy and eats and
thought how good it was to be together, and Moms thought
that it was wonderful to have such a good time even if she
wasn't in Puerto Rico where the grass was wet with *lluvia*.
Poppa thought about how cold it was gonna be tomorrow,
but then he remembered tomorrow was Sunday and he

wouldn't have to work, and he said so and Momma said "*Sí,*" and the talk got around to Christmas and how maybe things would get better.

The next day the Japanese bombed Pearl Harbor.

"My God," said Poppa. "We're at war."

"*Dios mío,*" said Momma.

I turned to James. "Can you beat that," I said.

"Yeah," he nodded. "What's it mean?"

"What's it mean?" I said. "You gotta ask, dopey? It means a rumble is on, and a big one, too."

I wondered if the war was gonna make things worse than they were for us. But it didn't. A few weeks later Poppa got a job in an airplane factory. "How about that?" he said happily. "Things are looking up for us."

Things *were* looking up for us, but it had taken a damn war to do it. A lousy rumble had to get called so we could start to live better. I thought, *How do you figure this crap out?*

I couldn't figure it out, and after a while I stopped thinking about it. Life in the streets didn't change much. The bitter cold was followed by the sticky heat; I played stickball, marbles, and Johnny-on-the-Pony, copped girls' drawers and blew pot. War or peace—what difference did it really make?

XXVI. RACE AND THE SEARCH FOR IDENTITY

Rican, Neo-Rican, Puerto Rican, Puerto Rican–American, Nuevo Yorrican, Boricua, Boriken, or PR? Who am I? The "search for identity" of a conquered, bewildered people in the midst of the race-conscious and racist society of their conquerors is not an easy one; it sometimes seems a hopeless one. Some years ago a child of Puertorriqueño parents, in a New York school, told an interviewer: "I am alien in two lands, I am illiterate in two languages."

In "Race and the Search for Identity," the New York-born writer and educator, Samuel Betances, a graduate student at Harvard University, explores a few of the racial blind alleys and psychological dead ends into which the American society forces the children of Puertorriqueños. His resolution of the white problem is his own, but the white problem is everyone's. (*The Rican*, Fall 1971.)

RACE AND THE SEARCH FOR IDENTITY

by Samuel Betances

Puerto Ricans are sometimes white, they are sometimes black, and they are sometimes Puerto Ricans—and so they are quite often confused. This holds particularly true for the second generation Puerto Ricans in the U. S. mainland. The single most crucial issue burning deep in the souls of many young, second generation Puerto Ricans in the United States is that of the wider identity—the search for ethnicity.

Puerto Rican youth in America in search of their ethnic identity have often faced the stark reality of having to relate to critical issues solely on the basis of black and white. In other words, it becomes impossible simply to be "Puerto Rican" or "Latin" or a "Third World Type" or "Spanish" in a society that demands categories based on black and white.

To a large degree, Puerto Rican youth who come from a racially mixed background believe that in America they can choose whether they want to be black or white. Some have decided not to suffer the plight of becoming black. It is hard for them to be a Puerto Rican without becoming black as well, the assumption being that one can choose with which group to relate.

Erik Erikson suggests that Negro creative writers are in a battle to reconquer for their people a "surrendered identity." He states:

I like this term because it does not assume total absence, as many contemporary writers do—something to be searched for and found, to be granted or given, to be created or fabricated—but something to be recovered. This must be emphasized because what is latent can become a living actuality, and thus a bridge from past to future.[1]

If what Erikson says is true, then the Puerto Rican adolescent's search for a wider identity becomes even more complicated in the light of some historical facts that are uniquely Puerto Rican.

Puerto Rico at present has no definite political status. The island is neither a state of the union, nor is it an independent nation. It is no more than a "perfume colony," as a critic of the present system has described it. Puerto Ricans are considered "Americans" by their Latin American cousins and "Latins" by the Americans. They have never been in control of their island and during a period of nineteen years, between 1898 and 1917, were citizens of no country.[2]

Dr. Román López Tames, a careful student of the Puerto Rican experience, has noted that there is insecurity in the island. Puerto Ricans are forever asking themselves, "What am I?" ("Que soy?"), and "What are we?" ("Que somos?"). He notes that "for the North Americans the island is hispanic, this is to say, strange sister to what they call Latin American." But on the other hand, "Latin American countries without having a very concrete notion about the island, quite frequently reject her considering her North Americanized, lost to the great family." [3] Puerto Rico has been likened by Dr. López Tames to the plight of the bat who is rejected by birds and by rodents, belonging to neither family in any concrete way, who is condemned to live a solitary life between the two worlds, misunderstood by both.

To some degree, the seeds of insecurity toward ethnicity are already planted in the minds of first generation Puerto Ricans. Thus, a youngster who has parents who have some doubt as to their own identity has to face new problems which indicate further that he is neither black nor white. He is neither American nor Latin American. He comes from an island which is neither a state nor a nation. Is it possible for Puerto Ricans to find their "surrendered identity"? Or is it not a fact that to some degree the historical experience indicates that there is nothing there which is latent, nothing that can come alive, nothing that can serve as a bridge from the past to the future, since Puerto Rico, as a geographical entity, has been molded in an experience of dependency, first to Spain and then to the United States?

Confusion, ambivalency, and contradictions are present in the lives of Puerto Rican adolescents as they relate to the issue of race and color. Some Puerto Ricans learn English very quickly and refuse to speak Spanish in hopes of finding acceptance in the larger society. Others who are dark-skinned deliberately keep their Spanish, lest they be mistaken for American Negroes. Still others will hide their dark-skinned grandmother in the kitchen while introducing their potential spouses to their lighter-skinned parents.[4] The more successful the Puerto Rican, the more "European-looking" his wife tends to be. It's an interesting commentary that the first book[5] out of East Harlem, *Down These Mean Streets*, based on the second generation experience, was written by Piri Thomas, a Puerto Rican who is very concerned with the crucial issue of identity. One chapter in his book is entitled, "How to be a Negro Without Really Trying." Others are, "Hung up Between Two Sticks" and "Brothers Under the Skin."

The migrant Puerto Rican, whose children are the focus of this paper, have brought with them certain experiences and outlooks on the issue of race and color that have influenced to some degree the lives of their children. The first generation grew up on an island which historically has experienced "whiteness" as a positive value and "blackness" as a negative one. "White is right," in Puerto Rico, too. While blackness may not be as negative as in America, it is still negative enough to be a source of embarrassment in many instances of Puerto Rican life.

Puerto Rico has a problem of color; America has a problem of race.[6] That is the critical difference between discrimination in Puerto Rico and in the U. S. mainland.

Discrimination in Puerto Rico is based on color. As such, color is a physical characteristic which can be altered and/or changed in several generations. Marrying someone lighter-skinned than oneself immediately alters the way in which the offspring of such a union would be described. A Negro–Puerto Rican who marries a non-Negro–Puerto Rican will have children which will be described as non-Negro.

If the pattern is continued through several generations, a Negro Puerto Rican can live to see his "white" great-grand-children. The negative physical element, color, can be eliminated or be made to play a less embarrassing role in the lives of those who seek to make things "better for their children."[7]

Not so in America where discrimination is based on the concept of race. It has to do with a deep-seated conviction about one group being superior to another. In the United

States, the element of racial inequality is prevalent. Racism has to do with the issue of the "purity of the blood," a kind of changeless, hereditary disease or blessing which is transmitted from parent to offspring. In America many gain their sense of being and power from their membership in the "superior" white race. The most deprived white man can think of himself as "better than any Nigger." It doesn't really matter what his position or educational background may be: "No matter how you dress him up, a Nigger is a Nigger," a racist will tell you.

To be black in America is such a serious handicap that a person with "one drop" of Negro blood is considered Negro. Negro blood is a kind of reverse and negative "black power," which haunts a person reminding him that he is inferior—at best, a mere shadow of a white figure. Such are the "deep-seated, anxiety-rooted, sado-masochistic drives" [8] which account for much of the racial problems in America. Is it any wonder that in the United States intermarriage is considered the unpardonable social sin?

Puerto Rican discrimination based on color as opposed to race can be labeled as a "milder" type of discrimination. It has, nevertheless, influenced the outlook of the people, including those who journeyed to the mainland with notions that blackness is a negative aspect in a person's life and whiteness is a positive value.

So that the non-Negroid Puerto Rican may look upon his darker skinned counterpart as a person with certain drawbacks, a descendant of slaves whose physical features, texture of hair and/or color of the skin may leave something to be desired. He is not necessarily someone to hate, to control, or to fear, but perhaps to avoid in certain social contexts.

And it is not always a matter of color that determines desirability in certain social contexts. Negroid features: full lips, kinky hair ("pelo malo") may play a much more crucial role in terms of desirability over light complexion in Puerto Rico. A man with "good" hair, but dark skin ("un trigueño de pelo bueno") may be more desirable than a light-skinned but kinky-haired individual. Color gives way to other physical characteristics at times. Distinction, however, may not be made verbally, so that when individuals refer to a person of "color," they may be really referring to "Negroid" features as opposed to complexion—although they may still relate to the question as one of "color."

Puerto Ricans believe that "trigueñas" or "morenas" (women of dark complexion) make better lovers than those who are non-dark. The belief that color plays a positive role in sex is somewhat different than the racist connotations found in such belief in America. One observer has noted, "this is not the expression of a neurotic fear of sexual insufficiency but an accepted and openly stated commonplace." [9]

Alex Rodríguez, a Puerto Rican spokesman in the city of Boston and past director of the Cooper Community Center in Lower Roxbury, was recently interviewed in the *Boston Globe* on the role of color and race in Puerto Rican life. Rodríguez noted that most Puerto Ricans, while identifying themselves as non-white, quickly learned the advantages of being "white" in a racist society. He suggests that in Puerto Rico, blackness is thought of as a beautiful trait. He used the following examples: "One of the most affectionate terms in Spanish is 'negra,' which means Dear or Darling, but literally translated means 'black one.' "

Rodríguez's example is used quite frequently by people of Latin America who would imply racial equality by citing it. The term "negrita" *does* imply intimacy and affection in the usage that Rodríguez gave it. But there is some difference between "intimacy" and "affection" with "equality" which should be considered. A Peruvian newspaper quoted Ve-large who held to the same interpretation on this matter as Alex Rodríguez. Pitt-Rivers brings focus to that difference:

The implication of racial equality that he drew from his examples invites precision. Such terms do not find way into such context because they are flattering in formal usage, but because they are not. Intimacy is opposed to respect; because these terms are disrespectful, they are used to establish or stress a relationship where no respect is due. The word "Nigger" is used in this way among Negroes in the United States, but only among Negroes. Color has, in fact, the same kind of class connotation in the Negro community as in Latin America: pale-skinned means upper class. Hence, Nigger, in this context dark-skinned or lower class, implies a relationship that is free of obligation of mutual respect.[10]

It is true that Puerto Rico has never had a race riot. But the assertion made by Puerto Rican spokesmen[11] that all is well in this matter of race and color in the island, or that Puerto Rico is one thousand years ahead of America on this issue is misleading. The fact that there is discrimination against those who would embrace the "Afro-Antillean cultured tradition" or those who are dark-skinned, certainly enough discrimination to make those who are black wish that they were not, indicates all is not well in Puerto Rico.

Those who damned the United States race riots and point to the superior culture which does not have race riots in Puerto Rico, have not been as zealous in explaining the problem of color that does exist in the island. As a result many citizens on the mainland, including such noted sociologists as Nathan Glazer,[12] believe the problem to be less serious than in reality.

The point being suggested here is that the problem of color is serious enough in Puerto Rican life to complicate further the second generation's search for ethnicity in the mainland. As the second generation looks toward the island and toward their homes, they don't find a people who have solved the problem of black and white. Instead they find further reasons for added anxiety, confusion, and feelings of uncertainty. Pointing out that Puerto Rico does not have race riots does not solve the problem of a youngster who must not only deal with a world outside of his home which is unsympathetic and at times cruel, but he also must confront his family and Puerto Rican neighbors who for reasons all their own seem to be making efforts toward concealment of color.

In the early part of 1970, sixty young second-generation Puerto Ricans were interviewed concerning this issue of race and color as it affected their search for ethnicity in the U.S. mainland. Thirty of the youth resided in the South Bronx in New York City; fifteen of them resided in the Division Street area of Chicago's Northwest Side; and fifteen lived in the South End of Boston. Their response to the questionnaire and their willingness to have their answers taped when requested, provided perspective in attempting to understand this very crucial issue. A close look at their responses indicates the problem to be much more complicated than previously imagined.

One young Puerto Rican in Boston, when asked how she was perceived by other people in a downtown store or in a crowded bus or walking through the busy streets of Boston, answered that most people would consider her "white." She quickly added, "an Eastern European type or Italian."

When asked how she described herself—"say that you were applying for a job and you had to fill out a blank which demanded some definition on your part"—she said, "Negro." Why? She explained that people on the streets tend to look at her very superficially. Since she has a light complexion and long, black hair, she could "pass" in that kind of situation. However, when applying for a job, she explained, employers tend to take a second look, even a third look, especially if the job requires one to be visible, like office work. By filling the blank "Negro," she felt the employer would probably say to himself that she was not really black. But he would probably be happy to hire such a nice, light-skinned, safe Negro.

On the other hand, if she filled in the blank "White," the employer would probably think her dishonest since she was not really white. He probably would not forgive her for trying to "pass." The chances of his objecting to one's describing oneself "Negro" are less than the other way around.

Here is the case of a nineteen-year-old Puerto Rican youth trying desperately to psyche out the society in which she lives, anticipating the moods of people she somehow must not offend if she is to make it in racially tense America in the 1970s. It is difficult to ascertain just what psychological price she and many like her are paying in their attempt to survive without arousing people's prejudices.

Several youths, when asked whether they thought people in America were prejudiced towards them because they were Puerto Ricans, answered, "no." They explained that prejudice stemmed from the fact of their dark skin color. Somehow in their minds they had carefully separated their skin color from their Puerto Ricanness.

Answering another question, this time on the issue of intermarriage between American Negroes and Puerto Ricans, one of the interviewees from New York answered:

Puerto Ricans are on the bottom of the social ladder in this country; blacks are even worse off. Blacks should not marry Puerto Ricans since two wrongs don't make a right!

While most of those interviewed said that when it comes to marriage it should really be up to the people involved, it would appear that the "two wrongs don't make a right" answer is closer to the feeling of those questioned. Deeper probing indicated that while most of them "prefer" not to marry American Negroes, they would not voice "opposition" to such marriages.

The question of intermarriage is a very difficult one for Puerto Rican youth to answer. Admitting that one has reservations, or voicing opposition to marriage with American Negroes, is in effect, admission of prejudice based on cultural and color differences. To agree even in principle with a stance against Negroes having a choice on who should be their potential spouses is to undermine the Puerto Rican position. If it is possible for a Puerto Rican to be prejudiced against Negroes in America, then it is possible for American-Anglos to be prejudiced towards Puerto Ricans, for similar reasons. This the second generation does not want.

What makes it difficult, then, is the fact that Puerto Ricans *do* express preference in regard to skin color. Deep inside they know that Americans have "legitimate" reasons for prejudice toward Puerto Ricans since they have, perhaps themselves, reasons why they discriminate against blacks. The feelings of insecurity are there.

Interestingly enough, second generation Puerto Ricans believe that even marrying a darker Puerto Rican than oneself is not desirable. Most of the youth simply stated that they expected to marry someone lighter-skinned, but not darker than themselves. Most of them know of Puerto Rican neighbors or had parents or relatives who would oppose their children marrying anyone, whether American Negro or Puerto Rican, who happened to be darker than they were, who could be described as "real black."

In the area of mutual cooperation with American Negroes in pursuit of better wages and against social discrimination, most Puerto Rican youth answered affirmatively. One youth in the Bronx voiced the opinion by stating that while Negroes experienced 100% prejudice, Puerto Ricans experienced about 99% prejudice; so they should work together. Five young Puerto Ricans in Chicago who had actually worked together in an organization with blacks were a little more cautious on the matter. They wanted to know what "together" meant. One young man in Chicago simply said that as long as there is a "fifty-fifty" cooperation at the top of such an organization that is all right, but not otherwise.

One response was somewhat bitter; a young man who obviously had some experience in black endeavors snapped at the question by saying:

When blacks need an extra pair of feet to march, they welcome the Puerto Rican cooperation. When they need an extra voice to shout against injustice, they welcome Puerto Rican cooperation. When they need another head to bleed in the struggle, cooperation is welcomed from their "Latin brothers." But when, as a result of the shouting, the marching, and the bloody head, there is an extra pocket to fill, the Puerto Ricans are suddenly not black enough.

When asked if Puerto Ricans should work with white Anglos in the same way that they would work with Negroes, most of them said, "yes." As one Puerto Rican put it, "Puerto Ricans should work with blacks and whites. The blacks have the power (aggressiveness) and the whites have the money; by working with both groups we can come out on top."

Another dimension in the trials of young Puerto Ricans' search for identity and ethnicity is the issue of just how black can a Puerto Rican become? Afro-American youth see their ultimate unity revolving around the issue of "blackness." The cry is "I am black and beautiful." Puerto Ricans who participate in all black meetings find themselves apprehensive when the anti-white rhetoric reminds them that the "white devil" is just as much a part of his experience as the heritage and concern which make it possible for him to be allowed into such organizations. As Piri Thomas puts it, "It wasn't right to be ashamed of what one was. It was like hating Momma for the color she was and Poppa for the color he wasn't." [13]

If one can be a "Negro" without really trying as Thomas would suggest,[14] then it is quite another matter to be "black." The politics of race in the black movement at times make a distinction between those who are described as "colored," those who are described as "Negroes," and those who are "black." If the society at large determines that racially mixed Puerto Ricans are Negro (using the "one drop" formula), where will the black movement place them? Can Puerto Ricans ever be "black" enough for such groups and still be Puerto Rican?

Puerto Ricans in Chicago, those who had some experience in black organizations, complained that the "black power" movement is too obsessed with "blackness" and not enough with "power," thereby writing off some potential energy from Puerto Ricans who up to that time wanted to embrace their African heritage.

Most Puerto Rican youth interviewed expressed pessimism about their ability to resolve the issue of race and color and identity in their own lives. They have felt that for too long they have been in the middle of blacks and whites receiving the worst from both sides. They were relieved to learn that other Puerto Rican youth were having similar problems over the issue of identity. Some were also glad to hear that an adult, the interviewer, was having a difficult time as well; that while the problem has not been resolved, one can still function and have self-respect. Perhaps that in itself is a very important beginning at resolving the destructive trauma which creates so much confusion in the lives of second generation Puerto Rican adolescents.

It's a good feeling to know that one is not alone when facing critical problems. If more Puerto Rican adults would but share some of their ambivalency and their confusion and end "the conspiracy of silence," it could lead more second generation Puerto Ricans to the conclusion that given the historical experience of Puerto Ricans in the island and in the "barrios" in the mainland, confusion and ambivalency may not be abnormal as all that.

At a time when the governor of Puerto Rico is desperately trying to coin the phrase, "Puerto Rico is our fatherland, but the United States is our nation," confusion and ambivalency may indeed not be as abnormal as all that!

Notes

1. Erik H. Erikson, *Identity, Youth and Crisis* (New York, W. W. Norton and Company, Inc., 1968), p. 297. The phrase "surrendered identity" was borrowed by Erikson from Van Woodward.

2. The U. S. Government declared the residents of Puerto Rico citizens on the eve of the First World War, in 1917.

3. Román López Tames, *El Estado Libre Asociado de Puerto Rico* (Oviedo: Publicaciones del Instituto Jurídico, 1965), pp. 14, 15.

4. Fortunato Vizcarrondo popularized the problem in his famous poem, "Y tu agüela, onde ejta?" Literally translated, it means, "And your grandmother, where is she?"

5. While Jesús Colón's book, *A Puerto Rican in New York: And Other Sketches*, was published in 1961, several years before *Down*

These Mean Streets, the treatment he gives his sketches suggests more of a first generation view of New York City rather than a second generation approach. Colón's formative years were spent in Puerto Rico; see pages 11 to 15 of his book.

6. Eric Williams, "Race Relations in Puerto Rico and the Virgin Islands," *Foreign Affairs* (1945, Vol. 23: 308). As quoted in Renzo Sereno's *Psychiatry*, "Cryptomelanism: A Study of Color Relations and Personal Insecurity in Puerto Rico," Vol. X, 1947, p. 264.

7. "Color is an ingredient, not a determinant of class. It can, therefore, be traded for other ingredients. It is something that can be altered in the individual life, but it is something that can be put right in the next generation." Julian Pitt-Rivers, "Race, Color and Class in Central America and the Andes," *Daedalus: Journal of the American Academy of Arts and Sciences* (Cambridge, Mass., Spring 1967), Vol. 96, p. 556.

8. Pitt-Rivers, *op. cit.*, p. 547.

9. *Ibid.*, p. 550.

10. Joseph Monserrat is guilty of this one-sided type of analysis. See his report, "School Integration: A Puerto Rican View" (New York, the Commonwealth of Puerto Rico, 1966), p. 5.

11. Gordon K. Lewis, *Puerto Rico: Freedom and Power in the Caribbean* (New York, Harper & Row, 1963), p. 286.

12. For example, Nathan Glazer writes in his book: "The Puerto Rican introduced into the city a group that is intermediate in color, neither all white nor all dark, but having some of each, and a large number that show the physical characteristics of both groups. (They) carry new attitudes toward color—and attitudes that may be corrupted by continental color prejudice but it is more likely, since this is in harmony with terms that are making all nations of a single world community, that the Puerto Rican attitude to color, or something like it, will become the New York attitude." *Beyond the Melting Pot* (Cambridge, Ma., M.I.T. Press, 1963), p. 132.

13. Piri Thomas, *Down These Mean Streets* (New York, Signet Books, The New American Library, Inc., 1967), p. 122.

14. *Ibid.*, pp. 124–126.

▼△▼△▼△▼△▼△▼△▼△▼△▼△▼

XXVII. LIFE AND DEATH IN EL BARRIO

El Barrio is the Mecca, the Casbah, the Harlem of the Puerto Rican communities in the United States. It is the *corazón*, the heart, and the *alma*, the soul. Nowadays, there are barrios in many cities, from Boston to Honolulu, from Chicago to Phoenix; but none compare to El Barrio, *the* Barrio. On the edge of Manhattan Island, in the gray city, on gray streets, in gray tenements, beneath gray skies, the dazzling array of the Puerto Rican spirit, rhythm, song, and human drama curses, and shatters, the grayness. In his unpublished novel, *Rhythm Section/Part One*, the barrio poet Víctor Hernández Cruz (1949–   ) (*19 Necromancers from Now*, edited by Ishmael Read, New York, Doubleday, 1970) re-creates the real and surreal life in the barrio. Though best known as a poet, in *Snaps* (New York, Vintage Books, 1969) Hernández Cruz's prose works have an imagery both unique and typical, which reflects and sets the style of many younger barrio writers. And yet the vignettes here included from *19 Necromancers from Now*—"#1 exploration," "#2 trans-atlantic flight," "#6 bodega," "#8 night writers (riding)," "#9 song & dance"—are the literary grandchildren of the old *cuento* tradition on the island, of the intimate, brief, poetic essay; it is only the social and grammatical syntax that has been transformed by city life.

#1 exploration

by Víctor Hernández Cruz

Borinquen is a heavy island. Full of fruits/soft windy days. From the beginning, O the men & women wrapped warmly in their skins. The night fire floats with the spirits, the songs follow the drumming/follow the songs is the timing. The foot steps seek the grass floor, rapidly change song into chant, goes into yelling. The fire moves to the east winds. The hiss of night clouds. Star message from far away solar system, reaches Caribbean islands loud & clear. Boricua is a great name, the hunters follow fish atop blue waves. Tonight the sun falls behind an orange sky, dotted with clouds. The evening smell of burning fish. From across many lands came traders/perhaps Incas or Aztecs. From the Caribbean islands that were fully peopled. Arawak is a pretty name, & god bless the rivers they bathed in. God bless the trees. & O the mighty creator who knows all knowledge/river spirits & mountains that talk. O the singing wilderness full of birds.

Amidst the old women is one who sees things in her nights. A certain glowing vision, a prophetic dreamer, who tells of evil coming. Who knows every plant & herb/who tells how to heal by the wondrous gifts of the creator. She sings her prayers, claps her hands, shakes off evil spirits. She talks to the young girls, & listens. & thanks all her spirits for her happiness, talks to them & helps them in return.

Among the men is one who can hunt. Who stands barefoot in the river & grabs the fish with his hands. He is loved by everyone & he is the father of sons. Thru ages & ages of stillness/good spirits have been encircling the land. & the food has grown tall & good. & the women grow dark & beautiful. One day a strange ship appeared off the island & everyone wondered & wondered what could this mysterious thing be. It came closer.

The old spiritualist woman said, could it be the ship I saw in my dream, could it be. The dream was bad & full of demons & terrible things.

Could it be the devil on the sea?

#2 trans-atlantic flight
by *Víctor Hernández Cruz*

Flight 262 leaves San Juan for New York or Nueva York as my uncle says. The propeller plane took off on time, weirdly floating up & down, above & under clouds. I fell asleep (or did i; that's what i was told). The dream was just as terrible as the flight. The stupid plane went into the eye of a storm halfway across the ocean.

How we got here, who knows, cept i remember the airport. Never had seen so many people excited in my life.

Now i want the dream:

Tropic Star Flight. Fought an eagle in the sky.

They woke me up to give me a special energy pill. They

told the passengers everything was cool/when vultures were splashing their peaks against the wings. I saw the plane (ship of metal) break open with flames & i swung into the air with a sword in my hand. Yelling warrior chants to the birds. Who came after me & i took cover behind clouds, until i got my set up right. & then wham came the edge of my sword ripping/& tearing shit out the beasts. Then i shot down & caught the two parts of the plane before they hit the ground & sawed them in the air with invisible string. & all these Puerto Ricans got here like that.

Some relatives of ours were waiting with heavy coats & sweaters.

& now the tropics behind/exchanged for cement geometric boxes. I felt the cold & knew it was not just the weather, even then, when i still could not say *hey man* right.

#6 bodega

by *Víctor Hernández Cruz*

It is on the corner; bananas hang by the window. It is by a restaurant (*comidas criollas*). The men stand inside & men gossip/taking occasional shots of Don Juan (sneaky pete).

In the bodega *La Perla del Caribe* the numbers man comes at 12/& home relief mothers come down with last nights dreams, which they play for a quarter or half a dollar (or however good the dream was).

En la Bodega you can buy exotic fruits & vegetables, coconut soda called Coco Rico. Long & short rice. Goya beans, pigeon eggs/cardboard ham. Ghost candles of all colors. Bad fish from Brooklyn.

& beer of all kinds, the best seller Schaefer. The police

came to have a can in the back & on Sundays to get some money.

Bodegas are sometimes set up a couple of doors away from each other on the same block. Some blocks can have as many as 6 bodegas.

They buy food from Brooklyn & Bronx warehouses. Some of it really goes out to lunch.

#8 night writers (riding)
by Víctor Hernández Cruz

The party was up the biggest building on Second Ave. Up two crazy Puerto Ricans house. The elevator did not work/the stairs didn't either. Painters like to throw parties, & they are mad happenings usually. He pointed to a gray frame & claimed it/the best in months does exactly what i want it to.

A guy named Dee, he stayed, dragged his ass from 110th street to stay a weekend in a museum world. Dee made it with a schoolteacher in the back seat of her car. Ramon fell asleep in a chair. Going down (again the elevator didn't work) going down the stairs the janitor was sweeping & cursing life in the world, Ballantine dreams come true. On St. Marks Place bells were ringing/people were blaring all their shit. The fake world of pale sheep lost in poverty/hiding from the machines that made them.

I walked toward Tompkins Square Park in the summertime style, my hands in my pockets. The tradition of playing drums in the open air was being practiced, drums were burning under the sky. The music made the trees seem red/as the wind went by them softly. 30 humans were crowded around the Conga players, some following along,

banging beer bottles & sticks together. The drummers spoke
to go/gods & spirits & americans just walked by blabbing
shit.

A timbale player showed up with his sticks/he tightened
up his skins & started talking too. He turned out, you could
hear it a block away, like nature non electric energy burning
thru the trees. Some of the people now started dancing.

Others were just leaning back, their lips parted.

& there was chorus:

> *Que suene la conga*
> *Que suene la conga*
> *Que suene la conga*
> *Ahora*

It got kind of chilly but it was really hot & sweaty. Many
people walked past the street party/only staying at the
nearby corner till the light changed. A woman held onto her
eyes as if the steady drumming would make them jump out.
Dogs were barking far off in the background. A man tried to
hustle dimes for his show/which he performs nightly. He
wanted sweet wine music, trum bak trum bak brak teeeee
tuu brak teeeee tuu came out so mellow/the drum language
of the streets.

I went back to St. Marks & there was Ramon his eyes
wide open 3 in the morning going home.

The trains are loud metal as the train sailed its magic
tunnels we wondered & stared at all the emptiness.

#9 song & dance

by Víctor Hernández Cruz

Summer Time is word singing time. *Rumba para bailar.*
Para gozar. Elements passing thru history. Pachanga lyrics.
Mulatta vén acá. Los cueros te llamen. Palm tree tale behind
maracas, behind guitars the tale of the pirates. La La La big
tall ships from europe brought nothing but rats. Word
mixing jump out the fire.

(Poetry is a very personal thing/all great poems have
been deeply alone.) Town gossip on the air/as Ramito sings
about the mountains.

Graciela sings about fire/*la rumba caliente. Las calles
están en algo.* Sweet street rhymes/the spreading Rumors.

(Popular poetry is songs)

As the Temptations as La Lupe.

Whose dance song ritual moves the spirit to come out.

Latin dance hall is religion/it is very ceremonial. Very
much in tune with Indian & African things.

As the dancers turn & jump & swing the chorus sings
them into lovely orbit.

▼▲▼▲▼▲▼▲▼▲▼▲▼▲▼

XXVIII. WHERE AM I AT?— THE YOUTH

If man is so perverse that he has to lose something before he cherishes it, that may in part explain why the lost youth of the urban barrios, who barely speak Spanish, do not know the island, being born more often in the U.S.A., ignored and forgotten by both societies, so determinedly hold onto a *puertorriqueñismo* they never knew. On the hot rods of Chicago there are more flags of Puerto Rico than in Mayagüez; in the high schools of Hoboken there are more militant *independentistas* than in Ponce. And yet, for all that, the third- or second-generation Rican is a child of anguish. "Where Am I At?" and "A Boycott" by the young Chicago law student Edwin Claudio, voice both the anger and despair, quest and loss of the youth who feels "I am nothing." In the bilingual poems of Jack Agüeros, a community leader on the Lower East Side of New York, "Canción del Tecato" and "El Apatético," the questions are the same, the answers but slightly different in tone; while in "The Straight-Jacket" by Migdalia Rivera, a young Chicago community activist, the question reechoes and the answer becomes an accusation. (*The Rican*, Fall 1971.)

Of all the cries of outrage by the younger barrio writers, none has been more widely printed and read than the *grito* of Pedro Pietri, whose "Puerto Rican Obituary" (*Palante, Young Lords Party*, New York, McGraw-Hill, 1971) has been passed from hand to hand in barrios across the land, in painstakingly handwritten copies. The relentless feeling of Pietri's writing has brought the comment: "He writes as Bertolt Brecht would have written, if he had been Puerto Rican."

WHERE AM I AT?

by Edwin Claudio

Where am I at?
I ask myself
In here or out there
But was in here where I wanted to be?
I, who is that
Patterns of change, changing who?

I
I, who is that
Physical self, physical who?

I
I, who is that
Do not ask for I as I am a
Mystery toward myself,
Caring in such a way that caring is
Not a degree of myself but a degree
Of others.

Can that be so bad?
So confused for words that is
This me on these lines
Or is it
Someone else, who I have never
Met,
That unknown that follows you like
A shadow, as if it was a shadow
Could be drowned out by darkness
So in the finals of all things
I am nothing
But that, which I
Hope will be another
You see my reader
I cannot see where
I am at.

A BOYCOTT

by Edwin Claudio

Like it happened:
  Ricans got together to say *No* to
  an unjust education which says
  you learn the anglo way of life
   Can you dig?
    Wife swapping in nice
    decent suburban homes.

Then we look back and ask how many said NO.
  Listen why don't you look
  at the SPIKS who thought

they were too COOL to walk out?
I mean they were
             "arctic cool"
             "zero cool"
             "ice-cream cool"
             "refrigerated cool"
I mean they were so COOL that they still even to this day
do not realize that they are being systematized. So you can
be your big COOL self.

Spiks, we are in the present and if you LADIES AND
GENTLEMEN don't think that this is your bag because YOU all
look so pretty to come to SCHOOL and do your thing

             then wake up because you
             might look "together" on the
             outside but in-deep
             that's where it counts.

CANCIÓN del TECATO

by Jack Agüeros

Hola Jack, ¿Como estás, bendición, y
Qué Broder? ¿Como está la familia y
Los muchachos? Y Pepe y Catalina,
¿Todavía los ve? Y el grupo,
¿Qué hacen?

No, qué va.
Ya yo no estoy en eso.
Mira Jack,
Dame acá una peseta.

EL APATÉTICO

by Jack Agüeros

Ay, mire Señor, el plás-
ter se cayó, hace un mes
esa agua cae a chorros, el
inodoro no funciona.

Se lo he dicho al lanlor, a los vecinos al anti-
poverty, al super, al maestro de mi hijo, al in-
vestigador, se lo he dicho a tomundo, a toaboca.

Cálmese Señor, me dicen que ya viene el
programa Model Cities.

Cerca de mi ventana rota
Perdido y prisionero en mi sobretodo
Veo las estrellas yo pen-
sando, porqué me pondrían
en este planeta fundido,
Me quedo, y me voy.

THE STRAIGHT-JACKET

by Migdalia Rivera

When one is damaged by a
society as cruel as this, one
must bandage the wounds. But a
sore without air doesn't heal;
it rots and spreads.

Air, yes, freedom—privacy, yes, privacy
to remove the bandage
and apply medication to that sore . . .

My wound has been a sore
with no time for care in
this long hard process of life.
Wrapped in this straight-jacket
                of pretense
my sore refuses to heal.

In my short but painful moments
                of reflections
I see my sore becoming a cancer.
You ask if it is malignant—
give me freedom today
and you shall have your
                answer tomorrow.

PUERTO RICAN OBITUARY

by Pedro Pietri

They worked
They were always on time
They were never late
They never spoke back
When they were insulted
They worked
They never went on strike
Without permission
They never took days off
That were on the calendar

They worked
Ten days a week
And were only paid for five
They worked
They worked
They worked
And they died
They died broke
They died owing
They died never knowing
What the front entrance
Of the first national bank
   looks like

Juan
Miguel
Milagros
Olga
Manuel
All died yesterday today
And will die tomorrow
Passing their bill collectors
on to the next of kin
All died
Waiting for the Garden
   of Eden
To open up again
Under a new management
All died
Dreaming about America
Waking them up in the middle
   of the night
Screaming: Mira! Mira!

Your name is on the winning
   lottery ticket
For one hundred thousand
   dollars
All died
Hating the grocery stores
That sold them make-believe
   steak
And bullet-proof rice and
   beans
All died waiting dreaming
   and hating
Dead Puerto Ricans
Who never knew they were
   Puerto Ricans
Who never took a coffee break
From the ten commandments
to KILL KILL KILL
The landlords of their cracked
   skulls
And communicate with their
   Latin Souls

Juan
Miguel
Milagros
Olga
Manuel
From the nervous breakdown
   streets
Where the mice live like
   millionaires

And the people do not live
   at all
Are dead and were never alive

Juan
Died waiting for his number
   to hit
Miguel
Died waiting for the welfare
   check
To come and go and come
   again
Milagros
Died waiting for her ten
   children
To grow up and work
So she could quit working
Olga
Died waiting for a five
   dollar raise
Manuel
Died waiting for his
   supervisor to drop dead
So that he could get a
   promotion

Is a long ride
From Spanish Harlem
To Long Island cemetery
Where they were buried
First the train
And then the bus
And the cold cuts for lunch
And the flowers

That will be stolen
When visiting hours are over
Is very expensive
Is very expensive
But they understand
Their parents understood
Is a long non-profit ride
From Spanish Harlem
To Long Island cemetery
Juan
Miguel
Milagros
Olga
Manuel
All died yesterday today
And will die again tomorrow
Dreaming
Dreaming about Queens
Clean cut lily white
    neighborhood
Puerto Ricanless scene
Thirty thousand dollar home
The first spics on the block
Proud to belong to a
    community
Of gringos who want them
    lynched
Proud to be a long distance
    away
From the sacred phrase:
    ¿Qué Pasa?

These dreams
These empty dreams

From the make believe
    bedrooms
Their parents left them
Are the after effects
Of television programs
About the ideal
white American family
With Black maids
And Latin janitors
Who are well trained
To make everyone
And their bill collectors
Laugh at them
And the people they represent

Juan
Died dreaming about a new
    car
Miguel
Died dreaming about new
    anti-poverty programs
Milagros
Died dreaming about a trip to
    Puerto Rico
Olga
Died dreaming about real
    jewelry
Manuel
Died dreaming about the Irish
    sweepstakes

They all died
Like a hero sandwich dies
In the garment district

At twelve o'clock in the
afternoon
Social security numbers to
ashes
Union dues to dust
They knew
They were born to weep
And keep the morticians
employed
As long as they pledge
allegiance
To the flag that wants them
destroyed
They saw their names listed
In the telephone directory of
destruction
They were trained to turn
The other cheek by
newspapers
That misspelled who
mispronounced
And misunderstood their
names
And celebrated when death
came
And stole their final laundry
ticket

They were born dead
And they died dead

Is time
To visit Sister López again
The number one healer

And fortune card dealer
In Spanish Harlem
She can communicate
With your late relatives
For a reasonable fee
Good news is guaranteed

Rise Table Rise Table
Death is not dumb and disable
Those who love you want to
    know
The correct number to play
Let them know this right
    away
Rise Table Rise Table
Death is not dumb and disable
Now that your problems are
    over
And the world is off your
    shoulders
Help those who you left
    behind
Find financial peace of mind
Rise Table Rise Table
Death is not dumb and disable
If the right number we hit
All our problems will split
And we will visit your graves
On every legal holiday
Those who love you want to
    know
The correct number to play
Let them know this right
    away

We know your spirit is able
Death is not dumb and disable
RISE TABLE RISE TABLE

Juan
Miguel
Milagros
Olga
Manuel
All died yesterday today
And will die again tomorrow
Hating fighting and stealing
Broken windows from each
    other
Practicing a religion without
    a roof
The old testament
The new testament
According to the gospel
Of the internal revenue
The judge and jury and
    executioner
Protector and eternal bill
    collector

Secondhand shit for sale
Learn how to say Cómo Está
    Usted
And you will make a fortune

They are dead
They are dead
And will not return from the
    dead

Until they stop neglecting
The art of their dialogue
For broken English lessons
To impress the mister bosses
Who keep them employed
As dishwasher porters
    messenger boys
Factory workers maids stock
    clerks
Shipping clerks assistant
    mailroom
Assistant, assistant, assistant,
    assistant
To the assistant, assistant
    dishwasher
And automatic smiling
    doorman
For the lowest wages of the
    ages
And rages when you demand
    a raise
Because it's against the
    company policy
To promote SPICS SPICS SPICS

Juan
Died hating Miguel because
    Miguel's
Used car was in better
    condition
Than his used car
Miguel
Died hating Milagros because
    Milagros

Had a color television set
And he could not afford one
    yet
Milagros
Died hating Olga because
    Olga
Made five dollars more on the
    same job

Olga
Died hating Manuel because
    Manuel
Had hit the numbers more
    times
Than she had hit the numbers
Manuel
Died hating all of them
Juan
Miguel
Milagros
Olga
Because they all spoke broken
    English
More fluently than he did

And now they are together
In the main lobby of the void
Addicted to silence
Under the grass of oblivion
Off limits to the wind
Confined to worm supremacy
In Long Island cemetery
This is the groovy hereafter
The protestant collection box

Was talking so loud and proud
    about

Here lies Juan
Here lies Miguel
Here lies Milagros
Here lies Olga
Here lies Manuel
Who died yesterday today
And will die again tomorrow
Always broke
Always owing
Never knowing
That they are beautiful
    people
Never knowing
The geography of their
    complexion

PUERTO RICO IS A BEAUTIFUL PLACE
PUERTORRIQUEÑOS ARE A
    BEAUTIFUL RACE

If only they
Had turned off the television
And tuned into their own
    imaginations
If only they
Had used the white
    supremacy bibles
For toilet paper purpose
And made their Latin souls
The only religion of their race
If only they

Had returned to the
   definition of the sun
After the first mental
   snowstorm
On the summer of their senses
If only they
Had kept their eyes open
At the funeral of their fellow
   employees
Who came to this country to
   make a fortune
And were buried without
   underwear

Juan
Miguel
Milagros
Olga
Manuel
Will right now be doing their
   own thing
Where beautiful people sing
And dance and work together
Where the wind is a stranger
To miserable weather
   conditions
Where you do not need a
   dictionary
To communicate with your
   hermanos y hermanas
Aquí se habla español all the
   time
Aquí you salute your flag
   first

Aquí there are no Dial soap
    commercials
Aquí everybody smells good
Aquí TV dinners do not have
    a future
Aquí wigs are not necessary
Aquí we admire desire
And never get tired of each
    other
Aquí qué pasa Power is
    what's happening
Aquí to be called negrito y
    negrita
Means to be called LOVE

XXIX. THE MASS OF THE PEOPLE

Where Peter Stuyvesant, the first governor of New Amsterdam, lies buried in a crypt in the walls of the Church of Saint Mark's in the Bowery, there is a Puerto Rican congregation. On the Lower East Side, where generations of the aristocracy of the American Revolution settled, and where later the Irish and the Italian and the Jewish immigrants settled, the new settlers from Puerto Rico have not only changed the neighborhood, they have changed the Masses in the old church. In these Masses and psalms, written in Spanish by Father David García and his parish of barrio poor, the refugees from Borinquen in the United States voice their pains and hopes. (Translated by María Cristina López Kelly.)

MASS OF THE PEOPLE, CHURCH OF SAINT MARK'S IN THE BOWERY

by Father David García

Beginning of the Rite

This service is for the People who united constitute a New Community. A People who is willing to meditate, believe, and participate in a New World where God is the power of Love, Community, Truth, and Justice.

Entrance Hymn

Greeting the People

THE PRESIDENT: We are here in the name of the Father, and the Son, and the Holy Spirit.

THE PRESIDENT AND THE PEOPLE: We are gathered here in the name of Jesus Christ and in the name of all those who have suffered in the struggle for Justice. In the name of Betances, Campos, Torres, Zapata, Bolívar, Ché, Martínez, and all the brothers and sisters among us and with us.

We are present here to demand a New World where men and women from the city and the fields may live and work together.

Kyrie

THE PRESIDENT AND THE PEOPLE: Lord, Lord, Have
mercy, have mercy on us.
 Christ, Christ, Have mercy, have mercy on us.
THE PRESIDENT: Lord have mercy and listen to our
prayers.
THE PEOPLE: Christ have mercy and listen to our prayers.
THE PRESIDENT AND THE PEOPLE: Lord have mercy and
listen to our prayers.

The Word

> Old Testament
> Psalm
> Epistle
> Gradual Hymn
> Gospel
> Homily

The Creed

THE PRESIDENT AND THE PEOPLE: We believe in one God,
Father Almighty, and in
Jesus Christ, His Son,
Who was born of our People.

Christ lived among us
Sharing our fate,
And for us he suffered bitterly
Until his death.

He rose the third day
Thus dominating his death,
He is now and forever will be
at the right hand of the Father.

The Holy Spirit
Who is the fountain of Life,
is in the Church of Christ
Imitating our love.

We believe that Christ will come
Distributing all His wealth.
In this manner we the faithful
believe in our Lord.

Prayer for the Faithful

THE PRESIDENT: Let us pray brother and sister aloud or in
silence for_____.

After each prayer, the people answer.

THE PEOPLE: We beg you, listen to us!

THE PRESIDENT: Oh Lord, listen to our pleas and accept
our prayer!

The Peace

THE PRESIDENT: The peace of the Lord be with you, but
remember that peace cannot exist where there is
oppression and not freedom.

THE PEOPLE: Peace, Power, Love!

The Offertory

—What must be milled
To become bread.
—Grapes must be crushed
To become wine.
—The people must be liberated
In order to change the world.

THE PRESIDENT:

With this wine and this bread
We offer to you, Our Father,

All our sorrows and our joys,
Our work and our homes.
—These gifts are the symbol
of our struggle for unity—
A struggle which is carried on
by men and women
in the fields and in the cities.
—We the people, offer you,
With the gifts at the altar,
All that is nature
In our yearning for freedom.

Thanksgiving

THE PRESIDENT: Let us give thanks.

THE PEOPLE: Yes, but why should we be grateful?

THE PRESIDENT: We give thanks to God and we praise all His history which comes to us in the Scriptures. We thank Him for all men and women who have fought for the liberation of the people, just as Jesus Christ fought in Israel.

THE PEOPLE: Yes, Let us give thanks to God!

THE PRESIDENT: Jesus Christ, a man on earth, walked among us in a world of conflicts and oppression. He entrusted us to remember His death, through which we were freed, and to fight for Him until He returned.

We remember His love for His people and His fight against hunger, sickness, and poverty.

THE PEOPLE: We remember His death, we live His example, we await His resurrection. We see Him in our brothers and sisters throughout Latin America, Africa and Asia; together with them we offer ourselves for their liberation and ours.

THE PRESIDENT: The night that He was betrayed, Jesus

Christ took the bread, broke it, and gave it to His
friends, saying:

Eat all of you, because this is My Body which
will be given to you.

In the same manner, He took the Chalice, Gave Thanks,
and gave it to His friends saying: Drink all of you,
for this is the Chalice of My Blood, Blood of the
new and Eternal Alliance. Do this in remem-
brance of me.

THE PEOPLE: Amen.

THE PRESIDENT: Send your Spirit of Life and Power, Glory
and Love among us, personifying this Bread and
this Wine, Your Body and Blood.

Together with all the men and women who have been,
are and shall be, Let us sing with joy.

THE PRESIDENT AND THE PEOPLE: Holy! Holy! Holy! Our
Father, creator of Heaven and Earth, Give us your
grace. Hosanna in the Highest!

THE PRESIDENT: Let us pray according to our faith and
hope.

THE PRESIDENT AND THE PEOPLE:

Our father who are in Heaven
Blessed be your name
Your kingdom come,
Your will be done, on earth as it
is in Heaven.
Give us this day our daily bread
And forgive us our trespasses
as we forgive those who trespass
against us.
Lead us not into temptation
But deliver us from evil
For yours is the Power and the Glory
Forever and ever. Amen.

Communion

THE PRESIDENT: Jesus Christ offers Himself for us at this
        supper.

THE PEOPLE: Let us partake of this meal.

THE PRESIDENT: The meal of God, for the people of
        God—

   Body of Christ (*He says this to each person as they take
   the bread.*)

   Blood of Christ (*He says this to each person as they take
   the wine.*)

Gloria

THE PRESIDENT AND THE PEOPLE:

        Glory to God in the highest
        And on earth peace to men.
        His good will lives in he
        who loves truth.

        We give praise and glory.
        We thank you ceaselessly,
        We adore you, we adore you,
        Our Heavenly Father.

        You who take away sin,
        Being the Paschal victim;
        You who never forget your people,
        Have mercy on us.

        Because you alone are holy,
        Jesus Christ have mercy,

        You who are seated at the
        right hand of God Our Father Immortal.

        Divine Spirit we always

invoke you, and in your love
We live in perfect unity.

Farewell

THE PRESIDENT AND THE PEOPLE: This meal has ended.
    Blessed are the people
    Who live in the name of the Lord.
THE PEOPLE: Amen. We are blessed.
THE PRESIDENT AND THE PEOPLE: Let us go in the name of
    the Lord to defend our people. Amen.

ORDER FOR HOLY MATRIMONY, CHURCH OF SAINT MARK'S IN THE BOWERY

by Father David García

This service is for the People, who united constitute a New
Community. The People who are willing to meditate,
believe, and participate in a New World where God is the
power of Love, Community, Truth, and Justice.

Brothers and sisters, and all those who fight for the
    People:
We are gathered here, in front of this group, in the midst
    of oppression, with the purpose of uniting in Holy
    matrimony this man and this woman, so that they
    may become one body in the struggle for libera-
    tion.
Matrimony is not something that should be taken lightly;
    this union will produce one of the greatest re-
    sources we can have: liberated children and
    liberated families, a very good example for the
    People.

Before declaring this couple man and wife, let us think about the Revolution.

First Reading

Silence

Second Reading

Betrothal
(*Name*), Do you take this sister as your wife, and do you promise to live together according to the wishes of God, that men and women be free? Will you remain with her till one of you dies?

Answer: I will.

The President asks the same questions to the sister, making the appropriate changes in the wording.

The President will then ask:
Who is giving this sister to be united in matrimony to this brother?

Everyone present answers:
We are.

I, (*Name*), take you, (*Name*), as my wife from this day on, in spite of the increase in oppression, fear, torture, and confusion. I also promise to continue fighting for the People until liberation is attained or until death forces me to be silent.

The wife will make the same promises to her husband.

The husband will give the ring to his wife, or they will exchange rings, saying:
With this ring I marry you,
With my body I will worship you:
Everything that I am and possess
I give to you.

ALL THE PEOPLE: Long live Free Puerto Rico!

Offertory

Ecclesiastics

Communion

When everyone has received Communion, the President will hold the hands of the married couple in his, and he will say:

          _____ and _____ have united themselves in matrimony and they have sworn in the presence of these brothers and sisters to commit themselves to the liberation of all the people who are prisoners under capitalism. Above all, they should never allow themselves to deviate from this path and work.

ALL THE PEOPLE: Yes.

PSALM 5,
LISTEN TO MY PROTEST

by Father David García

Listen to my words, O Lord, hear my moaning.
Listen to my protest.
Because You are not a friend of dictators
nor a partisan of their politics.
You are not influenced by propaganda
And You are not a partner of the gangster.

There is no truth in their speeches,
nor in their statements to the press.

They talk about peace,
while they increase the war production.

They talk about peace in their peace conferences,
And secretly they are preparing for war.

Their desks are covered with criminal plans and sinister
   files.
But You will save me from their plans.

They speak with machine-gun mouths,
Their shiny tongues are the bayonets.

Punish them, O God, abort their politics.
Confuse their memorandums, and stop their programs.

At the hours of the alarm signal,
You will be with me.
You will be my refuge the day of the Bomb.

You will bless he who doesn't believe in
the lies of their commercials and
their political campaigns.
You will surround him with love
as if it were a line of armored tanks.

PSALM 21,
WHY HAVE YOU FORGOTTEN ME?

by Father David García

My God, my God, why have You forgotten me?
I am a caricature of a man, the scorn of the people.
All the newspapers ridicule me.
I am surrounded by armored tanks,
Machine guns are aimed at me,

I am fenced in by wire, high-voltage fences.
They call my name all day,
I have been branded with a number.
I have been photographed at the wire fences
and one can count every bone in my body.

They have taken away all my identification
and I have been taken naked to the gas chambers,
while they divide my clothes and shoes.

I scream for morphine and no one listens,
I scream in a straitjacket,
I scream all night in the mental health ward,
    in the room for incurable cases,
    in the wing for contagious diseases,
    in the home for old folks.
I struggle in a bath of perspiration in the psychiatrist's
   office,
I suffocate in the oxygen tent.
I cry at the police station,
    in the prison yard,
    in the torture chambers,
    in the orphanage.
I am contaminated with radioactivity
    and no one comes near me.
But I will be able to talk about You
To my brothers.
I will praise You when my people
come together.
My hymns will echo in the midst of a great people.

The poor will have a banquet,
They will celebrate a great feast:
The birth of a New Nation.

NOTES ABOUT THE CONTRIBUTORS

(in order of their appearance)

JUAN de CASTELLANOS
(1522–1607)

A poet and chronicler, Juan de Castellanos was born in Alanís, a small town in the province of Seville, and died in Tunja, Colombia. He lived in Puerto Rico and was also familiar with several countries of the New World. His famous work, *Elegies of Illustrious Men of the Indies,*° is the longest epic poem in the Spanish language. The Sixth Elegy deals with the conquest of Puerto Rico and is dedicated to Ponce de León.

RICARDO E. ALEGRÍA
(1921–)

An anthropologist and folklorist who was born in San Juan, Alegría has been the executive director of the Institute of Puerto

° Most titles of works are given in English for greater clarity.

Rican Culture since its creation in 1955. He has developed an extraordinary activity in all aspects of the historical, artistic, and literary life of the country. Author of many books dealing with the prehistoric Indian cultures of the island, he is also known for his research on the feast of Saint James in Loíza Aldea, published in 1954 as *La Fiesta de Santiago en Loíza Aldea*. The tale included in this anthology has also been staged as a ballet.

CAYETANO COLL y TOSTE
(1850–1930)

Coll y Toste was a historian and author of many famous Indian stories and legends. Born in Arecibo, he studied medicine in Barcelona and took a prominent part in the political life of his time. His immense contribution to the culture of Puerto Rico is embodied in the research gathered by him. He was editor of the *Historical Bulletin of Puerto Rico* from 1914 to 1927.

DAMIÁN LÓPEZ de HARO
(1581–1648)

Bishop of Puerto Rico, he became famous in the island's literature for a letter written to his friend Juan Díaz de la Calle, describing his trip and the local conditions upon his arrival in San Juan. He inserts a sonnet in this long descriptive letter that is a sketch of the "tiny island" with realistic traits and not a little humor.

JUAN RODRÍGUEZ CALDERÓN
(1775–1839)

Poet Juan Rodríguez Calderón was born in La Coruña, Spain. A soldier, he deserted the Army, fled to France, and was exiled to the island of Puerto Rico toward 1797. He is reputed to have founded the town of San Lorenzo. A learned man and an adventurer, in his poetry devoted to Puerto Rico he reveals a grateful attitude and a precision in observing nature.

SANTIAGO VIDARTE
(1827–1848)

A Romantic poet, Vidarte was born in Humacao and died in Barcelona, Spain, where he was studying at the time. He is published in *The Puerto Rican Album* and *The Song Book of Borinquen.* Vidarte is considered the first important poet from the island.

LUIS LLORÉNS TORRES
(1878–1944)

Born in Juana Díaz and died in San Juan, Lloréns Torres was a poet, journalist, and famous lawyer who also cultivated the theater and the historical essay. He distinguished himself in the Modernist movement with his poetic theories of "panedism" and "pancalism." Among his works are *Voices of the Big Bell* (1935) and *Heights of America* (1940). We have selected for this anthology three examples of his literary output: a short poem,

"Vida Criolla"; an act of his play *The Cry of Lares;* and his famous poem to Bolívar. (See Part VII.)

MANUEL A. ALONSO
(1822–1889)

Born in San Juan, Alonso lived in Caguas and was educated in Barcelona, where he studied surgery. He died in San Juan. A "custombrist" writer, his principal work, *El Jíbaro (The Peasant)* (1849), constitutes an important contribution to Puerto Rican literature. Written in verse and prose, it reflects, with grace and spirit, the reality of town and country life, describes the language of the peasant and his traditions, and expresses the author's concern regarding education, the political situation, and social conditions in the land.

EUGENIO MARÍA de HOSTOS
(1839–1903)

Hostos, the great patriot and educator, was born in Mayagüez and died in Santo Domingo. He studied in Spain, and in his journeys through several American countries he was acknowledged for his superior qualities as a teacher, sociologist, and thinker. The author of numerous political, social, and educational books, he was also the author of a romantic novel, *The Pilgrimage of Bayaón*. He is considered one of the foremost Latin American essayists of the nineteenth century.

MARGOT ARCE de VÁZQUEZ
(1904–)

Essayist, literary critic and professor, born in Caguas and resident in Hato Rey, her literary life has been closely connected to her university chair. Her most important published works are *Garcilaso de la Vega* (1931), *Impressions* (1950), *Gabriela Mistral: Person and Poetry* (1958), and studies on José de Diego and other Puerto Rican writers.

RAMÓN EMETERIO BETANCES
(1827–1898)

Born in Cabo Rojo, Betances studied medicine in Paris, where he lived most of his life. A great intellectual, he became a translator from Latin, journalist, and fiction writer in French. He wrote a play, some poems, and the romantic novel *La Vierge de Borinquen* (1859). As a patriot, a revolutionary, and abolitionist, he was the author of many pronouncements and manifestos, and his "Ten Commandments of Free Men," (Saint Thomas, November 4, 1867) is considered a significant political document. Although his whole life was dedicated to the fight for Puerto Rican independence, he died without fulfilling his dream, as happened to Hostos and other of his contemporaries.

LOLA RODRÍGUEZ de TIÓ
(1843–1924)

Poet and patriot, born in San Germán, she lived in exile in several countries and died in Cuba. Her poetry is collected in several volumes: *My Songs* (1876), *Clarities and Mists* (1885), and *My Book of Cuba* (1893). In the struggle for independence, her name is linked to the Cry of Lares, since at that time she wrote the patriotic verses of *La Borinqueña*, the national anthem of Puerto Rico.

JOSÉ GAUTIER BENÍTEZ
(1851–1880)

A Romantic poet who was born in Caguas and died in San Juan, José Gautier Benítez is considered the most refined lyrical poet of the nineteenth century on the island. His work is collected in a single volume titled simply *Poetry* (1880), reprinted and prefaced by diverse critics on different occasions. His favorite themes were the fatherland and love.

FRANCISCO ÁLVAREZ MARRERO
(1847–1881)

A poet born in Manatí, where he lived until his death, Francisco Álvarez Marrero cultivated lyric poetry with delicate refinement and profound Romanticism. Manuel Fernández Juncos published his work *Flowers of a Broom Patch* and the play *God Everywhere* in a volume he titled *Literary Works of Francisco Álvarez Marrero* (1881).

PACHÍN MARÍN
(1863–1897)

Romantic poet Pachín Marín was born in Arecibo and died in the battlefields of Cuba. A patriot who fought for Puerto Rican independence and lived exiled in several countries, he founded a weekly, *El Postillón* and published several books, among which are prominent *Ballads* (1892) and *On the Sand* (1898).

JOSÉ MERCADO
(1863–1911)

A festive poet of great versatility, José Mercado was born in Caguas and died in Cuba. His work *Kindlings* (1900) has been highly praised. He used the pen name MOMO and distinguished himself in Puerto Rican journalism, having founded several newspapers. Besides his facility for writing satirical verses, he expressed in patriotic poems his love of Hispanic culture.

MANUEL ZENO GANDÍA
(1855–1930)

Novelist Manuel Zeno Gandía, born in Arecibo and died in San Juan, was a renowned doctor of medicine as well as a famous Realistic and Naturalistic fiction writer. His place in the literature of Puerto Rico is based mainly on the series of novels in which he describes the social and economic conditions of the island—*The Stagnant Pool* (1894), *Marten* (1896), *The Deal* (1922), and *The*

Redeemers (1925)—in which he presents the situation created during the first years of American political influence in San Juan.

MIGUEL MELÉNDEZ MUÑOZ
(1884–1966)

A prose writer, who was born and died in Cayey. He cultivated the essay, novel, and short story, and was a faithful interpreter of the lives and struggles of the peasants. Two of his works are *Stories of the Cedar* (1936) and *Stories of the Central Highway* (1941).

JOSÉ PADÍN
(1886–1963)

Essayist and educator, José Padín was born in San Juan and died in Hato Rey. He held the position of Commissioner of Education in Puerto Rico and later became one of the editors of D. C. Heath & Company in Boston. His labors as a writer are dispersed in magazines and newspapers, and in 1951 his essays *Persons on Things* was published, and in 1967 *Puerto Rican Sketches*.

NEMESIO R. CANALES
(1878–1923)

Essayist and humorist of the Modernist period, Canales was born in Jayuya and died in New York. His most famous work, *Paliques* (1913), reflects his free spirit and his leanings toward social satire. He also cultivated the theater, being the author of a work titled

The Galloping Hero (1923). He distinguished himself in journalism along with Lloréns Torres, with whom he collaborated in several undertakings.

ANTONIO S. PEDREIRA
(1899–1939)

Essayist, professor, and scholar, Pedreira was born in San Juan and died in Hato Rey. He was the initiator of a conscience of evaluation of Puerto Rican literature and culture that continues till the present. He was a distinguished university professor and the author of very valuable books of erudition: *Hostos, Citizen of America* (1932), *Puerto Rican Bibliography* (1932), and *Insularismo* (1934), his most famous work.

MARÍA TERESA BABÍN
(1910–)

(See "Notes About the Editors," following the Acknowledgments.)

CONCHA MELÉNDEZ
(1904–)

Literary critic and scholar, professor emeritus of the University of Puerto Rico, Concha Meléndez was born in Caguas. Her contribution to Spanish American literature has been recognized everywhere. At present she is engaged in compiling her *Complete Works*, which include, among others, *The Indianista Novel in Spanish America* (1934), *Signs of Iberoamerica* (1936), and *Pablo*

Neruda: Life and Work (1936). She has also written on many Puerto Rican writers, such as José de Diego, Enrique Laguerre, and René Marqués.

TOMÁS BLANCO
(1897–   )

Essayist, novelist, and poet, Tomás Blanco was born in Santurce. He studied medicine, but his whole life has been dedicated to literature and historical research. He represents the Puerto Rican intellectual who deeply feels a moral commitment to the homeland. He has also lived in Spain and traveled in Europe and the United States, where he has contributed articles published in many important journals and magazines. Among his most significant books are *Historical Synopsis of Puerto Rico* (1935); a novel, *The Bards* (1949); *The Infant's Christmas Gifts* (1954); *Letras para Cantar* (*Verses for Singing*) (1962), poetry; and *The Five Senses* (1955).

NILITA VIENTÓS GASTÓN
(1908–   )

Essayist, lawyer, and journalist, born in San Sebastián and residing in Santurce, Nilita Vientós Gastón has devoted her life to intellectual pursuits, and has distinguished herself as president of the Atheneum of Puerto Rico, as well as being the editor of the review *Asomante*. Presently she is the editor of a new review, *Sin Nombre*, and teaches courses at the University of Puerto Rico. She has published a critical study on Henry James, and her newspaper articles, *Cultural Index*, have been published by the University of Puerto Rico.

LUIS PALÉS MATOS
(1899–1959)

A poet who became famous for his book of Afro-Antillean themes, *Tun Tun de Pasa y Grifería* (1937), Luis Palés Matos was born in Guayama and died in San Juan. He cultivated poetry from the Modernist stage to post-Modernism and ultra-Modernism. With another writer, de Diego Padró, he created a movement that they called, in collaboration, Diepalism, by joining syllables of their last names. His complete work, *Poetry*, has been published by the University of Puerto Rico Press. It includes, besides Negro poems, his poems on patriotic and love themes. Palés Matos is one of the most famous Puerto Rican authors in Spanish American literature.

FRANCISCO ARRIVÍ
(1915–   )

Playwright, poet, and essayist, Arriví was born in San Juan. He has excelled in the theater as author and director of the drama festivals of the Institute of Puerto Rican Culture. His experience as teacher and radio commentator and his dedication to the development of a national theater are merged in his active and energetic work. Among his best-known plays are *María Soledad* (1947), *Bachelors' Club* (1953), and *Vejigantes* (1965).

JOSÉ A. BALSEIRO
(1900–   )

Essayist, poet, and novelist, Balseiro was born in San Juan. He has resided in the United States for several years, where he has been a professor in various universities. Some of his best-known works are the essays entitled *The Lookout* (musical and literary criticism; first volume, 1925) and *Expression of Hispano-America* (1968), the poetry *Nostalgia of Puerto Rico* (1946), and the novel *Human Gratitude* (1972). He is one of the best-known literary critics in Spain and Latin America.

LUIS MUÑOZ RIVERA
(1859–1916)

Politician, journalist, and poet, Luis Muñoz Rivera was born in Barranquitas and died in Santurce. His labors in the defense of rights and autonomy led him to occupy high positions in government, among them that of Resident Commissioner in Washington. His poetry is of a virile, combative essence, his most representative work being *Tropicals* (1902).

LUIS MUÑOZ MARÍN
(1898–　)

Luis Muñoz Marín—political leader, journalist, and poet—was born in San Juan. While studying and living in the United States he started to write poetry and to work as translator and journalist. He was active in Puerto Rico as a politician since his early youth, as a member of the Socialist and the Liberal parties, until the Popular Democratic Party came into being under his leadership. In 1948 he was elected governor, thus becoming the first Puerto Rican elected by the people for that post. His democratic credo is embodied in his ideal of the "free associated state" or Puerto Rican Commonwealth as represented in the Constitution of 1952. His speeches are written in a very personal and interesting prose style, and his poetry reveals his social consciousness.

JOSÉ de DIEGO
(1866–1918)

Poet and patriot, José de Diego was born in Aguadilla and died in New York. A defender of independence and Puerto Rican culture, he dedicated speeches and poems to the symbols of the homeland and the vernacular language of his country. His works are saturated with Romantic passion in Modernist verses of rhythmic intonations. Among his published works are *Jovillos* (1911), *Rose Apples* (1904), *Songs of Rebellion* (1916), and *Songs of the Kingbird* (1950).

GILBERTO CONCEPCIÓN de GRACIA
(1909–1968)

Doctor of Law, political leader, and writer, Gilberto Concepción de Gracia was born in Vega Alta and died in San Juan. After his initiation in, and separation from, the Nationalist movement, he became the first leader of the Puerto Rican Independence Party. He lived in New York and Washington, D.C., for many years, and he distinguished himself as a journalist and orator. As a member of the Puerto Rican legislature, and of Stacom (Commission on Status), he contributed greatly to the ideas and the laws enacted, but he finally resigned from Stacom when he realized there was a conflict between his ideal of independence and the commission's position.

PEDRO ALBIZU CAMPOS
(1891–1965)

Doctor of Law and political leader, Pedro Albizu Campos was born in Ponce, studied at Harvard University, and died in San Juan. Heir to Betances, he became the inspiration and leader of the Nationalist Party. He suffered imprisonment several times for his political activities, and he died shortly after he was set free. His style as a political orator, his fervent appeal to the people, his missionary and militant discipline, and his quest for independence contributed to make him a patriotic symbol for the new generations.

VIRGILIO DÁVILA
(1869–1943)

Regionalist and "custombrist" poet, who adopted the techniques of style and versification from Modernism, Virgilio Dávila was born in the town of Toa Baja, but lived the rest of his life in Bayamón where he was a schoolteacher, businessman, and farmer, and obtained the post of mayor. His most famous works are *Aromas of the Land* (1916) and *A Little Town of Yesteryear* (1917).

JOSÉ ANTONIO DÁVILA
(1898–1941)

Poet, doctor of medicine, and translator from English to Spanish and vice versa, Dávila was born and died in Bayamón, the son of

Virgilio Dávila. Some of his works are *Harvest* (1940), *Trinket Shop* (1941), *Tristan's Motives* (1957), and *Poems* (1964).

FÉLIX FRANCO OPPENHEIMER
(1912–   )

Poet and professor, Oppenheimer was born in Ponce. He has been an active poet in the movements with philosophical tendencies, such as Transcendentalism. His most important books are *Man and his Anguish* (1950) and *Of Time and its Figure* (1956).

FRANCISCO MATOS PAOLI
(1915–   )

Poet Francisco Matos Paoli, born in Lares, has suffered periods of imprisonment for his *independentista* ideas, and has been linked to the poetic vanguard movements, such as Transcendentalism and Integralism. Some of his books are *Dweller of the Echo* (1941), *Theory of Oblivion* (1944), and *Song to Puerto Rico* (1950).

FRANCISCO LLUCH MORA
(1925–   )

Poet and professor Francisco Lluch Mora was born in Yauco. He has taken part with other poets in vanguard literary movements and has been editor of the review *Atenea*. Among his most famous works are *Of Siege and Closure* (1950) and *From Clay to God* (1954); he is also known for his contributions to literary criticism.

EVARISTO RIBERA CHEVREMONT
(1896–)

A poet of great versatility, Evaristo Ribera Chevremont was born in San Juan and lives in the Condado section of Santurce. He has been a fount of inspiration and stimulus for many poets of younger generations. His poetry started with Modernism, but has advanced along renovating, vanguard lines toward the expression of his personal "I." Some of his works are *Color* (1938), *The Pensive Flame* (1954) and several anthologies that gather poems from diverse periods.

JULIA de BURGOS
(1916–1953)

Poet Julia de Burgos was born in Carolina and died in New York. She has been considered, by critics, one of the greatest of the women poets in Latin American literature. Her books are *Poems in Twenty Furrows* (1938), *Song of the Simple Truth* (1939), and *The Sea and You* (posthumous, 1954).

LUIS HERNÁNDEZ AQUINO
(1907–)

Poet, professor, and journalist, Luis Hernández Aquino was born in Lares. He belonged to the "atalayista" and "integralist" movements. He has collaborated actively in several magazines, and founded *Bayaón*. Among his works are: *Island for Anguish* (1943), *Voice in Time* (1952), *Still Water* (1939), and *Poems of the*

Brief Life (1940). He has done several scholarly studies on language and poetry, and in collaboration with other authors has prepared a number of anthologies.

GUSTAVO AGRAIT
(1909–   )

Poet, professor, and TV commentator, Agrait was born in San Germán. He has held posts in advertising firms, and has been in charge of a television program called *Cardinal Points*, in which he analyzes and presents problems of interest. He has published a thesis on the "Beatus Ille," poems in magazines, and *Variations on Obsessive Themes* (1932–1966).

FRANCISCO MANRIQUE CABRERA
(1908–   )

Poet and professor, born in Bayamón, Cabrera lives in Río Piedras and he is considered one of the best Puerto Rican lyric poets of the twentieth century. He is the author of the first *History of Puerto Rican Literature*, published in 1956. His poems have appeared in literary reviews and his book *Poems of My Land, Land*, was published in 1936.

JUAN AVILÉS
(1905–   )

Poet Juan Avilés was born in San Sebastián, but has lived in New York for over forty-five years. His poems are dispersed in newspapers and reviews. He has published three books: *Songs of Morning*, *Shadowless Roads*, and *Next-to-last Canto*, which gathers his poetry from 1921 to 1971.

OLGA RAMÍREZ de ARELLANO NOLLA
(1911–   )

Poet Olga Ramírez de Arellano Nolla, born in San Germán, lives in Mayagüez. Some of her works are *Deep Bed*, *The Fecund Rose-Garden*, *Sea of Poetry*, *The Land of Transparency*, and *Diary of the Mountain*. She is a deeply emotional writer whose main themes are nature and love.

JOSÉ P. H. HERNÁNDEZ
(1892–1922)

Poet José P. H. Hernández was a native of Hatillo, where he lived and died. A lover of music and literary gatherings, he led a tranquil life devoted to his creative labors. Among his works are *Couplets from the Path* (1919), *The Last Combat* (1921), and *Songs of the Sierra* (1925).

MANUEL JOGLAR CACHO
(1898–   )

Poet Manuel Joglar Cacho was born in Morovis but resides in Manatí, where he is a businessman. He showed a creative vocation from an early age, and has published beautiful books. Among these the critics have praised *Lazaro's Soliloquies* (1956), *Songs to *the Angels* (1957), *On the Paths of Day* (1958), *Last Furrow* (1960), and *The Thirsty Water* (1961). He has received several prizes for his poetry.

JUAN ANTONIO CORRETJER
(1908–)

Both poet and patriot, Corretjer was born in Ciales. From his youth he took part in the struggles of the Nationalist Party. He, along with other defenders of Puerto Rican independence, was detained in custody in Atlanta, Georgia, in 1935 for his political activities, and he has been imprisoned on other occasions for his rebelliousness; he has always acted according to his political ideal. His poetry is a manifesto against tyranny and a lyrical song to liberty. He has also been editor of the newspaper *Hispanic Pueblo* in New York. Some of his works are *Agüeybana* (1932), *Ulysses* (1933), *Love of Puerto Rico* (1937), *Song of War* (1937), *Native Land* (1951), *Praise in Ciales Tower* (1953), and *Witch Grass* (1957).

JUAN MARTÍNEZ CAPÓ
(1923–)

A poet and journalist who was born in Aibonito, Martínez Capó lives in San Juan. He has devoted his life to journalism and poetry, and his contributions to literary criticism have been maintained through weekly reviews of books he publishes in *El Mundo*. In 1961 his first book of poetry, *Voyage*, was published with a prologue by María Teresa Babín. He has continued writing poetry that he occasionally publishes in Puerto Rican literary magazines.

JORGE LUIS MORALES
(1930–   )

Poet and professor, Jorge Luis Morales was born in Ciales. He has shown from his early youth a consistent dedication to poetry. He is the author of *Metal and Stone* (1952), *The Window and I* (1960), and *Poetic Anthology* (1968).

VIOLETA LÓPEZ SURIA
(1929–   )

Poet and professor, Violeta López Suria was born in Barceloneta and lives in San Juan. She has published several books, among which are found *Drops of May* (1953), *A Few Stars in My Room* (1957), *Flood* (1958), and *The Skin Stuck to the Soul* (1962).

DIANA RAMÍREZ de ARELLANO
(1919–   )

Poet and professor, she was born in New York, where she teaches literature. She has published several books of poems, of which *I Am Ariel* (1947) and *Albatross on the Soul* (1955) are very well known. She has been awarded several prizes for her poetry.

CLEMENTE SOTO VÉLEZ
(1904–   )

Born in Lares, Clemente Soto Vélez became known in the 1930 decade as a poet of the "atalayista" group. As a follower of Albizu's National movement he was jailed in Atlanta, and after serving his term, he remained in New York City, where he has made his home. His first poems are included in all the anthologies concerned with the ultramodern movements in Puerto Rican letters. His most recent books are *Internal Embrace, Trees,* and *The Promised Land* (unpublished).

ANDRÉS CASTRO RÍOS
(1942–   )

Representative of a new generation, the author of *Just Death* (1967), Andrés Castro Ríos is one of the university students who became known in the magazine *Guajana.* His poems appear in two anthologies: *Anthology of Young Poets* (1965) and *New Puerto Rican Poetry* (1971).

CÉSAR ANDRÉU IGLESIAS
(1910–   )

A novelist and journalist, César Andréu Iglesias has been an active politician, defender of independence and socialist ideas. He was a visiting professor at Hunter College in 1970–1971, and presently he lives in Puerto Rico. For many years he worked as a columnist for the newspaper *The Impartial.* His most famous novels are *The Vanquished* (1956) and *A Drop of Time* (1958).

JOSÉ I. de DIEGO PADRÓ
(1896–   )

José I. de Diego Padró, novelist and poet, was born in Vega Baja and lives in San Juan. He created the "Diepalist" movement together with Palés Matos in 1921. His contribution to the novel is of great significance, for he advances existential techniques in the narrative and brings original insight to the art of the novel. In poetry his best-known works are *The Last Lamp of the Gods* (1921) and *Vagabond Epistles* (1952). His novels are *Absent-minded* (1961), *Time Played with Me* (1960), *The Minotaur Devours Itself* (1965), and *A Cowbell with Two Clappers* (1969).

JULIO MARRERO NUÑEZ
(1910–   )

A playwright and short-story writer, Julio Marrero Nuñez was born in San Juan, where he held the post of historian for the National Park Service. His love for old buildings in old San Juan, his dedication to the knowledge of military architecture as represented in El Morro fortress, Fortaleza palace and San Cristóbal fort, and so on, have provoked in his spirit the desire to narrate episodes about these sites. He is the author of the play *Borinquen* (1946) and *Stories of San Felipe del Morro* (1963).

ENRIQUE A. LAGUERRE
(1906–   )

A novelist and university professor, born in Moca, Enrique A. Laguerre has written short stories, dramatic works, essays, and newspaper articles. Among his most famous works are *The Flare-up* (1935), *Solar Montoya* (1941), *The 30th of February* (1943), *The Undertow* (1949), *The Fingers of the Hands* (1951), *The Labyrinth* (1960), *The Ceiba in the Pot* (1961), and his most recent, *The Fire and Its Air* (1970).

ANTONIO OLIVER FRAU
(1902–1945)

A short-story writer and lawyer, born in Arecibo, Antonio Oliver Frau lived in Lares and died in Ponce. His literary fame is based on his book *Narrations and Legends from the Coffee Plantation* (1938). In these stories he offers a vision of rural customs, with insight on economic questions and political changes affecting Puerto Rico.

WILFREDO BRASCHI
(1918–)

A journalist and short-story writer born in New York, Wilfredo Braschi is a professor at the University of Puerto Rico who has devoted his life to journalism. His book *Cuatro Caminos* (*Travel Chronicles*) was published in 1963. He later published *Metropolis* (1968), a collection of very interesting stories.

ABELARDO DÍAZ ALFARO
(1917–)

Short-story writer Abelardo Díaz Alfaro was born in Vega Baja, has lived in Caguas and Ponce, but has settled in Río Piedras. He writes programs for radio and television, inspired themes related to the traditional customs of his land. His most famous book is *Terrazo* (1947).

JOSÉ LUIS GONZÁLEZ
(1926–   )

A short-story writer, born in Santo Domingo, González has lived in Puerto Rico since childhood, although he has resided in Mexico for several years. He is an "engagé" writer with ideas of social redemption. Among his best-known books are *Five Blood Stories* (1945), *The Man in the Street* (1948), *Paisa* (1950) and *La Galería* (1972).

MANUEL MÉNDEZ BALLESTER
(1909–   )

A dramatist, journalist and novelist, Méndez Ballester was born in Aguadilla and has distinguished himself in politics, having held seats in the island legislature as a member of the Popular Party. His most important works are the historical novel *Cerrera Island* (1937) and the plays *Dead Time* (1940), *The Clamor of the Furrows* (1938), *Crossroad* (1958), *The Miracle* (1960), and *The Fair* (1963). He has collaborated in the press and on the radio with a column titled "The Human Condition."

LUIS QUERO CHIESA
(1911–)

A short-story writer and painter, Luis Quero Chiesa was born in Ponce. He moved to New York in 1929, and after a brief stay in Puerto Rico, settled in New York permanently. He was elected president of the Board of Higher Education of the City University of New York in 1972. His short stories have been published in magazines and newspapers, and there are three included in anthologies of Puerto Rican short-story writers: *José Campeche, The Protest,* and *Behind That Little Light.*

ROY BROWN
(1946–)

Singer and folklorist, Roy Brown was born in Florida, the son of a Puerto Rican mother and an American father. He came to live in Puerto Rico in 1950. He has studied in Ohio and at the University of Puerto Rico. He has become well known through the musical group "Taoné"; his compositions are inspired by his love of independence and have been classified among the new music of protest.

WRITERS FROM LOS BARRIOS OF
NEW YORK, CHICAGO, AND OTHER PLACES

Jesús Colón, a Puerto Rican community leader, intelligent and idealistic, who has spent most of his life in New York, famous for his library, which consists of a wonderful collection of Puerto

Rican documents and books; Piri Thomas, the renowned author of *Down These Mean Streets* (1967); Samuel Betances, a student at the Harvard Graduate School of Education; Víctor Hernández Cruz, author of *Snaps* (1969), born in Aguas Buenas in 1949, who came to live in New York in 1954 and has already become a poet whose work has appeared in important reviews and anthologies; Edwin Claudio, a law student in Chicago; Jack Agüeros, a community leader on Manhattan's Lower East Side; Migdalia Rivera, a young community leader in Chicago; Pedro Pietri, who was born in 1944 and whose "Puerto Rican Obituary" has been widely reprinted; and David García, a religious leader at the Church of Saint Mark's in the Bowery—are a group of representative Puerto Ricans who are expressing the anxieties, the frustrations, and the dreams of their people in verse and prose.

ACKNOWLEDGMENTS

The editors gratefully acknowledge the following sources:

"Let Me Tell You the Story," from *The Islands: The Worlds of the Puerto Ricans,* by Stan Steiner. Copyright © 1974 by Stan Steiner. Reprinted by permission of Harper & Row Publishers, Inc., New York.

"Revolt of the Borinqueños," from *Elegías de Varones Ilustres de Indias (Primera Parte: Elegía VI),* by Juan de Castellanos, from *La Gesta de Puerto Rico,* edited by María Teresa Babín, Ediciones Mirador, San Juan, Puerto Rico, 1967. Translation by Muna Lee. Reprinted by permission of the editor.

"The Renegades," by Ricardo E. Alegría, from *The Island Times,* San Juan, Puerto Rico, November 8, 1963. Reprinted by permission of the author.

"Guanina," by Cayetano Coll y Toste, from *Leyendas Puertorriqueñas,* Editorial Orión, Mexico, 1963. Reprinted by permission of the author's granddaughter and editor, Edna Coll.

"Sonnet," by Damián López de Haro, from "Carta del Obispo de Puerto Rico," 1644, from *Panorama de la Cultura Puertorriqueña,* edited by María Teresa Babín, Las Américas, New York, 1958. Reprinted by permission of the editor.

"To the Beautiful and Felicitous Island of San Juan de Puerto Rico," by Juan Rodríguez Calderón, from *Ocios de Juventud,* San Juan, Puerto Rico, and Lambert & Co., San Francisco (no date; about 1830?) and from *Memorias Geográficas, Históricas, Económicas y Estadísticas de la Isla de Puerto Rico,* San Juan, Puerto Rico, Oficina del Gobierno, 1832, Vol. IV, pp. 410–18.

"Insomnio," by Santiago Vidarte, from *Cancionero de Borinquen,*

Barcelona, 1846, and from *Cuadernos de Poesía*, Instituto de Cultura Puertorriqueña, San Juan, Puerto Rico, 1965. Reprinted by permission of the editor.

"Vida Criolla," by Luis Llórens Torres, from *Obras Completas*, Instituto de Cultura Puertorriqueña, San Juan, Puerto Rico, 1967. Reprinted by permission of the editor.

"The Puerto Rican" and "A *Jíbaro* Wedding," by Manuel A. Alonso, from *El Jíbaro*, Colegio Hostos, Río Piedras, Puerto Rico, 1949. Reprinted by permission of F. Manrique Cabrera, the editor.

"On a Paper Boat," by Eugenio María de Hostos, from *Antología Puertorriqueña*, by Manuel Fernández Juncos, 1907. Reprinted in *Obras Completas*, Instituto de Cultura Puertorriqueña, San Juan, Puerto Rico. Reprinted by permission of the Instituto de Cultura Puertorriqueña and the author's son, Dr. Adolfo de Hostos.

"Hostos, Exemplary Patriot," by Margot Arce de Vázquez, from *Impresiones*, Editorial Yaurel, San Juan, Puerto Rico, 1950. Reprinted by permission of the author.

"La Virgen de Borinquen," by Ramón Emeterio Betances, from *La Virgen de Borinquen*, Sociedad de Jóvenes Pro-Cultura Puertorriqueña, Ponce, Puerto Rico, 1970. Translated by Miguel Ángel Santana, director of French Department, University of Puerto Rico, from the original French ("La Vierge de Borinquen," Paris, 1859) into Spanish; and translated into English by Magali Soto and Stan Steiner. Reprinted by permission of the translators.

"The Cry of Lares" (selection), from *El Grito de Lares* (Editorial Cordillera, San Juan, 1967), a play by Luis Llórens Torres, from *Obras Completas*, Instituto de Cultura Puertorriqueña, San Juan, Puerto Rico, 1969. Reprinted by permission of the editor.

"Bolívar," by Luis Llórens Torres, from *Obras Completas*, Instituto de Cultura Puertorriqueña, San Juan, Puerto Rico, 1967. Reprinted by permission of the editor.

"The Song of Borinquen," "To Blanca María," and "Cuba and Puerto Rico," by Lola Rodríguez de Tió, from *Mi Libro de Cuba*, 1893, and *Claros y Nieblas*, 1885. Also included in Martín Gaudier, *La Borinqueña*, Ediciones Rumbos, Barcelona, Spain, 1959.

"Poem of Puerto Rico" and "Return," by José Gautier Benítez, from *Poesías*, 1880. Reprinted in *Poesías*, Editorial Campos, San Juan, Puerto Rico, 1955.

"Madrigal," by Francisco Álvarez Marrero, from *Obras Literarias de F. Álvarez*, San Juan, Puerto Rico, 1881. Reprinted by Carlos N. Carreras, *Los Poetas Que Fueron*. Complete anthology. *Poetas Puertorriqueños*, Vol. I. Ateneo Puertorriqueño, San Juan, Puerto Rico, 1922.

"The Nightingale" and "The Rag," by Pachín Marín, from *Vida y Poesía de Pachín Marín: Cuadernos de Poesía*, No. 5. Ateneo Puertorriqueño, San Juan, Puerto Rico, 1958. Selection and Prologue by María Teresa Babín.

"The Castilian Language," by José Mercado, from *Antología Puertorriqueña*, by Manuel Fernández Juncos, 1913, 1932.

"The Redeemers" (selection, chap. 10), from the novel by Manuel Zeno Gandía, *Los Redentores*, 1925. Reprinted by Club del Libro de Puerto Rico, San Juan, Puerto Rico, 1960.

"Two Letters," by Miguel Meléndez Muñoz, from *Cuentos del Cedro*, Ediciones Rumbos, Barcelona, Spain, 1957. Reprinted in *Obras Completas*, Instituto de Cultura Puertorriqueña, San Juan, Puerto Rico, 1963.

"Military Justice," by José Padín, from *Estampas Puertorriqueñas*, by José Padín, 1967. Edited by Theodore J. Parthenay, Appleton, New York, 1967. Reprinted by permission of the editor, Mr. Parthenay.

"Riches and Poverty," by Nemesio R. Canales, from *El Día*, Ponce, Puerto Rico. Reprinted in *Paliques*, Editorial Universitaria,

University of Puerto Rico, 1952. Reprinted by permission of the editor.

"The Land and Its Meaning," by Antonio S. Pedreira, from *Insularismo*, Biblioteca Autores Puertorriqueños, San Juan, Puerto Rico, 1934.

"Symbols of Borinquen," by María Teresa Babín. (From a book in preparation.)

"The Mountains Know," by Concha Meléndez, selected from *Psiquis Doliente*, Poems, 1923. Reprinted by permission of the author and courtesy of Patria Vientós.

"Serenade of the *Coquí*," by Tomás Blanco. Selected from *Los Cinco Sentidos*, Pan American Book Co., San Juan, Puerto Rico, 1955. Reprinted by permission of the author.

" 'Puertoricanists' and 'Occidentalists,' " by Nilita Vientós Gastón, from *El Mundo*, San Juan, Puerto Rico, February 19, 1955. Included in *Indice Cultural*, Editorial Universitaria, University of Puerto Rico, 1962. Reprinted by permission of the author and the editor.

"Black Dance," "Pueblo," and "The Call," by Luis Palés Matos, from *Poesía 1915–1956*, Editorial Universitaria, University of Puerto Rico, 1971. Reprinted by permission of the editor.

"Masquerade: Devil Masks" (selection), from *Vejigantes*, a play by Francisco Arriví, from *Máscara Puertorriqueña*, Editorial Cultural, Río Piedras, Puerto Rico, 1971. Translated by Dr. B. E. Coulthard. Reprinted by permission of the author.

"The Black Trumpet," by José A. Balseiro, from *Vísperas de Sombras y Otros Poemas*, 1959. Reprinted by permission of the author.

"What I have Been, What I Am, What I Shall Be," by Luis Muñoz Rivera, from *Obras Completas*, Instituto de Cultura Puertorriqueña, San Juan, Puerto Rico, 1968. Reprinted by permission of the editor.

"Give Us Our Independence," speech by Luis Muñoz Rivera to the U.S. House of Representatives, May 15, 1916, from *Status of Puerto Rico, Hearings Before the United States Puerto Rico Commission on the Status of Puerto Rico*, Vol. II, Doc. No. 108, pp. 141–6.

"The Pamphlet," by Luis Muñoz Marín, translated by Muna Lee de Muñoz Marín, from *An Anthology of Contemporary Latin American Poetry*, edited by Dudley Fitts. Copyright 1942 by New Directions Publishing Corporation, New York. Reprinted by permission of the author.

"A Good Civilization," speech by Luis Muñoz Marín to the Legislative Assembly, San Juan, Puerto Rico, January 15, 1960. Reprinted by permission of the author.

"No," "In the Breach," and "Ultima Actio," by José de Diego, from *Obras Completas*, Instituto de Cultura Puertorriqueña, San Juan, Puerto Rico, 1966. Reprinted by permission of the editor.

"A Revolution of Our People," speech by Gilberto Concepción de Gracia at Aguadilla, Puerto Rico, November 10, 1950. Reprinted by permission of Mrs. Concepción de Gracia and Gilberto Concepción Suárez.

"Everybody Is Quiet but the Nationalist Party," speech by Pedro Albizu Campos at Lares, Puerto Rico. From: *Habla Albizu Campos*. The Historic Speech of P.A.C., September 23, 1950. Commemorating the Rising of Lares. Paredon Records, New York, 1971.

"The Town," by Virgilio Dávila, from *Pueblito de Antes*, 1917. Courtesy of Patria Vientós.

"Nostalgia," by Virgilio Dávila, from *Obras Completas*, Instituto de Cultura Puertorriqueña, San Juan, Puerto Rico, 1964. Reprinted by permission of the editor.

"Letter of Recommendation (To the Proprietor of the Universe)," by José Antonio Dávila, from *Poesía Puertorriqueña*, Editorial Universitaria, University of Puerto Rico, 1954, p. 63.

"I Remember the Apostle," by Félix Franco Oppenheimer, from *Estas Cosas Así Fueron*, Editorial Yaurel, San Juan, Puerto Rico; 2nd edition, Club de la Prensa, San Juan, Puerto Rico, 1970. Reprinted by permission of the author.

"Invocation to the Fatherland," by Francisco Matos Paoli, from *Luz de los Héroes*, Ediciones Juan Ponce de León, San Juan, Puerto Rico, 1954. Reprinted by permission of the author.

"Fatherland," by Francisco Lluch Mora, selected from *Momento de la Alegría*, Ediciones Yauriquén, San Juan, Puerto Rico, 1959. Reprinted by permission of the author.

"The Wooden Wall" and "The Castilian Language," by Evaristo Ribera Chevremont, from *Antología Poética*, edited by María Teresa Babín, Department of Education, San Juan, Puerto Rico, 1967. Reprinted by permission of the author and the editor.

"Río Grande de Loíza," by Julia de Burgos, from *Poesía en Viente Surcos*, included in *Obra Poética*, Instituto de Cultura Puertorriqueña, San Juan, Puerto Rico, 1961. Reprinted by permission of her nephew, Joseph A. Burgos, Jr.

"Elegy Before the Ruins of Caparra," by Luis Hernández Aquino, selected from *Voz en el Tiempo: Antología Poética (1925–1952)*, Biblioteca Autores Puertorriqueños, San Juan, Puerto Rico, 1952, pp. 71–3. Reprinted by permission of the author.

"Find," by Gustavo Agrait, from *Variaciones Sobre Temas Obsesivos: Poesías (1932–1966)*, Ediciones Juan Ponce de León, San Juan, Puerto Rico, 1969. Reprinted by permission of the author.

"Batey," by Francisco Manrique Cabrera, from *Poemas de Mi Tierra, Tierra*, Puerto Rico Progress, San Juan, Puerto Rico, 1936. Reprinted by permission of the author.

"The Coffee Plantation," by Juan Avilés, from *Antepenúltimo Canto (1921–1971)*, New York, 1971. Reprinted by permission of the author.

"Island of Childhood" and "The Puerto Rican Wild 'Amapola,'" by Olga Ramírez de Arellano Nolla, selected from *Diario de la*

Montaña, Ediciones Juan Ponce de León, San Juan, Puerto Rico, 1967. Reprinted by permission of the author.

"Madrigal," by José P. H. Hernández, selected from *Canto de la Sierra*. Included in *Obra Poética*, Instituto de Cultura Puertorriqueña, San Juan, Puerto Rico, 1966. Reprinted by permission of the editor.

"To Saint John of the Cross," by Manuel Joglar Cacho, selected from *Antología Poética de Asomante*, Asomante, San Juan, Puerto Rico, 1958. Reprinted by permission of the author.

"Distances," by Juan Antonio Corretjer, selected from *Antología Poética de Asomante: Cuadernos de Poesía*, No. 14. Ateneo Puertorriqueño, San Juan, Puerto Rico, 1962, pp. 48–53. Reprinted by permission of the author.

"Peasant," by Juan Martínez Capó, selected from *Viaje*, San Juan, Puerto Rico, 1961. Reprinted by permission of the author.

"Hymn to the Sun," by Jorge Luis Morales, selected from *Antología Poética*, Editorial Universitaria, University of Puerto Rico, 1968. Reprinted by permission of the editor.

"Ode 1962," by Violeta López Suria, selected from *Antología Poética*, Editorial Universitaria, University of Puerto Rico, 1969. Reprinted by permission of the editor.

"To a Poet," by Diana Ramírez de Arellano. (From a book in preparation.) Printed by permission of the author.

"The Promised Land," by Clemente Soto Vélez. (From a book in preparation.) Printed by permission of the author.

"Four Voices of Puerto Rico," by Andrés Castro Ríos, selected from *Antología de Jóvenes Poetas*, Instituto de Cultura Puertorriqueña, San Juan, Puerto Rico, 1965. Reprinted by permission of the editor.

"The Collapse," by César Andréu Iglesias, from *Los Derrotados*, Club del Libro, San Juan, Puerto Rico, 1960, chap. 18. Reprinted by permission of the author.

"The Fish Sing," by José I. de Diego Padró, from the novel *Un Cencerro y dos Badajos*, (*A Cowbell and Two Clappers*), Ediciones Juan Ponce de León, San Juan, Puerto Rico, 1969. Reprinted by permission of the author.

"The Interpreter," by Julio Marrero Nuñez, from *Cuentos del Castillo del Morro*, Ediciones Juan Ponce de León, San Juan, Puerto Rico, 1963, pp. 61–77. Reprinted by permission of the author.

"The Cockfight" and "The Strike," by Enrique A. Laguerre, selected from *La Llamarada*, Tipografía Ruiz, Aguadilla, Puerto Rico, 1935. Reprinted by permission of the author.

"The Red Seed," by Antonio Oliver Frau, from *Cuentos y Leyendas del Cafetal*, Yauco, Puerto Rico, 1938. Reprinted by Instituto de Cultura Puertorriqueña, San Juan, Puerto Rico, 1967.

"The Hunchback's Zeppelin," by Wilfredo Braschi, from *Metrópoli*, Ediciones Juan Ponce de León, San Juan, Puerto Rico, 1968. Reprinted by permission of the author.

"Peyo Mercé Teaches English," by Abelardo Díaz Alfaro, from *Terrazo*, San Juan, Puerto Rico, 1947. Reprinted by permission of the author.

"The Letter" and "The Passage," by José Luis González, from *La Galeria*, ERA, Mexico, 1972. Reprinted by permission of the author.

"Crossroad" (selection), from a play by Manuel Méndez Ballester, from *Encrucijada*, Ediciones Rumbos, Barcelona, Spain, 1958. Reprinted by permission of the author.

"The Protest," by Luis Quero Chiesa, from *El Universal*, Guayaquil, Ecuador, December 28, 1954. Reprinted by permission of the author.

Songs of Roy Brown: "The Mind Is a Sleeping Soul," "Old Bastions of Borinqueños," "Paco Márquez," and "Monon," by Roy Brown. From: ALBUM *Yo Protesto*, VANGUARDIA, San Juan, Puerto Rico.

"The Odyssey of a *Jíbaro*," by one *Jíbaro*, from *The Islands: The Worlds of the Puerto Ricans*, by Stan Steiner. Copyright © 1974 by Stan Steiner. Reprinted by permission of Harper & Row Publishers, Inc., New York.

"Grandma, Please Don't Come," by Jesús Colón, from *A Puerto Rican in New York*, Mainstream Publishers, New York, 1961.

"Puerto Rican Paradise," by Piri Thomas, from *Down These Mean Streets* (chap. 2). Copyright © 1967 by Piri Thomas. Reprinted by permission of Alfred A. Knopf, Inc., New York.

"Race and the Search for Identity," by Samuel Betances, from *The Rican*, Chicago, Illinois, Vol. I, No. 1 (Fall 1971), pp. 4–13. Reprinted by permission of the editor.

"#1 exploration," "#2 trans-atlantic flight," "#6 bodega," "#8 night writers (riding)," and "#9 song & dance," by Victor Hernández Cruz, from *19 Necromancers from Now*, edited by Ishmael Reed, Doubleday, New York, 1970.

"Where Am I At?" and "A Boycott," by Edwin Claudio, from *The Rican*, Chicago, Illinois, Vol. I, No. 1 (Fall 1971), pp. 14 and 29. Reprinted by permission of the editor.

"Canción del Tecato" and "El Apatético," by Jack Agüeros, from *The Rican*, Chicago, Illinois, Vol. I, No. 1 (Fall 1971), pp. 3 and 15. Reprinted by permission of the editor.

"The Straight-Jacket," by Migdalia Rivera, from *The Rican*, Chicago, Illinois, Vol. I, No. 1 (Fall 1971), p. 18. Reprinted by permission of the editor.

"Puerto Rican Obituary," by Pedro Pietri, from *Palante: Young Lords Party*, by Michael Abramson and The Young Lords Party. Copyright © 1971 by Michael Abramson and The Young Lords Party. Used with permission of McGraw-Hill Book Co.

"Mass of the People, Church of Saint Mark's in the Bowery," "Order for Holy Matrimony, Church of Saint Mark's in the Bowery," "Psalm 5, Listen to My Protest," and "Psalm 21, Why Have You Forgotten Me?", by Father David García. Used with permission of the writer.

NOTES ABOUT THE EDITORS

María Teresa Babín, born in Ponce, is Professor of Spanish, Graduate Center, City University of New York, and Professor of Puerto Rican Studies, Lehman College, C.U.N.Y. At Lehman College, 1969–1972, she chaired the first department of Puerto Rican Studies in the United States. She has written many books, including: *Introdución a la Cultura Hispánica* (*Introduction to Hispanic Culture*) (1949), *El Mundo Poético de García Lorca* (*The Poetic World of García Lorca*) (1954), *Jornadas Literarias* (*Literary Journeys*) (1964), *Siluetas Literarias* (*Literary Silhouettes*) (1965), *La Cultura de Puerto Rico* (*The Culture of Puerto Rico*) (1970), and *The Puerto Ricans' Spirit* (1971).

Stan Steiner is the author of *The New Indians* (1968), *La Raza: The Mexican-Americans* (1970), and *The Islands: The Worlds of the Puerto Ricans* (1974). He has co-edited *Aztlan: An Anthology of Mexican American Literature* (with Luis Valdez, 1972) and *The Way: An Anthology of American Indian Literature* (with Shirley Hill Witt, 1972). He now lives in New Mexico.